AF540399

ROLE OF VOLUNTARY ORGANISATIONS IN TRIBAL DEVELOPMENT

ROLE OF VOLUNTARY ORGANISATIONS IN TRIBAL DEVELOPMENT

(TRIBAL LIFE IN INDIA—10)

Edited by

DEVENDRA THAKUR

D. Litt.

Former Professor, L.N. Mishra College of Business Management,
B.B.A. Bihar University, Muzaffarpur

and

D.N. THAKUR

Ph.D.

SECOND REPRINT EDITION

DEEP & DEEP PUBLICATIONS PVT. LTD.

F-159, Rajouri Garden, New Delhi - 110027

ROLE OF VOLUNTARY ORGANISATIONS
IN TRIBAL DEVELOPMENT
(Tribal Life in India—10)

First Published : 1994
Second Reprint Edition : 2009
Reprinted : 2011

ISBN 978-81-8450-113-1 (Vol. 10)
ISBN 978-8450-114-8 (Set)

Typeset by THE LASER PRINTERS
8/15, 3rd Floor, Subhash Nagar, New Delhi - 110 027

Printed in India at NEW ELEGANT PRINTERS
A-49/1, Mayapuri, Phase-I, New Delhi - 110 064

Published by DEEP & DEEP PUBLICATIONS PVT. LTD.
F-159, Rajouri Garden, New Delhi - 110 027 • Phones : 25435369, 25440916
E-mail : ddpubs@gmail.com • ddpubs@yahoo.com
Showroom :
2/13, Ansari Road, Daryaganj, New Delhi -110 002 • Telefax : 23245122

Contents

Preface

During post independence period through planning process special efforts have been made by the Government to bring about economic development of tribal people in India. But inspite of special efforts made during four decades of planning, tribal people have not come at par with other sections of the country. The present study aims at examining the role of governmental organisations in bring about economic development and in this context the role of voluntary agencies have also been analysed so that a comparative view could be presented to assess their relative contribution. In this project Santhal tribe of Bihar has been of special interest and Santhals form the focal point of study. Our choice for the detailed study of Santhals has been due to the fact that they are the biggest tribe in Bihar State and they also occupy the third position in tribes of India as a whole. As socio-economic change forms an essential/vital part of developmental process, study of socio-economic change of tribals assumes special significance in the present study.

Santhal is the third largest tribe in India. They are living in large number in present Santhal Pargana division of Bihar. They are also living in the Singhbhoom District. Santhals are also living in the plateau of West Bengal, Tripura and some parts of Nepal. They are settled tribe. Their living character is non-nomadic like other tribes. They choose their settlement near forests, hills, etc. They have their own style of living. They own Panchayati way of living which is so rigid that it hinders their movement in other areas. Thus, they are living in isolated state of living. So special efforts need to be made to bring about social change.

Now the question is as to what has been done for their

upliftment and how the socio-economic development agents are functioning in this regard ? The Government endeavours to bring about development through plan projects which are implemented by the bureaucratic machineries. Voluntary agencies through their works have also played an important role in this regard.

The project under study has answered a number of questions like: which of the two is more efficient? Are both of them necessary for the economic development and social change of tribal people? Efforts have been made to examine these points in this study. Efforts have also been made to use Socio-economic Survey Technique utilising random sampling method so that a quantitative analysis could be presented. Development of tribes in India and Bihar has been presented in brief in the introduction chapter. This is followed by the indepth study of Santhals so as to determine their present economic level. Thereafter the role of voluntary agencies in tribal development in general and Santhals in particular has been dealt with.

After determination of the level of growth of tribes, specially Santhals the project has experimented case study technique to determine quantitatively the role of Government organisation and voluntary agencies. Their field of working in socio-economic areas has been measured and compared.

Finally, a comparative view has been presented so that it becomes easier to say which of the two is better, or both are co-ordinate to each other.

We are grateful to the Government of India and Ministry of Welfare for selecting us to undertake this study. We convey our sincere thanks to various departments of Government as well as other institutions which helped us in conducting the study.

We are indebted to all the research workers and other staff working for this project for their honest efforts. We record here our sincere gratitude particularly to Dr. Banshidhar Prasad Singh, Head of the Department of Economics (B.U.), Dr. Bachaspati Thakur, L.N.M.U., Darbhanga, Smt. Sumat Uraon, Ex-Minister, Welfare, and Mr. Rambilas Paswan, Ex-Minister of Labour and Welfare, Government of India.

Muzaffarpur

DEVENDRA THAKUR
D.N. THAKUR

Tribes in India

The Constitution of India has defined "Scheduled Tribes" as such tribes or tribal communities or parts of or groups within such tribes or tribal communities as are deemed under Articles 342 to be Scheduled Tribes for the purpose of this Constitution. The 212 tribes declared by the President in exercise of the powers conferred by clause (i) of Article 342 of the Constitution of India in the different States of India, constituted 5.36 per cent of the total population of the country in early fifties.

The tribal habitation in India can be demarcated in three tribal zones: North-eastern, Central and Southern. The northeastern zone consists of sub-Himalayan region and the mountain ranges of north-eastern-India. This zone is inhabited by tribes like the Gurung, Limbu, Lepha, Garo, Khasi, Naga and others. The Central Zone consists of the plateau and mountainous belts between the Indo-Gangetic Basin to the north and Krishna river in the south. The main tribes found in this zone are the Santhal, Munda, Oraon, Ho, Bhil, etc. The southern zone consists of the peninsular India, south of the river Krishna. Tribes like Chenchu, Kota, Toda, Malayam, etc., inhabit in this zone.

The tribes sometimes called aboriginals because of their being the earliest inhabitants of this country, not only belong to different stages of culture, but they vary from area to area in regard to size of the population, language, racial types, socio-economic organisation, etc.

The largest concentration of tribal people anywhere in the world except perhaps Africa, is in India and it is interesting to note that there are six hundred and thirteen tribes inhabited all-over India. There are as many as thirty tribes only in Bihar, but among them four tribes can be treated to be significant; Munda, Oraon, Santhal, and Ho. An alphabetical list of the tribes of Bihar, is as follows:

An Alphabetical list of the Scheduled Tribes in Bihar

1.	Asur	16.	Kheria
2.	Baiga	17.	Kharwar
3.	Banjara	18.	Khona
4.	Bedia	19.	Kisan
5.	Bathudi	20.	Kara
6.	Bhumij	21.	Karwa
7.	Binjhia	22.	Lohara, Lohra
8.	Birhor	23.	Mahli
9.	Birjia	24.	Mal Paharia
10.	Chero	25.	Munda
11.	Chik Baraik	26.	Oraon
12.	Gond	27.	Paharia
13.	Gorait	28.	Santhal
14.	Ho	29.	Sauria Paharia
15.	Karmali	30.	Savar

Source: Scheduled Tribes and Scheduled Area in India, Government of India, 1978, p. 6.

In Table 1.1, we have tried to arrange the State-wise figures of tribal population in India from different sources. In this table when we look at the figures of tribal population in India as a whole we find that the number of tribal people in India as in 1951 was 2,25,11,854 and it was 3,01,72,221 in 1961. The growth in tribal population was 76,60,367 that is 32.23, per cent. But in the following decade, i.e., 1961-71, the growth in tribal population was 78,94,997 and the percentage of growth was 26.17. This fact obviously reveals that there is a decreasing trends in the growth rate of tribal population in India which may be due to poor, economic conditions of the tribal people.

TABLE 1.1

Tribal Population in India

Sl. No.	State/U.T.	1951	1961	%age of growth 1951-61	1971	%age of growth 1961-71	1981	%age of growth 1971-81
1	2	3	4	5	6	7	8	9
1.	Andhra Pradesh	1149918	1324368	15.17	1657657	25.17		
2.	Assam	1554801	2064316	32.80	1606648	22.19		
3.	Bihar	3880097	4204784	8.87	4932787	17.31	5810867	17.80
4.	Gujarat	2092556	275446	31.68	3784422	35.58		
5.	Himachal Pradesh	27925	108194	287.40	141610	30.89		
6.	Karnataka	80402	192096	138.92	231268	20.39		
7.	Kerala	132767	212762	57.89	269856	26.60		
8.	Madhya Pradesh	4814128	8673410	37.87	8387403	25.59		
9.	Maharashtra	1660852	2397169	45.21	2954249	23.27		
10.	Manipur	194239	249048	28.22	334466	34.30		
11.	Meghalaya	N.A.	N.A.	—	814280	—		
12.	Nagaland	2,633	343697	66.83	457602	33.14		
13.	Orissa	3009580	4228757	40.84	5071937	20.00		
14.	Rajasthan	1774278	2351470	30.16	3125506	32.92		

(Contd.)

TABLE 1.1 *(Contd.)*

1	*2*	*3*	*4*	*5*	*6*	*7*	*8*	*9*
15.	Sikkim	N.A.	N.A.	—	52056			
16.	Tamil Nadu	136376	251991	84.78	311515	23.62		
17.	Tripura	192293	360070	87.25	450544	25.13		
18.	Uttar Pradesh	N.A.	N.A.	—	198565			
19.	West Bengal	1566868	2054081	31.00	2532969	23.31		
20.	Andaman & Nicobar	N.A.	14122	—	18102	—		
21.	Arunachal Pradesh	N.A.	N.A.	—	369408	—		
22.	Dadar & Nagar Haveli	N.A.	51269	—	64445	25.70		
23.	Goa, Daman & Div.	N.A.	N.A.	—	7654	—		
24.	Lakshadweep etc.	13485	23391	73.45	29540	26.29		
25.	Mizoram	N.A.	N.A.	—	313299	—		
	India	2511854	3017221	32.23	38067218	26.17**		

Sources: (i) A Statistical Hand Book of Tribal Welfare and Development,
(ii) Tribal Sub-plan Area, and
(iii) Census of India, 1981, Series 4, Bihar, Paper of 1982.

The impact of migration and resettlement on the growth rate of tribals in States like Himachal Pradesh, Karnataka, Tamil Nadu, Tripura, Nagaland and Lakshadweep during 1951-61 is almost obvious. A large scale migration of the tribal people from one State to the other seems to have occurred as a result of distress, growing poverty and allied factors (the so called push factors). It might have also occurred on account of better opportunities in other States and abroad (the so called pull factors). But the decreasing trend in general population of the Indian tribes is, surprising which draws the attention of the population experts, planners and policy-makers. The growth rate of the tribal people of Bihar during the years 1971-81-1981-91 is 3.14 and 17.80 per cent. It apparently discloses the fact that our endeavours in the field of tribal development was not satisfactory.

TRIBAL WAY OF LIVING

Many tribes, very often, live by hunting, fishing or gathering. But these are in-sufficient to satisfy their needs. The aboriginal inhabitants of the Andaman Islands, however, depend upon these entirely for their livelihood. They have no trade relation with others; and are much isolated from one another that the Onge of little Andaman do not understand the language of the Jarawas of the Great Andaman or of the inhabitants of the North Saninel Island, all of which are close by. Each of these groups satisfies all its needs completely with the help of local resources and exercise considerable ingenuity in maintaining themselves on these island although technologically they are very poorly equipped.

The Andamanese fish very little with nets. They use bows and arrows and spears for the purpose. There are coral reefs round some of the island where the water is shallow and crystal clear. It is very easy to spot the fish and turtles from their canoes in shallow water, while turtles' eggs can be collected easily from the beaches of a few of the lonely island. Shell-fish of various kinds and crabs are also gathered for food. But it is interesting that so far as the Onge are concerned, they do not shoot birds for meat, although the bird population is not small. It has been suggested that they do not do so far losing their arrow in the thick vegetation which cover the island.

The food which the Andamanese eat by simple boiling is

never enriched by salt. If meat cooked with salt is offered to them, they reject it forthwith. Honey is one of their favourite foods and from January to March, they spend long time in gathering honey from hives. There is some kind of leaf, called tongee, the juice of which is mixed with saliva and be smeared over the body. This prevent the bees from stinging men who come to loot their hives.

In the midst of warm, rain drenched forests of Tripura, Manipur, Nagaland, Mizo district and NEFA, there live a number of tribal communities who depend principally upon a rather simple form of cultivation. The same method is also applied to vogue among some of the tribes of Orissa and Madhya Pradesh, while, outside India, it is practised in northern Burma, Sumatra, Borneo and New Guinea, as well as in parts of African continent.

In areas where it is practised in India, a village community control a certain measure of land, consisting of mountains and valleys, and puts a small parts of it every year under cultivation. Ploughs and cattle are not employed, but axes or bill hooks and digging sticks are the only implements used for the purpose. After winter, a portion of the hill-side or jungle is first marked off for cultivation. It is cleared by lopping off the undergrowth and branches of trees, which are allowed to dry in the sun for some time. Shortly before the rains set in, the dry leaves and bushes are set on fire. Farmers take care that the fire does not spread into the forest. When the fire dies down, the ashes are lightly spread over the ground where necessary. The fire kills the weeds and insects, and the ashes fertilise the ground. Then the farmer walks over the field with a digging stick or bill-hook in hand, makes a hole in the ground, sows a few seeds and covers it over with earth by pressing it down with his toes. As the rains come, the seeds begin to sprout and the harvest is gathered as each crop ripens.

In Nagaland or NEFA, the land may, thus, be used for only one season or two, while in more crowded places like Orissa, it may be used for three seasons and then left for a number of years to recuperate. The period of recovery may vary from three or four to ten years; it all depends upon the needs of the farmer and the pressure of population in the locality.

This process of shifting the area of cultivation has many names. In Assam, it is known as Jhum or Jum; in Orissa as Podu, dahi or Kamana; Penda in Madhya Pradesh and so on. Those who practice this from of cultivation do not themselves move from place-to-place to form new settlement,. What they do is, every family goes on adding a fresh patch of forest every year, while a patch which has been used several times is left free to recuperate. The villages themselves remain in the same place, generation after generation.

Shifting cultivation of the tribal people in India has become tied up with the economy of the market, i.e., with the requirement of the peasant population, of both tribal and non-tribal origin, which live nearby and which pays for goods and services in cash. Unlike the hunting and gathering of the Andamans, it has become ancillarly to a larger peasant economy and lost its independent status. Yet, whereever possible, the tribal communities continue to practice it for many of the hill sides. This is more or less, the only practicable method of land utilisation. When we consider the thin population of the area for which it is not possible to convert the hill slopes into terraced field for growing wetland paddy.

The process of slow and continuous contact between the tribal communities, who practised a comparatively simple form of production, with peasants and artisants with greater specialisation must have gone on for centuries. There is no doubt, that the chief attraction for the tribes, when their system began to fail them, as in the case of the juangs in Orissa,[1] was greater promise of food which the more advanced method held.

Among the Apatani tribes in NEFA, fields have been terraced and indigenously irrigated by diverting hill streams. But the Apatani, like the Newar of Nepal, use only the hoe and no plough or animals for cultivation. In the mountanous regions of Himachal Pradesh terraced farming is carried on with plough and bullocks. In some of these areas, there are no specialised castes of artisans; in other such castes are present.

Although such basic information is not available, we know from our specific knowledge about such tribes as the Juangs of Orissa, or the Gonds of Madhya Pradesh or the Santhals of Bihar and Bengal, how the majority of them have eventually come within the orbit of the present civilization of the Hindus and how also they have finally come to be largely classified under the categories of cultivators, agricultural labourers and workers in certain other primary types of occupation.

In the census of 1961, 11.59 per cent among the workers belonging to the Scheduled Tribes were classified as 'cultivators' who owned some land. 10.58 per cent were 'Agricultural labourers' who did not owned land; while 11.08 per cent were engaged in the primary occupation of mining, quarring, forestry, gardening, fishing, hunting, rearing of livestocks, etc. The Santhal of Bihar, Orissa and Bengal, the Mundas and Oraons of Bihar and the Gonds of Central India have, thus, largely given up their attachment to more primitive forms of production and taken to work which affiliated them with the more prosperous communities living in the neighbourhood. These tribes are, thus, no longer self-contained, as primitive Andamanese fishing and gathering people happen to be.

SOCIAL INSTITUTIONS

Men do not live alone, and in order to meet their needs of food and shelter, companionship and love, recreation and play, they form into associations, build institutions through which such needs are satisfied.

The first institution which one should name is of course, the family. It is present among all people in the world. Family is formed through marriage; and each tribe or community has its own rules regarding the choice of mates. There rules of proferance and of avoidance. Whom to marry and whom not to marry. And the rules vary from one tribe to another in a wide variety of ways. There are, however, a number of special or exceptional examples which may be described on account of their uniqueness.

As a rule, most families consists of husband, wife and children. But among some tribes in the Himalayas, one wife may have several husbands. The same custom was prevalent among the Todas of the Nilgiri in Tamil Nadu. Their shortage of women was formerly due to the customs of female infanticide. That custom no longer obtains there and the original practice of some men having a common wife is reported to have been replaced by some men having more than one wife in common. This does not imply, however, that sexual relations are promiscuous. Actually, strict rules are observed by parties concerned; and when a child is born, its paternity is established by means of social ceremony instead of on biological considerations.

The reason why such an extraordinary examples of marital relationship has been described is for the purpose of emphasizing the fact that the code of sexual conduct which one community believes to be natural may be very different from that of another, which may consider its custom to be the most natural one instead. All codes or moral or approved behaviour are man-made, i.e., artificial. And one of the benefits which one derives from a study of the lives of people other than one's own, is that prejudice are loosened and one begings to realise that there are hardly any accepted codes of behaviour which are common to all people in the world. The tribal folk of Chhotanagpur, Orissa, Madhya Pradesh and Assam share a certain institution unrelated to the family, but which has a great bearing upon the sexual life of tribes like the Oraon, Juang, Maria, Gond, Naga and the like. These tribes have an organisation of the youth of the village where they club together, and have certain rights and duties in relation to the rest of the community. Among some tribes there are two dormitories, one for boys and another for girls; while among the Oraons, for example, there is only one for boys.

The youth's dormitory several purposes in the village. The hut in which it is housed may serve to accommodate guests, while the old and the young frequently meet there for gossip and recreation. Riddles are often exchanged while the ancient lore of the tribe may also be passed on from one generation to another in the evenings. The dormitory, thus, serves as informal kind of school. But it is chiefly used by the boys and sometimes also by the girls to seek one another's company in singing, dancing and love making. Pre-marital sexual intemicy is not forbidden among quite a few tribes provided the rules of avoidance in the choice of mates are not transgressed. Young men and women, thus, grow up without many of the inhibitions and repressions to which sophisticated communities are generally subject. This is perhaps the reasons why most tribal communities in India have been able to reserve their joy of life, in spite of the appalling poverty from which some of them suffer.

One interesting point may be referred to hers. Small tribal communities have often come under the influence of their powerful Hindu neighbours. This sets up a desire among them to fall in step-up with the practices of the latter. As a result some of them already given up a few of their customs and taken to the imitation of Brahminical people. Some are now ashamed of admitting the existence of their youth's dormitories, and some have even given up the beautiful dances of their men and women because the superior Hindus look askance at them on that account.

There are a few more elements in the family life of tribal communities to which attention should be drawn. Young men and women may choose their own mates; but this can also be the responsibility of parents. When a bride is selected a compensation has to be paid to her parents, as they are on the point of losing a working hand in the family. Among a few tribes, the so called 'bride price' may be high and may entail an amount of bard labour before one can accumulate the necessary funds. There are three ways in which the difficulty can be overcome. The bridegroom may elope with this chosen bride, in the hope of securing the approval of the elders concerned later on. Or, he may serve in the house of his prospective father-in-law as a labourer, and thus, in the course of a few years, earn his right to the hand of the daughter. Another possibility is the arrangement of two simultaneously when the sister of the bridegroom is married to the brother of the birde. In such cases, the dues may be largely written off against each other.

Marriages can be of long or of short duration Divorce or separation is not uncommon, marriages of widows and of divorced men and women may be quite frequent. So, the partnership of men and women in a family is of looser nature than in an orthodox Hindu home. Yet there is no reason to believe that the emotional relationship between husband and wife in any tribal society suffers in quality on that account.

Next to the family comes the clan. The clan is composed of a number of families, Often bearing a common designation and which believe that they have all sprung from a common ancestor. Marriage is usually forbidden within a clan. Among some tribes, a custom is to regard certain others as Bandhu or friendly or related clans; and no marriage takes place between the two. There are other clans from which spouses are chosen according to prescribed rules. When a clan is described as a friendly or related clan. Something like the rules of incest which are applicable in the cases of the family is thus, extended to a longer unit of organisation.

Clan organisation has much to do with marriage but it also ensures co-operation between members when economic assistance is needed, or when a death takes place in the house. Among the

Juang of the highlands of Keonjhar in Orissa who practice shifting cultivation. Villages are usually inhabited by members of a single clan. But when they adopt the more advanced technique of plough cultivation, change naturally begins to take place.

The Munda tribe of Chhotanagpur had a simple kind of political organization of its own. Two officers-one secular and the other religions, looked after the affairs of the village. There was moreover, a bigger chief the Manki, whose jurisdiction extended over larger territory, and to whom the village chief was subordinate. This arrangement survived for sometime even after the land came under British rule; and then the power of these chiefs became considerably reduced.

It is believed that the Bhumej of the neighbouring districts of Manbhum were originally of Munda affiliation. When in the past they come fully under the economic influence of their Hindu neighbours, the upper class among the Bhumej formed place in Hindu society as Kshatriyas. They claimed royal descent and married among neighbouring royal families. In the similar manner, it has been reported by anthropologists from several parts of eastern and middle India that sections of tribal people thus, branched off and political do dominance over their compatriots, and this by following the model set by Hindu society. The growth in members and an accentuated contact at many levels with a politically better organized community thus, led to development in tribal society, different from those which had been found sufficient when numbers were small, and distinctions into classes on account of differences in wealth and power were of a feeble nature.

CULTURAL ASPECTS OF TRIBAL LIFE

The tribal population in India belong to various sages of cultural development. Elwin divides the tribes into four classes according to their sages of cultural development. The purest of tribal groups comprising about two or three millions have been placed in the first class. These Highlanders do not merely exist like so many villagers, they really live. Their religion in characteristic and alive, their tribal organisation is unimpaired, their artistic and choreographic traditions are unbroken, their mythology still utilizes the healthy organisation of tribal life.

Geographical considerations have largely protected them from the debating contact of the plains.[2] The Second category of tribes, according to Elwin's classification has been experiencing contact with the plains and consequently has been undergoing change. This group, though retaining their tribal mode of living exhibits the following characteristics in contract to the first group: (i) instead of communal life, this group live village life which has become individualistic. Their communal life and traditions, are only preserved through their village dormitories; (ii) in contract to the class-I Tribe, the members of those of class-II do not share things with one another; (iii) are cultivation has ceased to be a way of life for them; (iv) the members of these tribes are contaminated by the life outside. They come in contact with the groups living on the periphery, who live a more complex, viz., civilized life; (v) the members of these tribes are less simple and less honest than the members of the tribes belonging to class-I.[3]

The tribes who belong to the third category constitute the largest section of the total tribal population, about four-fifth of it. Members of this class of tribal groups are in a peculiar state of transition. According to some investigations, they are tribal in name but have become 'backward Hindus' constituting a sizeable section of the lower rung of Hindu society; one section is described as Christian. These tribes have been appreciably affected by external contacts. They have been exposed to the influence of economic and socio-cultural forces of Hindu society. They have been also subjected to missionary influences.

The tribals of fourth category according to Elwin consist of the old aristocracy of the country represented today by great Bhil and Naga chieftains, the Gond Rajes, a few Bishevar and Bhaiya landlords, Karku noblemen, wealthy Santal and Uraon and some highly cultured Mundas. They retain the old tribal names and their clan and totem rules and observe elements of tribal religion through they generally adopt the full Hindu faith and live in modern and even European style.[4] According to Elwin, tribal of this class have won the battle of culture contacts. It means that they have acquired aristocratic traditions, economic estability, affluence, outside encouragement, acertain arrogance and self-confidence characteristics alike of ancient families and modern enterprise.[5]

Though tribal culture differs from tribe to tribe. The Sauria

Paharia observe many a ritual which mark important stages in the Agricultural clander. During the latter half of the months of Bhado (August-September), on getting the maize crop from the field, villagers worship in the 'Jaherthan'. The whole village contributes for a he-goat and one or two chickens. These are sacrified to the villages deities by a 'Kotwar'. Only after observing this ritual can they eat maize. It is similar to 'Nabanna' observed by Hindus after harvest of Aghani paddy, the main crop like maize of Sauria Paharia. The most important annual worship of the Suria Paharia is the 'Sailani Puja' in honour of 'Kando Gosai' in the month of 'Magh' (December-January-February) or 'Chait' (March-April). The God is taken out from his abode and sacrifices are offered to him. It is also similar to 'Debothan' in Hindus. Every sixth year, the villagers offer a buffalo to this deity, the ritual being known as 'Karra Puja'.

Festivals connected with hunting are observed among the Hill Kharia and the Oraon. The 'Phagun' or the spring festival among to Hill Kharia consists of two parts: one is the ceremonial hunting expedition and the other is the ceremonial conceration of the first fruits, the first flowers and the edible leaves and other products of the season. Before the performance of this ceremony, no fruits of the new season may be eaten. All the adults male population of a Hill Kharia settlement join in a ceremonial hunting expedition under the leadership of the Dehuri. In the evening, when the party returns, the hunters are entertained to a feast cooked by women. The game is divided between different Kharia families of the settlement in production to the number of members in each family and the whole night is spent in singing, dancing and merry-making. The morning following the Dehuri and the villagers worship at the seat of the village deity. The expenses of the worship and the sacrifices are met by contributions made by the entire village community.

Each of the Chhotanagpur tribes has a series of festivals. For the Oraon the first festival is 'Sarhul' which is celebrated in the month of 'Chait' (March-April). It is festival of the spring and is celebrated at the time when the Sal tree blossoms. Until the celebration of this rite, no Oraoq of the village may gather, or eat or use the new fruits. Flowers and edible leaves of the seasons. The 'Sarhul' festival is so important that its date is fixed by the Village Panchayat and its ceremonies extend over several days.

All the villagers take part and go in procession to the sacred grove of the village where the village deities are worshiped. The 'Pahan' and his assistant officiate at the rites and the leader of the youths dormitory has important duties to perform on this occasion. The expenses of such communal festivals are large but all the villagers contribute in cash and kind. Singing and dancing continue at the village Akhara for several days.

The next important festival is the 'Karma' which is celebrated by tribals and non-tribal with equal enthusiasm in the month of September. A branch of 'Karam' tree is planted in the Akhara and offerings are made to it. The day as well as the preceding night are spent in fasting but in the evening every one meets at the 'Akhara' and spends the night in dancing and singing round the 'Karam' sapling brought from nearby jungle. The story of the two brothers Karam and Dharam is recited by the 'Pahan'. People in the village on this occasion, give themselves up completely to merry-making.

The Santhal and the Kharia hold village festivals on the occasion of the sowing of rice. The Hindus have similar festival for first transplantation of paddy seedlings by the head of the family. The Ho also publicly worship the village deity Desauli and his consort before sowing rice. The Oraon and the Santhal observe the Hariari or festival of green rice plants in the month of Asarh (July) after the rice, millet and cotton seeds have been sown in the field. There can be no transplantation of seedlings, till this ceremony has been performed. The village elders fix a day for its celebration and fowls for sacrifice are collected from the villagers. On the day of Hariari festival, the Pahan and his assistant offer sacrifices and make offerings to the village deities on behalf of the village community.

The Kadleta or Kadlota festival is celebrated by the Munda in Asarh (July), just before the transplantation of rice seedlings and on this occasion sacrifices are offered to the village deities in the sacred grove in the presence of the assembled villagers. Among the Oraon this festival is celebrated one month later.

The Kharihan Puja is celebrated among the Munda, Oraon and Kharia just after the harvest. This ceremony is intended toward off the evil eye from heaps of harvested grain. The ritual is performed by village priest on behalf of the village community.

The Chief festival of the Santhal called 'Soharai' is celebrated after the rice harvesting in December-January. This festival lasts for five days and ritual includes the sacrifice of fowls to the village defties by the Naek. The gods of the cattle-shed are also worshipped at this village fastival and so are the ancestral spirits. During the five days of the 'Soharai' festival, the Santhal indulge in a veritable Saturnalia, giving themselves up to dancing, eating, drinking, singing and sexual license.

Among the Ho, the chief festival is the 'Maghe Parab'. It is celebrated in December-January and also extended for five days. The Deuri performs all the rituals. All the offerings are sacrificial. Animals are contributed by the villagers. Each Ho village fixes a different date for the celebration of 'Maghe Parab' so that guests from other village may arrive. This festival, which is an occasion for dancing and singing provides opportunities for youngmen and women of different villages to come together and seek amorous adventures. Older writers like Dalton have written of the licentiousness and debauchery indulged in during this festival, but the picture they have drawn is exaggerated.

In some villages influenced by Hindu contact some Hindu festivals are also celebrated with great eclat. Somewhere the 'Phagu' festival coincides with the 'Holi' festival of the Hindus. Besides the Hindus of the village, the tribals sprinkle coloured water over their friends and neighbours. In the evening a gola dance is organised in the Akhara in which persons of different communities participate, some as dancers and others as spectators. Similarly 'Dasahra' festival is celebrated by all the communities. Recently the Munda have come to join the Ramanavmi festival. On this occasion the 'Mahabiri Jhanda' is taken out in a procession.

Thus, we see that all the people in a tribal village combine for the performance of rites and for the worship of their gods on village basis. Only the village with its hierarchy of secular and sacredotal functionaries provides a framework for enactment of the great seasonal rites and times of danger and stress for the propriation of gods and spirits and the protection of its inmates.

More than the tribes as a whole or even the exogamous clan, the village is animated by a spirit of ready co-operation the service of the gods and it is through such constant co-operation that it assumes a certain mystic unity. Most of the deities worshipped during the seasonal rites are the gods of the village territory rather than gods of its individual inhabitants and it is probably on account of this that they can be worshipped through the traditional machinery operated by hereditary priests and headman, who again act not in their individual capacity but as representative of the village community.

The tribal concept of pleasure—their pre-occupation with pleasure activities such singing, dancing drinking, story telling, etc. realized through cycles of festivals and their happy go-lucky spontaneous nature sharply contrast than with their non-tribal counterparts. Many anthropologists have praised them for their commitment to such persuits of pleasure. Archer is full of praises for the Santhal when he states, 'free from sickness, the Santhals have poise, buoyancy and a quite extraordinary zest for life. An air of exhilaration surrounds all that they do."[6] But some have wrongly equated the tribal concept of pleasure with hedonism which is obvious from Man's comment on the Santhal. "They seem to carry out to the full the principle to set, drink and be merry and care not for the morrow."[7] But the tribal concept of pleasure is an invaluable possession of tribals. It is responsible for their optimistic nature, extraordinary zest for life and their freedom for psychosis and neurosis. It constitutes their main source of strength which serves as a cushion to absorb the suffering and frustration arising from poverty and exploitation.

Most of the tribals in India have rich tradition of oral literature. Many of the songs of tribal communities of India as well as their folk-tales have been published by anthropologists. Sarat Chandra Roy, who was one of the earliest among them presented a number of Mundari songs, along with their English translations, in his book entitled. "The Mundas and their Country" in 1912. The recent translations and transcreations of their poems by one great poets and scholars have brought to general notice their great aesthetic and literary values. Some of these poems are at par with the poems of some of the greatest poets of the world. Their folktale and their myths of creation have also been praised all over the world. Frazer, for instance, praised the Santhal myths of creation as it combines the principles of creation and evolution and found in it the confirmation of his thesis.

RELIGIOUS ASPECTS OF TRIBAL LIFE

Tribal religion in India seems to have a common feature, that all beings are endowed with a living spirit. Animals, plants, rivers, mountains are exception to this rule. The dead who have apparently left us are yet with us, and it is through remembrance of offerings that we have to renew our relationship with them on due occasions. The dead are again reborn in the shape of offsprings in the present generation. The span of man's comradeship is thus, extended to encompass all that he sees around him, as well as those whom he loved and has apparently lost. All these are common with Hindu religion.

What is significant in the tribal religion or 'animistic' beliefs of our brethren, the Mundas, the Oraons or the Santhals, is that the whole world, peoples by spirits thus, rendered holy. In the forests where some of the more isolated communities live, a few trees are never touched or cut, for they represent the primal grove, Pipal tree is also considered sacred and abode of Basudeo, a Hindu god. It is never cut down. They are symbolic of the whole forest which men, under the pressure of needs, have had to cut down. The mountains are holy; and there are rocks of extraordinary shape of even colours, which are taken as proofs of their sacredness.

If the spirits dwell everywhere and in all are at peace with them, men enjoy freedom from illness and a long life. If anyone falls ill, the general belief is that some relationship has been violated, when, by means of trances or particular magical ceremonies men or women skilled in the art decide what should be down by sufferers. And when this is done, health is once more believed to be restored.

Among more sophisticated communities, certain places, probably enclosed by a well covered by a roof, are marked off as specially sacred. But among the 'animistic' tribals of India, all places are holy as they are the seats of spirits. Some have accused the so called animals of living in perpetual fear of ghosts and spirits. But there does not seem to be any particular justification for this. All men have their hopes and fears, and to single out a few elements of tribal religions and say that the latter are born only of fear is doing grave injustice to them.

A faith which establishes man's kinship with all that he sees, around him, a faith which releases some of the creative forces within him, which burst forth in simple, loving ceremonies or occasionally in beautiful, lyrical poems or songs, or in art which is direct and not trammelled by sophistication, can hardly be accused of being barren and destructive in its influence upon the human spirit.

There is one thing which has happened to tribal folk after their contact with men of other faiths. It is true that these tribes are poor, devoid of formal education, and oppressed by fears which arise out of lack of modern knowledge. But in this respect they suffer from disabilities similar to those which the poorer classes among the non-tribal people are also subject. Christian missionaries have worked these for more than a century, Firstly, because they offer a more fertile field for developing a truly religious life than nominally Christian and poverty-striken classes in the countries from which the missionaries themselves come. For many missionaries work in their home country is less rewarding than work among the simpler and more responsive inhabitants of tribal India.

Christianity has undoubtedly brought the message of a richer life, a wider companionship and a new sense of dignity to converts. But it is interesting that the Christian religion has always been attended by the benefits of modern western civilization. And this was particularly so during the period of British rule when this converts felt closer to the British rulers than to their be nighted country-men. The western way of life spread among those who could afford to do so, while education, improved habits of living and reliance upon modern medicine got introduced wherever, Christianity was able to enter. Yet it might be worthwhile asking the question whether Christianity and westernization in India were necessarily identical with each other. Perhaps they are not. For there can be Christian religion which does not necessarily draw men and women away from their own civilization. Yet, up-till-now, the principal agent of westernization, often regarded as modernization, among the tribal folk has been Christian missionary enterprise. It is only after independence that Christianity has been swing in round to a point of view when allegiance to one's native culture is being encouraged.

Obviously, a relation of tribal folk to Hinduism or Christianity has been quite different. For at least Hinduism has not been a proselytizing religion. The indigenous population of India is supposed to have contributed in the past generously to the building up of what is known as Hinduism. The tribes retained the principal elements of their faith and practice, though these were modified to a greater or less extent. In addition, they shared some of gods and goddesses, and even participated in the social festivals and ceremonies of their Brahminical neighbours. Without any effort on the part of he latter for conversion. That participation did not turn them into Hindus. One might indeed say that tribes can be regarded as being fully absorbed in the Hindu fold if Brahmin perform Brahminical ceremonies for them during the three critical events of birth, marriage and death. If the latter are still celebrated by tribal rituals, then the communities are still true to their own faith in spite of the fact that, in outer fringes of their culture, they participate in some of the ceremonies of their Hindu neighbours. A parallel might be drawn from the example of relationship between Hindus and Muslims in India in the past. Even now there are a large number of shrines dedicated to Muslims saints in Bihar. Uttar Pradesh, Delhi and Rajasthan where both Hindu and Muslims devotees offer worship without any detriment to their religious affiliations. In the past and not so very long ago, Muslims used to join in the celebration of the spring festival called 'Holi'. And, Hindus in similar manner used to play prominent part in the performance of the Muharram by carrying the 'Tazia' or by an exhibition of their skill in play with 'lathi or quarter-staff. Such participation was largely in common festivals i.e., on a social place, and did not mean that one community had adopted the faith of another.

The relationship of many tribal communities to either Hinduism or Budhism is of this nature unless they been very deeply drawn into the Hindu social system. In Kinnaur in Himachal Pradesh, or the Mompas of Kaneng in Arunachal, many of the Scheduled Tribes, i.e., those who have been listed for special treatment under the Constitution, have, thus, come very close to either Hinduism or Buddhism or to both. Yet they have retained a custom like polyandry which marks them off from the rest of their neighbours.

After independence, when tribes, listed in a schedule under the Constitution, have gained access to certain statutory benefits, a new movement has started among even the westernized converts to Christianity to re-discover and re-affirm their tribal identity and separateness from those who are not included in the schedule. There is nothing wrong in such endeavour. But while describing the religions of the tribal communities in India, we have to indicate not only the character of their indigenous faiths and practices, but also the many-sided changes to which they have been subject through the contact and influence of their more prosperous neighbours. Sometimes they have been attracted towards westernism through the devoted help of western missionaries. And now a new trend has begun among them of new unification between Christian and non-Christian or 'animist', so that there 'tribal' identity may be reaffirmed, and in the process a salvage takes place of as much of their tribal culture and religious faith is consistant with the demands of modern life.

CIVIC ASPECTS OF TRIBAL LIFE

Among all tribes of India, especially Bihar, the village is a well defined political and administrative unit. The unit and solidarity of the village emerge most clearly in relation to government. Whether it is a large permanent settlement among the Santhal, Munda, Oraon, or Ho or a small frequently shifted settlement as among the Hill Kharia or Suria Paharia, it is governed by an administrative mechanism which not only regulates life within the village, but orders the villagers' relations with the world outside.

This machanism functions through its officers who are known by different designations among the various tribes under review. In the simpler societies the ordering of the social, political and ritual relations of the village are in the hands of one man. But in the more complex societies, we find a differentiation of function and authority vested in two headmen each with its own field of interest and prescribed duties. A primary differentiation of function splits village affairs into secular and sacredotal spheres of activity with a headman responsible for each and among some tribes, differentiation is further emphasized by the assistants to help each headman in the discharge of his duties.

In Hill Kharia villages, there is only one village headman who combines in his person the social as well as religious leadership of the village. He maintains peace and order within his settlement. Unlike among other tribes his position has not been recognised by Government. He is also the priest in whose hands rests the maintenance of harmonious relations with supernatural powers. His position and functions will be dealt with at the appropriate place.

Earlier authorities on the Suria Paharia mention four officers, viz., the Sinyare (Headman), Bandari (Messenger), Kotware (Incharge of arrangements for the punch) and Giri (the most influential ryot).[8]

Now a days we find only the headman caled the Manjhi. He is responsible for all secular affairs. The Manjhi is generally elected by the villagers and is often the most influential man of the village. The Manjhi is responsible to the divisional headman called the Sardar.

Among the Oraon and the Munda, the differentiation of functions is more pronounced that among the Sauria Paharia. The Secular headman known among the Oraon, as Mahto and among the Munda as 'Munda'. Previously the relagious headman or the Pahan was the head of the village and performed both secular and religious duties. His assistant was the 'Mahto' among the Oraon and 'Munda' among the Munda.

In most Oraon villages, the Mahto is elected once every three years by villagers assembled at the Akhara. The Mahto is the representative of the village. In some villages, the post of the Mahto is hereditary. Everywere the Mahto enjoys rent free service land during the tenure of his office. The Mahto settles all disputes over the amount of rent due to landlord. Formerly, the Pahan as the representative of the village community could together with the Mahto settled all uncultivated vacant land within the village border of which the village community was the joint owner. But now-a-days such settlements are made by Government Revenue Officials and the Mahto or his agent has no right to settle such lands.

All that has been said for the Oraon village headmen holds true more or less of the village headman of the Munda. The Ho headman is known as the Munda and the office is generally hereditary but if a Munda is dismissed his heir loses his right of succession and a new Munda is selected. The Munda weilds great influence in the social life of the village. All disputes other than those relating to worship and the tribal group as a unit are heard by him. With the assistance of clan elders, he decides the dates for village festivals. He attends marriage parieys and advices villagers on their duties and rights. Fi the village is a single-clan village, the importance of the Munda is considerable, but in multi-clan village, he must exercise great caution and tact in securing the smooth working of the village machinery.

Among the Senthal, as among the other tribes, headmanship is an indigenous institution. The Santhal headman is known as Manjhi. The Manjhi is the head of the village people. All the people will have to follow his lead. In ordering and inviting. In calling and restraining, at the name giving, at the initiating festivals, at religious instruction and worship, in connection with rice and curry, with bear and liquor, with spirits and mountain spirits, in quarrelling and squabbling, in strife and dispute, when there is hunger and thirst, with landlords and money lenders, when crime and misdeeds occur, in connection with theft and stealing, with medicine and witchcraft, with wenches and strumpets, when there is a fighting and killing, murder and wickedness, in grief and sorrow, in calamaties and danger, in illness and pain, at dying and falling away, in ceremonies connected with death and disease, at cremation and at final funeral ceremonies, in connection with all this the Manjhi has responsibility.[9]

Traditionally the Manjhi is elected by the entire village community. He is the representative of the village in both internal and external matters. Sometimes the officially recognised Manjhi is a non-Santhal and then villagers elect an official called Hand-i-Manjhi who is responsible for social matters in the village life while official duties are left to the Government nominee. The Manjhi is considered so important that in certain villages deceased Manjhis are worshipped at a shrine called Majhithan.

The local usage the headman is variously known as Manjhi. Pradhan or Musagir, but these terms are now used synonymously, The appointment of the Manjhi now lies with the Deputy Commissioner, who must satisfy himself that his nominee will be acceptable to the villagers.

The first and foremost duty of the Manjhi is the collection and punctual payment of the village revenue to the Government. The duty of keeping irrigation works in repair, maintaining village roads, boundary marks, camping and grazing grounds in the joint responsibility of the Manjhi and the villagers.

The Santhal Manjhi has two assistants. The principal assistants the Parmanik is chosen by the Manjhi himself. If the Manjhi dies without any male issue or brother, the Parmanik may succeed him. The second assistant is the Jog-Manjhi. His duties lie in the social sphere. He is the guardian of tribal morality; and is head responsible for clan in cost of the union of a Santhal with a non-Santhal. In addition to Parmanik and Jog-Manjhi, there is a 'Gorait' who is the village meassenger of the Santhal. He summons the villagers at the call of he Manjhi.

Thus we see that the different tribes with their villages of varying size and character are administered by a number of officers each with clearly prescribed duties. The corporate unity of the tribal village is maintained and strengthened by the existance of village officers who not only organize village affairs on a community basis and assist Government in the collection of revenue and in the maintenance of law and order at the village level, but also acts as liaison between the authorities and the people in the village. Tribal custom has endowed these functionaries with influence and authority and even where they have not been grafted on the present administrative machinery, their influence and prestige often exceeds that of the officially recognised head of the village.

ECONOMIC ASPECTS OF TRIBAL LIFE

It is almost obvious that the tribal communities in India is extremely backward and poverty striken. It is because a number of communities have continue in the pastoral of shifting cultivation stage of economy even till today. As the pressure of population further grew agriculture advanced the forest receded into the background. With longer land-mass coming under settled cultivation, it was possible to grow a variety of crops in different fields. But, inspite of all, the economic condition of the tribal people cannot be said to be much improved. The area under cultivation as proportion of the total reported area in some of the districts of Bihar reveals this fact. The reported area of cultivation is 50.5 per cent in Ranchi. 18.9 per cent in Singhbhum and 13.2 percent in Palamau which is decidedly much lower. Agricultural productivity is according to one study,[10] between Rs. 750 to Rs. 1000 of output in value terms per hactare. Productivity per worker varies below Rs. 500 per annum and during 1960's productivity per worker is intimated to have declined by as much as Rs. 140 per worker. The gross annual agricultural income per head of agricultural population is, therefore, extremely low.

Agriculture in the tribal region has remained backward due to natural, technological as well as institutional factors. Whereas the acidic soil certainly act as a constraint on increasing productivity by indigenous methods, inadequacy of irrigation facilities, lack of adequate extension facilities and concentration of land ownership, etc. hold the realisation of the potential that exists in its, agriculture. The main agricultural produce in the area is rice. The share of rice in the total agricultural income in Palamau was 49 per cent, in Ranchi 92 per cent and 96 per cent in Singhbhum in 1971. The yield per hectare in the three districts in 1970 was 677 Kgs. 762 Kg. and 863 Kgs. respectively.[11]

Tribal economy is intimately connected with the forests and their economy. The forest regions are, generally, inhabited by the tribal communities who are at one of the earlier stages of economic development compared to other communities in the country. These regions, therefore, are comparatively under developed though they have rice natural resources.

As the population engaged in collection of minor forest produce is believed to be essentially tribal and dependent mostly on agriculture for major part of its income, the low level of agricultural income makes it furthermore dependent upon the forest produce.

Forest in Bihar covers about 17 per cent of total land area against the all-India average of 23 per cent. In Bihar, the bulk of these forest lies in the Chhotanagpur region. In Ranchi district, forest covers 13.2 per cent of total reported area whereas in Singhbhum and Palamau the proportions go up to 33 per cent and 44 per cent respectively. However, the share of forest in total land area has been dwindling, yet the per head forest area in these three districts is about four times of the average per head forest area in the State.

Timber and fuel are the major forest produce in Bihar. At present the standing stock of timber is estimated at about Rs. 600 crores, at current prices. Among the minor forest produce, which includes every thing other than timber, the production of lac in value terms is very important. In 1978-79 when the production of stick lac in Bihar touched its historically lowest level, the value of stick lac production was estimated at about Rs. 2 crores. Distributed over about 5 lakh workers it would amount to an average of about Rs. 40 per worker for the year. But the production of stick lac, however, has witnessed a spectacular decline unlike other forest produce.

Outlays for forest development in Bihar have been rather meagre and it has remained a net revenue earner for the State. During 1977-78, the gross revenue of the forest department was about Rs. 17 crores of which about 10 crores was direct contribution to the State exchequer.

Considering the above figure related to tribal economy, it can be said that tribal economy is intimately connected with forest because their way of living is forest based. The relationship has been recognised but has not been articulated in terms of clear policies and programmes. The tribal economy and the forest, economy, therefore, have tended to drift apart with adverse implications to both. In some cases forest have suffered tremendous loss, while in others the tribal economy has been shattered. In spite of these, tribal economy, in general, is characterised by the close relation between the economy and the habitat. Not being powerful enough to modify the surroundings, the tribal learn to adapt themselves to it. Primitive society has tried to work out some kind of adjustment between material needs and the potentialities of the environment.[12] This is nowhere more clearly evident than in the adjustment of he tribal ness and effort to the forest that we set them. The tribal dependence on forest for food, fuel, house building materials, agricultural implements and minor produce for barter and market exchange also is considerable.

Here is also a point of consideration in this respect. The forest regions are sparcely populated generally inhabited by the tribal communities who are at the earlier or pre-stages of economic development compared to the other community in the country. These regions, therefore, are comparatively underdeveloped, though they have rich natural resources. These dormant resources have to be activised for faster regional growth.

Tribals are partially nomadic and partially settled one.

Nomadics dependence on forest is vital. They maintain their little material needs through minor forest products. Semi-settled and semi-nomadic tribe utilises inside forest semi-open land for their shifting or settled cultivation, but the settled tribals who settle generally near the forest utilises minor forest products and they are agricultural also. Besides this they have traditional undeveloped animal husbandry and poultry farms. If land is owned by the community, then animal husbandry is personal, even in the case of nomadic or semi-nomadic tribal. Animal rearing is related to draft animal for animal power. Bullock is the only draft animal in the tribal belt of Bihar. For making purposes, cows and goats are reared. They are mostly traditional of low milk yielding variety. The purpose of animal rearing for protein purpose lies in realing of cow, goat, pig, sheep and cock.

Minor forest products which are used by tribal are forest leaves, fire-wood, mahua flower, sabai grass, munje chirannje, fruits, flowers and other ingredients, for self-consumption and also for barter and exchange, Karujia, for only exchange, Non-edible and edible mahua seed for self-consumption and sale purposes. Besides this there are two rare minor product which are most closely related with the tribal economy. They play and will also play increasing dominant role in future. They are lack and tasar silk cocoons. Lac is a rare forest product by some insect. It is grown on forest trees.

Lac is a versetile industrial intermediate goods, a unique natural resin. Besides inner consumption it is a expertable goods also. Export earning out of it is 5 to 24.3 crores rupees. It is evident from lac export earning figure from 1970-71 to 1974-75 (See Kamal Narain Kabra, Dependence and Dominance. India Institute of Public Administration, New Delhi, p. 20) Tribal share in collection of raw lac is around 82 per cent. The another important forest produce is tasar silk cocoon. According to the report of District Industrial Centre, Ranchi, the tasar silk cocoon is annually collected of Rs. 121.0 lakhs annually from the forest belt of Chhotanagpur and Santhal Pargana. Tasar cocoon is reared on sal tree. State Government under the scheme of Tribal development and silk development plan have started 12 seed rearing centres of tassar silk insects. It appears from the report of the State Government of Bihar, 1983 that rearing through silk cocoon is increasing year by year. Tasar silk cocoons are counted in Kahn,

80 per cent tribals are responsible for its total collections, 20 per cent collection work is in hands of non-tribals but the raw silk cocoons trade is still in the hands of big traders of Bangalore, Bombay and Ahmedabad. Thus, it appears that tribals are distressed to sell this product and are exploited heavily.

Industry occupies the second position in terms of employment in the tribal region. A little more than 9 per cent of the work force is engaged in industrial activities, in both house-hold and non-house-hold sectors. The work force employed in other than house-hold industries varies from 1.2 per cent in Palamau to 11.85 per cent in Singhbhum. Ranchi has only as little as 4.13 per cent employment in non-house-hold sector. These employment figures, however, include a good number of migrant worker.

On the other hand, Ranchi accounts for 45 per cent of the regional work force in house-hold industries, whereas Palamau employ only about one sixth of the total work force of this region in this sector. The total employment in manufacturing and processing activities, however, is only 3 per cent of the total work force in Palamau; 7 per cent in Ranchi and 13.3 per cent in Singhbhum.

Trade and commerce alongwith transport employ about 5 per cent of total work force-concentration being in Singhbhum district (50.75 per cent) followed by Ranchi (35 per cent) and Palamau (14.25 per cent).

Collection of local produce is carried out through 'haats'. 'mandis', 'melas', etc. which are held over more than 500 centres within the tribal region of Bihar. State regulation of market is confined to looking after law and order and the collection of auction prices. Only Ranchi town has a regulated market. A sizeable number of markets are controlled by local bodies as well.

The tribal region of Bihar exports agricultural commodities, forest produce, minerals, iron and steel, engineering goods, some manufactured articles and transports equipments. Its import consists of foodgrain, vegetable, oil, sugar, manufactured and processed consumers, goods, and raw materials such as coal, steel alloys, etc.

The forest area and its surroundings are rich in minerals while economy starts to dig it economic activities in that area increases and the economic activities in tribals are benefited. The benefits in the shape of employment both regular and irregular increase their standard of living. It also has impacts on their social way of living. Their ethnic aloof character starts diminishing and becomes under within the main stream of the country. With the start of new activities naturally industrial belts emerges which generally invites and attracts tribal labour force to participate. Participation in industrialisation and mining operations may be migratory from both sides and seasonal in nature. But it definitely adds in their employment potentiality and consequently in their earning. Industrial towns and mining centre brings a new way of life in modernity in the tribal areas.

Surfaced road mileage per lakh of population in Bihar, is 20.61 miles whereas it is 36.72 in Ranchi, 41.01 in Palamau and 22.31 in Singhbhum. However, road mileage per 1000 Km. of area is below the average of 6.68 miles for Bihar ranging between 4.04 for Singhbhum to 5.23 miles in Ranchi. This indicates the large area of the tribal region of Bihar have low population density and poorer road coverage.

As on March 31, 1971, only 9.96 per cent of villages in Bihar were reported to have electricity whereas in Ranchi it was 3.08 Palamau 8.60 and Singhbhum only 1.70 per cent.

From the above-mentioned facts it is almost obvious that the tribal region of Bihar is extremely backward with large proportion of the population depending upon backward agriculture and for subsidiary employment on forest produce. The organised sector in industries though well developed in areas of the tribal region of Bihar and using modern techniques is not integrated with the economy of the region and provides employment to only a small section of local work force. The Industrial sector uses local fuels and mineral resources, but their location in the region does not seem to have affected the economy of the region and provides employment to only a small section of local work force. The industrial sector uses local fuels and mineral resources, but their location in the region does not seem to have affected the economy of the local people in any significant way. As a result, the bulk of population remains unemployed and underemployed with low incomes and dependent on backward agriculture and forest produce. To improve the economic condition of the tribal people, development of agriculture and social forestry need to get the topmost priority. The development of industries is also required which utilize the local produce as Sabai grass, cocoons, wood, leafs, etc. and thereby, increase employment as well as the demand of the forest produce. Such a development strategy instead of creating pockets of highly sophisticated industries, will be integrated with the principal resources and sector of the tribal economy and hence, will be more effective in raising the standard of living of the tribal population.

NOTES AND REFERENCES

1. Juango is a minor tribe in Orissa. Originally they were semi-settled tribe. Traditionally their acquired land won a Community land in which they were cultivating jointly with very poor capital but with the start of development efforts the old tradition had been broken. Tribal and their Development—A study of two tribal Development Blocks in Orissa, National Institute of Community Development Blocks in Orissa, National Institute of Community Development Hyderabad, p. 13.
   For further reference see L.P. Vidyarathi and B.K. Ray. "Tribal Culture in India", pp. 109-10. Concept Publication, New Delhi. For Further reference see J.N. Sinha, "Rural Employment Planning Dimensions and Constraints," *The Economic and Political Weekly*, Vol. XIII. Nos. Sund 7, Annual No. 1978, p. 297.
2. Elwin, Verrier: The Aboriginals Bombay, 1943. p. 8.
3. *Ibid.*, pp. 8-10.
4. *Ibid.*, pp. 10-11.
5. *Ibid.*, p. 11.
6. Archer, W.G. "The Hill of Flutes, Life, Love and Poetry in Tribal India, A Portrait of the Santhals," p. 290.
7. Man, E.G. "Santhalia and the Santhals," p. 17.
8. Bainbridge, R.B., "The Surias of the Rajmahal Hill Memoirs of the Asiatic Society of Bengal. "Vol. I, No. 2, 1907, p. 84.
9. Bodding, P.O., "Tradition and Institution of Santhal", p. 104
10. Draft sub-plan for Tribal Region of Bihar, 1974-79, p. 15.
11. *Ibid.*, p. 14.
12. Majumdar, D.N. Races and Culture of India, Allahabad, p. 67.

Socio-Economic Change of Tribes by Government and Voluntary Agencies

POLITICAL AND NATURAL DEMARCATION OF SANTHAL PARGANA

Santhal Pargana was created as a separate district in the year 1855 by ceding portions of Bhagalpur and Birbhum district which was the result of Santhal in surrection 1954-55. The district of Santhal Pargana was one of the three districts comprising Bhagalpur division and was situated between 23.45° and 23.30° North Latitude and between 86.0° and 88.0° East Longitude covering an area of 14,206.0 Sq. Kms., bounded on the North by river Ganga, on the south by the district of Dhanbad and Burdwan (West Bengal). On the west by the district of Giridih, Monghyr and Bhagalpur and in the East by Maldah, Murshidabad and Birbhum (West Bengal). Administratively it was located in Bhagalpur Division in the state of Bihar up to 1981 census.

But, the State Government has upgraded Santhal Pargana as a division consisting of four newly created district; namely,

Dumka, Deoghar, Godda and Rajmahal after 1981 census. There are altogether forty-one Blocks in the division now and all are under IRD Programme.

Santhal Pargana division may be divided into three natural divisions, which consist of hills, dales and the fertile alluvial plain. The hilly portion is streching from the bank of the Ganges in the North to the border of Bengal in the South. It includes the Rajmahal as well as other hilly covering entire Damin-i-Koh area. The hills and slopei are covered with forests which was once very dense, but scanty now. The valley has cultivable land, yielding mostly paddy. The second portion consists of the upland, undulations, long ridges and depressions. It covers almost half of the division including Dumka, Deoghar, Jamtara, Pakur and part of Godda region. Intensively cultivable land is available in this belt. There are high hills and lofty peaks. The third region is a narrow strip of low and fertile alluvial plain lying between the Ganges and the hills. The principal range in the division is that of the Rajmahal hills which rise 1000 to 2000 ft. On the Southern bank of the river Ganges. These hills stretch Southward almost upto the border of West Bengal. The Western range passes through Godda and Dumka and the Eastern range runs parallel to the loop line of the Eastern Railway up to Patna, where it bends westward to join the Western range. These hill ranges enclose between them about 5120 Sq. Kms. of hilly track 3,471 Sq. Kms. of which are known as Damin-i-Koh.

The Southern and South-Eastern parts of the district lying west of the hills are uplands. The main line of the Eastern Railway travels this plateau, some 1000 ft. high right from its entry into the district near Chittaranjan up to a little beyond Jasidih junction. The monotony of the region is broken by protruding hills here and there.

The river Ganges forms the northern boundary of the division. Proceeding towards western corner and running eastward, it takes a turn to the South and then onward forms the Southern boundary in Rajmahal. The Ganges is the largest and the most important river of the division.

The Barakar is another important river of the division which forms the south-western boundary. It originates in the division and finally merges with Damodar river in West Bengal. In addition to these two rivers, there are Mor and Ajai rivers. Mor is known as Mayurakshi. It originates from Deoghar. The river Ajai has its origin in Monghyr, but it runs through Deoghar and Jamtara and finally joins the river Bhagirathi in West Bengal. Other rivers of the division are Gumani, Bansloi, Palsi and Brahmani.

This division was once very rich in forest reserves, but now it is benefit of its jungle wealth to a great extent. There has been large-scale destruction of forest in the past few years. However, the Forest Department has started afforestation. The most common tree of the area is Sal and some inferior quality of teak.

Moreover, there are also Semal, bamboo, Jackfruit, Mahua, etc. Sal and Semal logs are exported in large quantity to neighbouring districts and also to places outside Bihar. Among the forest products are lac, Sabai grass, tassar silk cocoons and Mahua flower and seed.

The Santhal Paragana was a Sanctuary of wild animals. But due to large scale destruction of forests and wanton killing has reduced their number considerably. Tigers have vanished and leopards are rarely found. Bear are seen only in deep forests. Besides these, there are barking deer as well as monkeys.

The highlands along the eastern boundary of the division are made up of volcanic rocks including the greater portion of Rajmahal hills. Among the minerals found in the district are coal, building stones, road, metal, lime, china clay, fireclay, iron, copper, lead, bauxite, etc. There are a number of coal fields in Santhal Pargana. The Rajmahal hills are the source of building stones and road metals. Pakur chips are quite well known and are used extensively all over Bihar as well as in neighbouring states. Small deposits of copper ore and lead of inferior quality are also found. Glass-making silica is made out of sand-stone available near Mangal Hat.

This division is located in the tropical region. The climate in the undulated table land and in the hilly area is moderately extreme type. It has hot dry summer, good rainy season and cool winter. The average annual rainfall of the division is nearly 1,377 mm.

SOCIO-ECONOMIC CONDITION OF THE DIVISION

Santhal Pargana is pre-dominantly a rural division. The total population of the division is 3717528 according to 1981 census, out of which rural population is 3461435 and urban population is 256093. The density of population is 262 per Km. The main occupation of the people is agriculture. The scheduled tribes from 36.8 per cent of the total population.

LAND USE PATTERN

The division is predominantly agricultural in nature. The main occupation of the people is cultivation as over 26 per cent of the population of the district is either working as agricultural labours or as cultivators. The main agricultural crops of the division are Kharif and Rabi.

The district of Santhal Pargana is predominantly agricultural in character. The main occupation of the people is cultivation as over 25 per cent of the population of the district is either working as agriculture labours or as cultivators. Kharif and Rabi are the main agricultural seasons in the district.

The soil of the district is red sedentary. This is an inferior soil and can be used for cultivation of crops like maize, Kurthi, Kodo, etc. In the northern portions of Godda, Rajmahal and Pakur sub-divisions grey soil is found. This is of alluvial origin and is of a heavier texture. But even in the hilly and undulatory regions, rich alluvial soil with organic matter washed down from the upland is found in valleys and at places on plains. It is quite fertile and suitable for paddy cultivation. In the narrow strip of land between the Ganges and the Rajmahal hill ranges, rich alluvial diara soil is found. It receives silt every year. Light and friable, this soil is suitable for both bhadai (early Kharif) and rabi cultivation.

Paddy is the main crop of the district especially the winter rice. Maize is an another important crop grown in the district. On account of non-availability of proper irrigational facilities, rabi crops are not grown very extensively. Vegetable growing is a late introduction'in Santhal Pargana and is confined to the neighbourhoods of the towns only. Orchards are also maintained for the production of fruit such as mango, papaya, guava, jackfruits, etc. Linseed is grown mainly in Godda and Rajmahal, where it usually forms a second crop to rice, ground-nuts, sweet potatoes and Khesari are also widely grown. Sugarcane is raised in areas having assured irrigation. Jute is cultivated in parts of Pakur and Rajmahal sub-divisions.

IRRIGATIONAL FACILITIES

Irrigation is generally provided to wheat and sugarcane crops. Maize grown in bari and homestead land is also irrigated. The most common source is the well and the popular device is latha. A major part of the district being rocky, it is difficult to dig wells. Rocks are generally found 10 to 15 ft. below the surface except in the alluvial region. Slopes are steep and sub-soil water level in uplands fails as the summer approaches. Wells, therefore, are not a very dependable source of irrigation. The undulatory nature of the land makes it possible to store rain water by bunding. Seepage ponds are also found. Apart from being dependent upon rains, these are by no means adequate. The result is that failure of rains invariably involve failure of crops except small in pockets.

The district of Santhal Pargana abounds in rivers and rivulets and it has immense water resources. If exploited, the rivers can supply water for irrigation and electricity for power generation. During the pre-independence days, no tangible steps were taken for taming the rivers. But during the post-independence period the Government has taken various steps to utilise the river resources, the Mayurakshi Left Bank Canal, the Jamini Kola Irrigation Scheme etc. being the important canal systems commissioned. The irrigation potential of the district has increased during the recent past through the adoption of various life irrigation schemes and other minor, medium and major irrigational projects in all the sub-divisions of the district.

INDUSTRIALISATION

The district of Santhal Pargana is mainly inhabited by Santhals and the Paharias. The Santhals mostly use handloom fabrics, and this explains the existence of the large number of units in this category. The district of Santhal Pargana ranks first in the State in this group of industry. Poverty and backwardness of the people may be responsible for the large-scale use of earthen ware and earthen pottery. There are large jungle tracts where the manufacture of materials from bamboo, cane, leaves and other allied products is apt to flourish.

The traditional cottage and village industries practised by the

Santhals and the Paharias constitute tassar rearing, village blacksmithy and carpentry, handloom weaving, rope-making, careas flaying, stone wares, bidi-making, earthen ware, pots-making, etc.

Among the large industrial establishments of the district, mention may be made of the following:

(i) Pharmaceutical works of Dabur Private Ltd., near Deoghar.
(ii) Bihar Silica Works, Madhupur.
(iii) Metal Press Works, Sahibganj.
(iv) Railway Wagon Factory, Jasidih.
(v) China-clay-factories, Mangalhat (Rajmahal).

Besides the above, a number of small-scale industries has also been set up in the district. With the establishment of an industrial estate at Jasidih, the district is expected to be industrialised faster. The availability of its coal, copper, china-clay, fire-clay, sabai grass and bamboos underscores the industrial potentiality of the district. The district is close to Dhanbad and hydel power is available from Maithan and Massanjore. Quick transport, however, is the only problem. Rail communication is not adequate in the district. But there are good roads and industries can thrive.

LIVESTOCK

The district of Santhal Pargana has one of the largest livestock population in the State Stray Cattle are a common site in the district. However, this cannot be taken as an index of the prosperity of cattle wealth. Despite the large population of cattle, the yield of milk in the district is very poor. Except in parts of Deoghar and Godda sub-division, milk supply is extremely low. A typical cow or bullock of the district is a low, rickety cattle wearing a gloomy look. Milch-cows are limited in number, even these that do give milk yield very little.

There has been a concerted effort on behalf of the State Government to improve the breed of the cattle by way of distribution of steed bulls of Haryana and Thaparkar varieties. In order to grade up the cattle quickly and also at low cost, artificial insemination centres with sub-centres have been opened at various places in the district.

There are a number of veterinary hospitals and dispensaries spread over the entire district. Treatment, prevention and suppression of diseases of the livestock are the main functions of the veterinary institutions.

The livestock population according to the 1977 cattle census is indicated below:

Cows	901,774
Buffaloes	211,310
Bulls and Bullocks	718,228
Sheep	243,860
Goats	952,763
Pigs	239,894

Poultry is an important subsidiary occupation of the tribals. In order to improve the ordinary breed, the Government have taken up the poultry development scheme. A number of poultry development centres and extension centres have been opened in the district. There is a vast scope for the development of poultry in Santhal Pargana.

Fisheries

The extensive bed of the river Ganges at Sahibganj and Rajmahal offers one of the best fields in the state for collection of fish spawn and fishing. There are a number of displaced fishermen who are experts in their line. The spawn of Rohu, Ketla, Mirgal, Catfish and Hilsa is collected from the Ganges in flood season. The collected fish spawn is in great demand in other parts of Bihar and West Bengal. Fish spawn collected is stocked in specially prepared nursery tanks. The spawn develops to fry and fingerling stage within a fortnight and then it becomes ready for stocking in tanks.

The fish trade of Rajmahal and Sahibganj has considerable turnover. It has an assured market in Calcutta. There has, however, been very little of fishing development on the big tanks of the district.

Communication Facility

Roads: Until 1857 there was only one proper road which existed in the district. It was the Bhagalpur-Suri road which passed through the district. But there is now a net-work of good roads in the district. All the sub-divisional head quarters and most of the development blocks are connected with the district head quarters by block topped all-weather roads. No important place in the district is left unconnected by a good metalled road. There are two road-links with Calcutta through Jamtara and Suri. Patna, the State head quarters, is connected both *via* Bhagalpur and Chakai. The Jamtara-Dumka-Sabibganj road provides a link with Assam after ferry across the Ganges and is quite busy. A large number of buses ply on these roads.

Railways: The district is deprived of adequate railway communication. Rail lines only cutflank it. The main line of the Eastern Railway traverses close to the South Western boundary of the district and the loop line moves along the northern and eastern extremity of the district. The district head quarters has no rail link and only four of the six sub-divisional head quarters have railway stations.

Waterways: The only navigable waterway is the river Ganges. The railway maintains a ferry steamer service between Maharajpur Ghat (Sakrigali Ghat) and Manihari Ghat (Purnia). The Zila Parishad of Santhal Pargana has three Ghats, ferreies on the Ganges at Rajma, Sakrigali Ghat and Maharajhapur Ghat. Large cargo boats play on the Ganges and are used throughout the year. Smaller boats are also used for ferrying people across.

Airways: There are two small landing grounds. One at Dumka, the district head quarters and the other at Deoghar, the head quarters of the sub-division bearing the same name. No regular air transport services operate from these two landing grounds. These are used by small planes belonging to the State Government.

TRADE AND COMMERCE

The district has a good system of roadways which are very important for trade and commerce. The river Ganges provides water link also for such purposes. The railways do carry a certain percentage of the load but not so much as the roadways. Even Dumka, the district headquarter, has no direct railway connection.

The chief imports of the district are linseed, mustard seed, tobacco, raw cotton, sugar, refined and unrefined molasses, salt, kerosene oil, coal coke, gunny bags, gram, wheat and maize. The chief exports are paddy, maize, jawar, sabai grass, road metals, hides, raw fibres and minerals.

The chief centres of wholesale business in the district are Sahibganj, Madhupur, Deoghar, and Dumka. Sahibganj is by far the most important place for trade and commerce in the district. Wholesale trading in foodgrains is mostly carried on in Sahibganj, Dumka and Deoghar. The number of haats is quite large in the district. The haats are held once or twice a week. The haat is a primary market for the tribals who purchase grains and other commodities of day-to-day consumption.

ELECTRICITY AND POWER

The district receives most of its power supply from the Bihar State Electricity Board through the Damodar Valley Corporation.

All the 12 towns of the district have electricity. In the rural areas, however, the pace of electrification is comparatively slow. Out of 10.015 inhabited villages in the district only 585 villages (5.848) were electrified up to 1979. However, the State Government is making all efforts to electrify as many villages as possible under the Rural Electrification Scheme.

SOCIAL AND CULTURAL EVENTS AND NATURAL AND ADMINISTRATIVE DEVELOPMENT

As mentioned in the beginning, the district of Santhal Pargana has very recently been split up into 4 district, viz., Dumka, Deoghar. Godda and Sahibganj under State Government notification. This administrative change has not been taken into account for the purpose of this census since it took effect after the 1981 Census Operations. The present volume, therefore, deals with the old Santhal Pargana district as such.

The major social or cultural event has taken place in the district of Santhal Pargana during the 1971-81 decade.

Fair and festivals are held regularly in the district. The most important seasonal fairs are held at Deoghar and Basukinath on the occasion of Shivaratri Shravana Sombari and Shri Panchami. Besides, fairs are also held in different parts of the district of the occasion of the Durga Puja atd Diwali Festival. Hijala Mela held for seven days in the month of February near Dumka is also very famous.

VOLUNTARY AGENCIES ENGAGED IN ECONOMIC DEVELOPMENT AND SOCIAL CHANGE IN TRIBAL BELTS WITH SPECIAL REFERENCE TO SANTHALS

Considering the premitiveness and traditional living condition of tribes in the period of freedom struggle a few voluntary agencies have emerged to change their socio-economic condition. It was the inspiration of M.K. Gandhi which has brought up Dr. Rajendra Prasad, Amrit Lal Thakur, L.M. Shrikant, etc., in this field. They organised on the pattern of Gujrat Adim Jati Sevak Sangh on all India level and two sister organisations in Bihar namely, Santhal Paharia Seva Mandal with headquarter at Deoghar and Adim Jati Seva Mandal, Nivaran Ashram, Nivaranpur, Ranchi. Besides this Akhil Bhartiya Vanvasi Kalyan Ashram, Ram Krishna Mission are also emerged in this field. Very recently Badlao, an organisation to create employment in Santhal tribe at the border of Bengal and Bihar at Mihijam was organised.

In response to Gandhi's wave tribals themselves have organised a movement type voluntary organisation called 'Sadahar' in Santhal tribe and similar organisations have emerged in the Munda and Oraon too. It is macro-life purification wave following Ahimsa in major way and the principle of life is self-sufficiency. They are using own spun cloth and avoiding liquor and other harmful food drink and beverages. This wave of super-idiology has influenced tribal life and inspired Adim Jati Seva Mandal and Santhal Paharia Seva Mandal to serve for their betterment.

After independence the pattern of working of these voluntary organisations has gone a sea-change. More bureaucratisation has emerged in their office and their pattern of work. Although voluntary workers were paid around roughly one-third in relation to similar workers in the bureaucratic set-up of the State Government. Workers were more devoted to the principle in comparison to bureaucrats. Therefore, their work in the limited field is more efficient and effective in comparison to similar work done by bureaucrats. A glaring example of the type can be seen in the problem of settlement of nomadic Paharia tribe in Bihar.

Santhal Paharia Seva Mandal has succeeded in giving permanent settlement of nomadic Moriya Paharia tribe where Government has failed in this direction. Government has built pucca settlement colonies in the present Dumka district. But the nomadic Paharia has refused this opportunity of their permanent settlement. In the fields of primary education, tasar (a variety of silk cocoon production) and health care and advice services, the experience has been similar.

During the plan-era which starts from 2nd October 1952 the voluntary organisations have also started work on the basis of some projects. They managed to get sanction from the Government and the Government is contributing generally from fifty per cent to cent per cent expenditure of their schemes on the basis of consideration of their importance.

In the following chapter the contribution of voluntary agencies in the field of tribal development will be examined. Comparative study of the efforts of the Governmental agencies in implementing schemes of tribal development will also be made so as to ad-judge the contribution of governmental organisation *vis-a-vis* that of voluntary agencies.

It is not out of place to mention here that workers of the voluntary organisations who have opted to work in these organisations are committed and devoted workers. They are more firm in their principles than those who are hankering for earning. They gather under a symbolic banner for bringing about a change in the society through their services. Only for nominal wage they work enthusiastically to bring about a change in the society. But, on the other hand, the development workers of the Government are working only for work shake, some how or other, they are in a mood to fulfil their target without considering the substance. Naturally, the work done by voluntary organisations are expected to be sound and solid while that of Government agencies are not so. Generally, it is the administrative punishment that compels a Government worker to do while voluntary organisation worker's working pattern is self-inspiration. It is commitment that compels a voluntary worker to work while bureaucrate work by direction. So individual touch *vis-a-vis* human touch is lacking in Government work. But, with the start of planning era, there change that has been observed in the voluntary organisation workers. They are dogging the Government pattern, their nature and altitude and grasping Government workers malady. To the extent, they are following Government pattern in their organisational pattern, their working pattern results are similar as that of Government. Hence, a hypothesis "voluntary organisations engaged in tribal development are following the Government pattern of functioning. Therefore, a voluntary organisation engaged in tribal development is following the pattern of Government. *An effort has been made to test this hypothesis imperically* and justification of the hypothesis will certainly then speak why voluntary organisations are following Government pattern of working.

This has been observed only in the working pattern of Santhal Paharia Seva Mandal, Adim Jati Sevak Sangh and Adim Jati Seva Mandal, but not in the case of Akhil Bhartiya Vanvasi Kalyan Ashram, Ram Krishna Mission reasons of which have this that those organisations are political and missionary respectively. Their workers are totally devoted and committed. Generally they are not accepting government contribution and subsidies, but they are accepting foreign assistance with the permission of Home and Foreign Affairs Ministries. In this light empirical test in the universe will be done and cause and effect relationship will be established.

Socio-Economic Condition of Santhal Tribes

The Santhals call themselves simply Hor, meaning mén and state that they were formerly called Kharwar. It is only since 1917, that a Santhal has learned to tell a Shangu, what his name and sect is prior to that, as a rule he would simply say 'Manjhi'.[1] It is generally believed that the previous form of the word Satal might have been as 'Santhal' or Santhal they might have been called 'Sangtar' or Santar' also. There is in fact, difference of opinion about the proper form of the word Santar. The earliest mention of them appears to be contained in an article entitled 'Some extra-ordinary facts, customs and practices of Hindus by Lord Teign Mouth (Sir John Shore), which was published in the Asiatic Researches of 1795. In this article, they were designated 'Sanntars' and described as a rude and illiterate tribe residing in Ramgur (Ramgarh), the least civilised part of the company's possessions who have reduced the detection and trial of persons suspected of witchcraft to system.[2] The first mention of the Santals in the (Santal Parganas) district occurs in Montgomery Martin's Eastern India (compiled from Buchaman Hamiltons' manuscript) which contains the agents of the zamindars and it is only among the rude tribe called Saungtar, and in Bengalese part of the district that a kind of chief tenant is employed to transact the whole affairs of the community.[3] Further mention about the Santals at this early time has been obtained by Mr. Mopherson from the unpublished manuscripts of Buchaman Hamilton, in which it is stated, the Saungtars are a tribe that has a peculiar language, so far as I would learn, about five hundred families are now settled in the wilder part of the district. This, however, is late event, and they came last from Birbhum in consequence of the annoyance which they received from the Zamindar. The original seat of this tribe as far as I could learn from them, is Palamau and Ramgarh. They are very expert in clearing forests and bring them into cultivation. But seldom endure to pay any considerable rent, and whenever the land has been brought into full cultivation and the customary rent demanded, they retire to the wastes belonging to some other Zamindars. A whole village always more atonce and their headman (Manjhi) makes a bargain with the new landlord for the whole agreeing to pay a certain sum for as much land as they can cultivate.[4] By 1827, the Santals has got as far as the extreme north of Godda Subdivision, Mr. Ward when demarcating the Dmin-i-Koh finding three Santal villages in Patsunda, 27 villages in Burkop. His first impression of the Santals is interesting. There are, he wrote within this described line, two or three villages established by the race of people called 'Sautars'. These people are natives of Singhbhum and adjacent country, their habits and customs are singular.[5] Sir Herbert Hope Risley, a well known anthropologist, mentions Santhal, Sauntars, a large Dravidian tribe classed on linguistic grounds as Kolerian which is found in Western Bengal, Northern Orissa, Bhagalpur and Santhal Parganas. According to Mr. Skefsurd the name of Santal is a corruption of Santal.[6] We find some important reference about the Santals in the work of Indian author, too. Swami Shivanand Tirtha mentions in his book 'Nagvans' when some people of Nagvans immigrated from the mountain of plain foothill forest they were called Santhal.[7] In this way we find that Saunthar, Sonthal and Santal have commonly been used for the tribe presently living in Santhal Pargana and some parts of Bengal and Orissa.

Mr. W.B. Oldham is of opinion that the name is an abbreviation of Samantawala, Samanta, he says is another name given to Modern Silda Parganas in the Midnapur district whence the immigrants Santals was discovered by Mr. Ward in 1828 deposed that they had come. It may be mentioned that the Silda Pargana is known locally as Samantbhumi, but by the Santal (who elide them) as Sanbhui, the tradition being that the country was so called because it was conquered by a Samant Raja I.C.C. General of the emperor of Delhi. There are moreover, signs of fairly old Santal settlement in the Pargana and around about is a dense population of Santals accounting for over one-third of the inhabitants. There is also a tract called Samantbhum in Bankura district which the Santals claims to have colonised. In this way, we find that being the inhabitants of Samantbhum, when they settled in Santhal Pargana, they were known as Sauntal. That Sant and Saunt are to be derived from the originally Sansteking word, Sananta seems to be very probable. There is no doubt that the word itself is of Aryan Origin. If a translation of the word is sought, the original meaning would be something like 'borderman' but as they have probably got the name in the way mentioned, the meaning implied by the users of the word would not be that they are Sauntars.[9]

HISTORIC BACKGROUND

The sacred lore of the Santals describes their originally home to be the land of Hihadi-Pipadi. That it was due to Madho Singh, they fled away from their homeland and immigrated to Champagraha.[10] But the traditions of the Santhal represents them as a race wandering from one land to another until they found their present home in Chhotanagpur and the adjacent district. On the basis of these traditions several theories have been put forward to account their origin. One authority traces their origin in Central Asia holding that they entered India from the north-west. Another believed that they entered from the north-east. A third theory regards them as being pushed from the Central alluvial valley of the Ganges to the hills of Chhotanagpur under the pressure of the Aryans. A fourth theory credits them with having settled near Mirzapur after coming from the north-east and then being depressed to Chhotanagpur. Whether the Santhal came to the Chhotanagpur plateau from the east, north-west or north-east cannot, however, be conclusively proved on the basis of legend alone.[11] About the middle of the eighteenth century, Chhotanagpur was the chief habitant of the Santal. At the end of that century as the jungles were being cleared and the pressure of population was keenly felt, they moved up towards the virgin forests in and around Rajmahal Hills. The introduction of permanent settlement in 1970 in that area induced that landlords to pay more attention to land improvement and reclamation for which the Santal were increasingly used.

In 1832, the Government set apart a total area of 1,366 square miles in the Santhal Parganas for the settlement of the Paharia, another hill tribe of the area. The Santal, however, settled in this area known as Damin-i-Koh (skirt of the Hills]. Thus from the middle of the last century Damin-i-Koh became the main concentration of the Santals.

The Santals are, in fact, the descendents of one of several Mundari-speaking people who, prior to the establishment of British control in India, formed the dominant population in a large part of the Chhotanagpur region. This is a region of rugged hill ranges and, historically of dense forests, penetrated by several major streams of which the Damodar river is most frequently mentioned in Santal mythology. In Midnapur district of West Bengal, some three hundred miles south and west of Damin-i-Koh, lay the land of Sant from which the Santal most probably gained their name.

In this homeland the ancestors of the present Santals developed an interest in wet rice cultivation. This interest in permanent agriculture was added to their love of hunting and dependence upon forest products for livelihood. Opportunities to possess rice fields or to hold them in the face of aggressive non-Santal land speculators were limited. As the Chhotanagpur area was penetrated by other agricultural populations, the Santals became land hungry people early in the nineteenth century. It was not difficult to induce the Santhal to leave their homeland for cultivable area elsewhere. The hunger for land seem to have been the basic motivation for the investment of life and labour in the migration to the Damin-i-Koh.

Capital resources required for the migration included labour, life-support during the period before harvest, and tools, animals and seed necessary for the agricultural operation. Labour was plentiful and organised under village leaders. The investment in labour tended to be group investments rather than individual or family investments. This was enhanced by the cooperation necessary for the continuing arduous work of preparing rice fields and cutting channels for irrigation. Life support during the migration and the period before the first harvesting came similarly from collective enterprises. The Santals able to exploit the forests along the route of migration and surrounding their new settlements for meals and vegetables. Their hunting usually involved large scale operations which characteristically involved considerable co-operation. There are also indications that the gathering of forest products was done in groups. It was only for iron tools, draft oxen and seed grains that the Santals had to go outside lending agencies for their capital resources. Under the protection of officers of the British East India Company, the Santals went to the traditional agricultural moneylenders of non-Santal villages for loans for their tools, animals and seed grains. Though the Santals were dependent on the non-Santal moneylenders after their migration, it seems erroneous to assume that their migration depended on moneyed capitalists. It seems apparent that leadership and authority, like their labour and life-support enterprises, were indigenous to migrating Santals.

The collective and cooperative experiences of the migration and settlement in Damin-i-Koh tended to reinforce earlier trends in Santal Society. The great interest in wet rice cultivation and permanent agriculture formed a focal economic interest in Santal culture. Egalitarian organization became the basic principle of Santal political and social relationships. Indigenous leadership was esteemed in Santal villages life and in inter-villages relations.

In addition to the experiences involved in the investment made by the Santals in their migration and settlement in the Kamini-i-Koh they also experienced conflict before the new land was theirs. They did not find the Damini-i-Koh totally unoccupied and their movement into the area was not uncontested. They had to fight with non-Santal rivals to achieve their dominance in the territory. In the conflict their success was partly because of their technology as competent hunters and as masters of the forest and partly due to their effective social organisation and leadership.

The few poor scattered settlements of other agriculturists who had managed to penetrate into the forests of the Damin-i-Koh made no effort to contest the ambitions of the Santals. It was the Maler or Mal Paharias who attempted to prevent the immigration.

The Santals were not the first to challenge the Malers' right to their forests. Soon after the East India Company took control of Bengal, a devastating famine disorganised the village communities which lay within reach of the marauding Malers who immediately took advantage of the situation. This brought to the attention of the Government of Bengal which promptly sent company troops to protect the rent paying agriculturists. The British established a military presence in Raj Mahal hills, but the pacification of the Mal Paharias did not involved any serious cultural change for them. The first officers-in-charge of pacification were men of exceptional humanity. The followed policies which provided early precedents for later dealings of the British with the Santals. They gave recognition to the traditional Maler leaders, and promised the preservation of their traditional customs, which requiring only that Maler themselves from a peace-keeping organisation. Under the early British officers the Maler contained in possession of their forest rights in Damin-i-Koh.

After the first years of the pacification, however, the authorities in Calcutta began to call for revenues from the Damin-i-Koh and Raj Mahal Hill areas. Local officials tried to persuade the Maler to alter their patterns of food production, to substitute permanent farming for their slash and burn methods. When the Malers failed to responded to these efforts, relation between the authorities and the Malers became strained. Company officials decided that the area of the Damin-i-Koh should be opened to migrant of more productive habits. The Santal fulfilled this role.

The British authorities encouraged Santals migration into the Damin-i-Koh. However, they did not provide any effective protection for the new settlers against the attack of the Malers who claimed prior rights to the forests of the area. The Malers could not mount any massive resistance to the Santhals, for the peace-keeping corps subsidized by the British was untrained for concreted efforts against other people. Inspite of this, the Malers carried out their usual guerilla tactics over a long period of time against the new Santal agriculturists in the area.

This outcome of the conflict was determined by factors of technology and social organisation. In both the Santals were found to be superior to the Malers. The Santal were not purely agriculturists they were familiar with the forests and could not meet appropriately the guerilla type tactics of the Malers. The capacity of the Santal leadership for maintaining their social organisation while keeping the morale of their people during their physical encounters with the Malers proved more than adequate.

The Santal become the dominant population in the territory leaving the Malers as a minority in the Damin-i-Koh for more than a century. It should be noted that in addition to the fact that early Santal migrants were able to match and defeat the Malers, the massive number of immigrants within a few years resulted in 'no contest' between the two ethnic groups.

In 1887 a British Civil Servant, James Potent was assigned to the development of revenue resources in Damin-i-Koh. In 1833 only some 3,000 Santals resided in less than 50 villages in the area. By 1851 only fourteen years later, the Santals numbering about 83,000 settled in more than 1,400 villages. Fertile valleys were cleared of sub-forests and became highly productive paddy land. The Damin-i-Koh began exporting rice and vegetable oil to Calcutta markets. Most notably according to records of the East India Company, amount of collectable taxes in the Damin-i-Koh increased from rupees 2,000 in 1838 to nearly 44,000 in 1851.

But before the process of assimilation could be completed, the Santal rose in violent rebellion. The rebellion, the 'Hoel' of 1885, is regarded by the Santals as an event of crucial importance to their history. The social scientists can give it no less importance. The rebellion resembles in some respect as 'nativistic movement'. According to the record of the Santal Rebellion, the traditional leadership did not participate eventual outburst of violence. This was effected by visionararies with claims to supernatural powers. Although rebellion did not have all the Characteristics of what Wallace had called 'religious' revitalization.[12] Santals over a wide area were inspired towards 'Sagai' (actual 'oneness') and a determination to regain the status achieved by their settlement in the new land, at whatever personal cost.

Reports of a widespread discontent appeared in 1854. In village and 'Pargana' councils there were frequent discussions of the plight of all Santhals. The three most noted complaints were: (a) the fraudulent manipulation of the moneylenders, who falsified accounts, committed prejury in court actions and corrupt Government clerks and police officers with bribes; (b) the rapacity of tax collectors and landlords collecting taxes; and (c) the cruelty of the police.

Excitement mounted as the dry season passed and food resources dwindled. Suddenly, in a village not far from Barhait a climax was reached. According to the most widely accepted version of events, two brothers, Sida and Kanhu reported that they had received a visitation from the creator god of the Santals, the awesome 'Marang Buru' who had never been known to appear in any form to any man before. The brothers reported that they had been visited by the god for seven days in succession, and that at the last visit Marang Buru had given them a book with black white pages on which to write commands to the Santals to avenge their oppressions. News of he miraculous and repeated visitations spread quickly. Blank white pages began to circulate through the Santal villages, for an wide, symbolically commanding the people to draw up their bills of indictment and to take action against those who had stolen the land which was rightfully theirs. It is a measure of the Santal desparation that the supernatural visitation involved their most awesome, unapproachable and ultimate deity. It also seems significant that 'black white' pages were the particular symbols chosen to be circulated among the traditionally non-literate people. Their one major difficulty in dealing with money lenders and courts was their illiteracy. The people who had been oppressed through the written 'white pages' of the non-Santal world produced their own book of record and determined that the condemnation of their exploiter would be appalled out in details upon its pages.

On June 30th 1855, in the season when normally the cultivators should have been preparing their fields for the coming of the annual monsoons, ten thousand Santals gathered in an encampment just outside the village where the visionary brothers, Sida and Kanhu, were living. As Dutta reports, "the divine order that the Santals should get out of their oppressors' control was announced by the brothers to the crowd, and the Santal declared their determination to do away with the Bengali and up-country mahajans and banyas, to take possession of the country and set up a Government of their own." It is significant that, as Dutta reports, in the midst of this crescendo of furore and clamour, letters were then written by Kirta, Badhoo and Sano Manjhi at Sida's direction addressed to the Government, to the Commissioner, the Collector and Magistrate at Bhagalpur, the Collector and Magistrate at Birbhum, to the Daroghas of Thana Digbee and

Jikeree (Raj Mahal) and to several Zamindars and other; from the Darogahs and Zamindars replies were called for within 15 days.[13] The traditional leaders of the people, the three headmen, at a very brink of the rebellion wrote formal complaints to Government Officers. These documents represent a last attempt to achieve the kind of adjustment and reconciliation the Santal generally manage to achieve in their own judicial processes. The summary commands to the police officers [Darogahs] and land tax collectors (Zamindars) to appear before the Santals indicates that these functionaries required immediate trial and condemnation for their deeds of personal mal-treatment and exploitation.

Almost immediately thereafter violence broke out. A small carvan of money lenders was proceeding for a weekly market when they were met by a large group of excited Santals near the village of Barhait. The Santals in their fury attacked the carts and their occupants leaving five money lenders dead. A police patrol was sent to apprehend the two leaders of the Santal, Sida and Kanhu and bring them to trial for the murder of five moneylenders. The leader of the patrol found himself out numbered and attempted to reason with Santals. When he tried to slip away the crowd went out of control and only two of the 20 policemen survived. These two were able to report the violence to superior officers. Presently some 30,000 Santals armed with axes, hunting spears, bows and arrows were on the march. The rebels were not seeking to destroy the British regime although a few British officials were killed in isolated areas. The prime target were the individuals known to Santals as responsible for their losses and degration, number of moneylenders, many land tax collectors and particular policemen notorious for their rapacity. A succession of episodes marked the next four months, until, after the monsoon season had ended and the cool weather had begun, martial law was declared on November 10, 1855. With fourteen thousand troops armed with modern weapons General Lloyd and Brigadier General Bird threw a cordon around the Santal population. The 'Hool' was suppressed in sixty days at the cost of some 10,000 Santal lives.

Though the British authorities crushed the rebellion with decisive military force, the result of the rebellion favoured the Santals and brought redressal to many of the complaints which had prompted their violence. It brought a significant change in the relationship between the Santals and the economic and political system of British India. It may be said that the precedents set by authorities who had pacified the Mal Paharias a half century earlier were applied to the Santals. Since the Santal population concerned was a much larger, a tax paying and productive one, the British were more thorough in dealing with the Santals than in earlier situation. Mr. Phail reports that "the Santal grievances were so fully redressed that some of the newspapers of the day complained that the Government was encouraging rebellion by granting everything the rebels had asked for. Actually, as Mac Phail declares, a "lesson in Government . . . had been taught not by the Government to the subject people, but by a subject people to its Government", the lesson being that Government cannot ignore the welfare of its people or remain blind to the profound social and cultural dislocations."[14]

Administrative changes were made. The first measure taken was the establishment of a distinct administrative area in which Santal interests were to be guarded. An area of 5,000 sq. miles was carved out of the existing districts of Bhagalpur and Birbhum, and called explicitly the Santal Parganas.

This was declared a 'non-regulation district', meaning that the usual judicial and bureaucratic procedures of British India would not be applicable to the Government of the new district. The administrative centre was moved to the village of Dumka which was located almost in the middle of the Santal population and somewhat isolated from the non-Santal interests, surrounding the area. The Officer placed in charge of the new district, Mr. Ashley Eden, was a man known for his awareness of indigenous needs, and his ability to improvise procedures of administration suitable to a special settings.

The next important measure was the establishment of a new role of the Santal village headman, whatever may have been the excesses of the rebellion, the reputation of the Santal village headman as a responsible leaders, was not tarnished. They were not regarded by authorities as redical extremists, but as individuals capable of maintaining orderly government in their own established villages. The headmanship became the primary office of administration in the district of the Santal Parganas in Bihar. The headman was designated by the Government as the Pradhan of the village. This gave to the traditional headman responsibilities of collecting land rents and taxes, and transmitting them to the Government treasury. It formalised and gave Governmental recognition to the headman's leadership in judicial proceedings whether conducted personally or in concern with the villages councils. It made the headman responsible for law and order in the village; with the duty to report to the police forces in the area any disorder or trespass in the village confines. In these roles we see a new definition of traditional responsibilities, a formalisation and legal recognition of the roles implicit in Santal Society. To preserve the Santal headman in his status it was decreed that in all villages defined as 'Santal Villages', the headman must be a Santal. From the traditional status and administrative role, the Santal village was recognised as the smallest official political unit of Government in the Santal Parganas.

To protect the economic basis of Santal society, special regulations in the Santal Parganas Governed the transfer of land rights. It became illegal for a Santal to transfer ownership of land to a non-Santal. To establish Santal ownership a thoroughgoing revenue settlement was carried out by responsible authorities. Officers toured the villages and in consultation with the village, the headman and their councils, the right of Santals to their land were carefully examined and injustice of the pre-rebellions years were corrected. Most of their land was returned to the original Santal settlers or their heirs. Protection of these rights became one of he responsibilities of the village headman and his village council.

During the period which followed the rebellion and reorganisation, the East India Company was displaced from its control of the Indian Government by the British Parliamentary control, the rights of the Santals in the Santal Parganas were stabilized and became practically the traditional rights of the people.

During the period of British parliamentary control in India, the Santal experienced a number of changes in the environment. But these did not seriously alter the cultural norms and values relating to village organisation. Notable influences towards change included the extension of Christian missions into the Santal Parganas and the development of institutions for secular education in the district. Santals were given opportunities to move out from the village milieu. Some enlisted in the army corps used by the British during the First World War, a good many joined the movement of labour into the tea plantations of Northern India and lesser numbers left into village to work on construction crews for the railway systems. These movements out of the village were usually limited to a few individuals or families. Economically it was not a period of great prosperity.

The control of the British Parliament in India ended with the establishment of Indian independence. For the Santals, perhaps, the most significant event in the years after independence has been their inclusion in the special status of "Scheduled Tribes" under the provisions of the Indian Constitution. This has been possible because the nationalist movement which led to independence early recognised the special difficulties of the people called "aboriginals". The nationalist leaders gave a new name to the "aboriginals", they called them the "Adivasis"—original inhabitants. The nationalist movement made much of the plight of the "Adivasis" and promised redress. The result has been the special legislation for Scheduled Tribes.

SOCIO-ECONOMIC CONDITION—A COMPARATIVE PICTURE

In the democratic system of India, the Santal, like other "adibasis", have rights to the reserved places in the representative bodies and Governmental bureaucracies. They have been given special consideration when funds have been sent to bring health and educational facilities into their villages. Their opportunities for advancement of life as individuals have been protected. But these efforts to improve conditions of life have tended to dissipate the authority of the Santal traditions and substitute outside interests.

As far as the relation of the Santal and non-Santal is concerned it can be said that it is now, mostly confined to economic and political activities. Other forms of social contact are minimized. To the Pandits and the Shah the Santals are a special types of outcaste whose ritual status is highly impure, because they eat all types of meat, drink rice wine and liquor, conduct public dancing is mixed groups, i.e., male and female, practice widow re-marriage, and generally disregard other taboos necessary to Hindu purity. They are consequently, untouchables, contact between the lower class of Hindu community and the Santals take place somewhat more freely. These menials are sometimes employed for their services by the Santals, but social interaction of any type is highly reticent.

Conflict over control of land has polarized the dominant Hindu Shah and the Santals. The Santals do not try to hide recentment and distrust over the Shah and it appears to have one predominant interest in the Santals, their desire to gain possession of whatever Santal land became available. The interest of the Santals in the Hindu way of life is minimal. They seem to enjoy watching the Hindu festivals but remain confined to the role of spectators.

The relations between the Santals and the Bengali speaking weavers are less reticent, but again most interaction is confined to economic and political activities.

The Santals have in fact, developed a strong sense of ethnic identity out of their historical experiences. They regard themselves as special people. Their name for themselves 'hor-hopon' which signifies sons of mankind. Hor-hopon, therefore, carries the implicit meaning 'the true men'. The use of this term indicates a linguistic-cultural community with a self-conscious feeling of identity as a people with distinct ethnic and cultural characteristic closely associated with the 'hor-hopon' is the geographical concept of 'hordism' which signifies Santal country. A Santal villager says, 'Noa hordisom Kana', meaning, "this is Santal country" and in doing so he makes a distinction between areas occupied by Santals and by other people.

It is a matter of perversive anxiety among Santals that so much of the 'hordisam' has fallen into the hands of non-Santals. It troubles them that many Santal villages non-Santal populations have been admitted to permanent residence, but it is more distressing to realise that in some village even the control of the Santal headman has been lost. Where a non-Santal has been appointed, or elected, the village Choudhary (the non-Santal equivalent of Manjhi headman), it is generally felt that the village area has ceased to be a part of 'hordisam' even if the Santals are living in the village. The loss of villages to non-Santals has given a sort of patch-work character to 'hordisam'. Many villages do not refer to the Santal Parganas as 'hordisam' only those areas under Santal headman and Santal village councils are considered as the component of 'Hordisam'. The idea of 'hor-hopen' and 'hordisam' explicitly reveals the nature of the relation between the Santal and non-Santal people which can be concluded to be confined more to the economic and political fields than to the cultural bounds.

JUNGLE AND HILL LIFE OF THE SANTAL

The Santal people differ from the non-Santal in many respects. The Santal people, generally, live in a deep valley or on an indulating plateau or hill slope or precariously perched on a hill top which is, very often, surrounded by a clump of trees. If a Santal village is situated in the midst of a dense forest or scarb jungle, it is difficult to find the way to it. The non-tribal village, on the other hand, is comparatively more easily accessible. It is situated on a plain surface.

The Santal village is smaller than the non-Santal village. The average Santal village comprises forty to eighty house-holds. The settlements of the shifting cultivators is still smaller, but the number of shifting cultivators in the Santal is very small in comparison with the other tribes.

The mainstay of the Santal is agriculture. Rice, Maize, mullets, beans and vegetables are the chief crops produced. But in addition to these, about eighty-two varieties of wild plants, seventy varieties of fruits, seven varieties of resins, thirty-one varieties of mushrooms and seven varieties of jungal millets are gathered at one time or other.[15] Wild foods are collected by Santal women who work together in groups.

In the work of reclaiming land and clearing new jungles, the Santal have a very few equals in India. They live in villages consisting of a long street with a single row dwellings on either side. Each dwelling has a pig-stay, cattle shed on one side of the rectangular or square compound. Inside the principal hut of each dwelling a small space in one cornor called 'Bhitar' is set apart as the abode of ancestral spirits. The huts have no windows. The walls are made of thin sticks plastered with mud, rafters of sal wood and roof of bamboo. It is thatched with Sabai grass which is only found in the forest and sometimes, it is thatched with paddy straw also.

To be closely related with the hills and the forest for a long time, the Santals are very fond of hunting. It is the duty of the young Santals to participate the group hunting. When the Santal hunters go on hunting, their wives perpetually pray for their well-being, in that period. They avoid any kind of decoration. They do not even put vermillion on their fore-head.

The day on which the Santals go on hunting is full of pleasure and enthusiasm. Not only the inhabitants of the village, but of the entire locality assemble at one place and select the spot for hunting. When the spot for hunting is decided, the hunters encircle the entire area. Some of them stand behind the tree and some start to beat drums. The Santals are generally very skilled archers. It is, therefore, very difficult for a wild animal to escape from their arrows.

The Santals, in the past were engaged in collection of forest produce, hunting, fishing and cultivation on hill slopes. Their main trading craft was extraction of oil and manufacture of lime. But at present, most of them are engaged in cultivation.

SANTAL AND PLAIN SETTLEMENT

The Santals are one of the largest Scheduled Tribes of India. They are spread over a wide area in Bihar, Orissa, West Bengal Tripura and Assam. Of the total Santal population of the 49.46 pet cent resident in, Bihar, 37.90 per cent in West Bengal, 12.46 per cent in Orissa, and Tripura occupies the lowest position with 0.06 per cent to its credit. The Santals have distinct areas of concentrations where they have built up a tradition of their own through centuries. These areas are Santal Parganas, Singh-bhoom and Manbhoom districts in Bihar, the district of Mayurbhanj, Saraikela and Kharsean in Orissa and the district of Purlia, Midnapur, Bankura and Birbhum in West Bengal.

Prior to the present settled agriculture on the plain land that is found in the Santals today, their most popular method of growing crops was shifting cultivation. This is quite natural as shifting cultivation makes and stage of transition from hunting and food gathering to settled agriculture. Now, when majority of Santal population are engaged in settled agriculture, there are some Santals whose life depend on shifting cultivation. According to 'Draft Sub-Plan for tribal region of Bihar, 1974-79, the number of families engaged in shifting agriculture only in Dumka Meso area in about 10,000. Inspite of all it is a bare fact that most of the Santals are now settled agriculturists whether as share croppers or as small farmers.

LAND

More than one-half of the total Santal population are found only in Santal Parganas. This region is characterised by an undulating terrain, with isolated peaks and a number of hill streams which swell immediately after a spell of rain, but thereafter, become only a strickle. The district has generally an elevation between 500 to 600 feet including the Rajmahal bills. As regards soil types, red type yellow and light gray catenary soil predominate in Santhal Parganas. The acidic upland soils are reddish while the low land soils are of light to medium texture. Reddish yellow to yellow and grayish yellow, deep catenary soils are found in Santhal Parganas in the area adjoining the coal belt of Hazaribagh and Dhanbad, while yellow to red yellow and black catenary soil occur on Rajmahal trap rocks. The land-use statistics of the Santhal Parganas as shown in Table 3.1.

The tribal areas are characterised by comparatively lower proportion of land area being available for cultivation, on account of a higher proportion being covered by hills and forests and undulating rocky barren terrains. Further, even out of the land classified as cultivable, only a smaller proportion is actually tilled, the area left as cultivable waste, current or other follows, being considerable. The proportion of net sown area to cultivable area in the Santhal Parganas is 54.2 per cent. The proportion of net sown area is less because of the comparative infertility of the cultivable land leading to large areas being left fallow. This is particularly true of the uplands where the soils are acidic and deficient in time. Poor fertility is also the result of heavy soil erosion and in large parts deep rivers formed by the cascading turbulent hill streams are a common sight.

Rainfall

The Santhal Parganas has comparatively better rainfall than other parts of Bihar. The normal rainfall is around 1350 mm. About 85 per cent of the rainfall is received during the period from June to September. The late September rains known as Hathia, are

TABLE 3.1

Land-use of the Santhal Parganas (1970-71)

(Area in lakh acres)

Forest	*Barron land*	*Land put to non-agri-cultural uses*	*Cultivable waste land*	*Miscel-laneous tree crops and groves*	*Permanent pasture and other gra-zing land*	*Current fallow*	*Other fallow land*	*Net area sown*	*Total area*
3.60	2.36	2.79	2.40	0.33	1.56	4.67	3.22	14.19	35.12
10.3%	6.7%	7.9%	6.8%	1.0%	4.4%	13.3%	9.2%	40.4%	100%

Source: Draft Sub-Plan for Tribal Region of Bihar, 1974-77, p. 15.

crucial for the paddy crop, particularly in this area where assured irrigation is not available.

Irrigation

According to the Annual Season and Crop Report, 1970-71, area irrigated by various sources in the Santhal Parganas is as follows:

TABLE 3.2

Area Irrigated by Different Sources in the Santhal Parganas

(in thousand acres)

Canal	*Tanks*	*Tube-wells*	*Other wells*	*Other sources*	*Grand Total*
1	2	3	4	5	6
14.6	82.8	0.5	7.7	22.78	128.3

Source: Draft Sub-Plan for Tribal Region of Bihar, 1974-77, pp. 26-27.

Even if all sources are taken into account, the percentage of net irrigated area to net sown area is 9.02 in the Santhal Parganas.

Land Tenure System

Till the abolition of intermediary interests through the Bihar Land Reforms Act, 1950 by area-wise notifications issued in 1956, the Government collected revenue from the landlords (Zamindars). But large rural areas in two districts were handled as Government Estate and these require special mention. One was the damin area of Santal Parganas comprising ten blocks in which the tribals are in the majority. The other was the Kolhan area of Singhbum district, extending over ten blocks.

The association of village functionaries, either hereditory or elected, with the collection of land rent is peculiar to Santhal Parganas where the Pradhan collects rent, retains a portion of it for his services and makes over the rest to the landlord now the State Government. The office of a Pradhan is elective only in a limited sense; the son of a Pradhan can lay claim to succession, but has to be generally acceptable to the raiyats of the village. If he is not acceptable, then the vacant post is filled by election.

Even since the abolition of Land Reforms Act, 1950 a view

has been canvassed that the Pradhan or the Manki-Munda system has outlived its utility; that these functionaries with partly heritable rights are also like intermediaries and that they ought to be replaced by servants of the State Government, as in the rest of the State. This view however, overlooks the fact that, specially in tribal villages, these traditional functionaries are not merely rent-collectors but have an important place in the village community and are honoured members of the traditional tribal Panchayats or similar bodies. Certain improvements can definitely be effected particularly since the election to the post of a Pradhan. Often in the villages where tribals are not in the majority, has become the occasion for political activity commonly accompanied by bitter rivalry.

Tenancy and Pattern of Holdings

For the Santhals, a separate Act is in force in the district of Santhal Parganas which is known as the Santhal Praganas Tenancy (Supplementary Provisions) Act, 1949. The provisions of this act are more restrictive since no raiyat whether tribal or non-tribal, can effect a transfer of his holding, except where such a right has been conceded by the record of rights and only to the extent of which the right has been conferred. Even where the rights of transfer his land only to another Adivasi raiyat who is resident in the same Tappa or Pargana. Simple mortgages cannot be effected. Usufructuary mortgages not exceeding a period of six years, can be effected only by non-Adivasi Raiyat. Adivasi raiyat do not have the right of effecting over usufructuary mortgages. The provisions of the Act have not so far been amended so as to provide in particular, the facility of effecting simple mortgage in favour of financial institutions.

The distribution of occupational holdings for the Santhal Parganas and for the State, according to the Agriculture Census, is shown in Table 3.3. The smallest category that is less than 0.5 hectare, is being held by a proportionately less number of holders in this district. Even the highest category of 20 hectares and above the percentage of holder is less than the State average. While it is thus shown that the average size of the holdings in the district is larger than that of the State, yet one has to bear in mind that the quality of the land is not the same and the yield is poorer in this district than in other areas of the State.

TABLE 3.3

The Distribution of Occupational Holding in the Santhal Parganas
(Size of holdings in acres and holdings in percentage)

	0.1	1-2.4	2.5-4.9	5.0-12.4	12.5-49.9	50 & above	Unspecified
Santhal Parganas	6.59	30.44	34.08	24.35	3.91	0.04	0.59
Bihar	7.73	28.83	30.60	26.57	6.78	0.12	0.37

Source: Draft Sub-Plan for Tribal Region of Bihar, 1974-90, p. 46.

The first conclusion in the previous paragraph regarding the smaller proportion of the smallest holders is further reinforced by the above figures; the proportion is even less in the case of the Santals. But, on the other hand, large holders among them are also found to be smaller; in other words, even the Santhal Parganas, the large holders appear to be only the non-Santals.

By and large the Santals are cultivators who hold the tenancies under the Government, after the abolition of intermediary interests by the Bihar Land Reforms Act. The position is indicated in the Table 3.4.

TABLE 3.4

Percentage of Distribution of Santal Cultivators According to the Category of Land Possessed

	Owned or held from Government	*Held from private person or institutions for payment*	*Partly held from Government & partly from private persons or Institutions*	*Total*
Santhal Parganas	88.86	1.14	10.00	100.00
Bihar State	85.07	2.24	12.69	100.00

Source: Draft Sub-Plan for Tribal Region of Bihar, 1974-79, p. 46.

Problem of Land Alienation

Inspite of the restrictive provisions in the tenancy laws regarding transfer of raiyati rights Santals have been losing their lands to non-Santals over the decades. We have to distinguish between land taken away from the Santals, under the process of law, as illegal transfers, particularly in the rural areas, generally in favour of the money lenders, who come in possession after giving loans to the Santals and, thereafter, continue in possession on the ground that the loan has not been repaid. As regards alienation, reference has already been made to the provisions now available under the law for restoring illegally alienated land to the Santal owners. It may, however, be mentioned that the magnitude of the problem is not precisely known, as there has been no survey in this regard. It may be mentioned that Tenancy Act in Bihar envisage survey and settlement operations for the preparation of records of rights and these were to be taken up at intervals mainly as measures to prepare a list of holdings which will have a legal presumption of correctness and thus enable the raiyats to establish their claim in the court of law. Revisional survey operations are, therefore, a must if the extent of illegal alienation has to be correctly ascertained.

A Comparative Review of the Settled Santhals

Compared to North Bihar the density of population in South Bihar is low, which is inevitable in an inhospitable region of hills and forests, offering very little fertile land for prosperous cultivation. Yet the per capita net sown area is only slightly higher and because of low availability of irrigation, the gross cultivated area per head increases to a much lesser extent that the State average. The comparative figure shown below:

TABLE 3.5

	Per capita net cultivated area (acres)	*Per capita gross cultivated area (acres)*
North Bihar	0.34	0.46
South Bihar	0.38	0.53
Four Tribal Districts (Ranchi, Palamau, Singhbhum and Santhal Parganas	0.50	0.56
Bihar State	0.37	0.48

The comparatively poor yield from the lands in the tribal region can be seen if we work out the value of agricultural output per acre of gross cultivated area. The figures are Rs. 497.6 for North Bihar, Rs. 417.6 for South Bihar, Rs. 376.7 for the four tribal districts and Rs. 442.8 for the entire State.

On the four tribal districts of the State Santhal Parganas is shown to be among the poorest in the State excluding Palamau. Inspite of it, the infrastructure facilities in this district are poor, as can be seen from the fact that they rank lower than the State average is such indicators as percentage of gross irrigated area to gross sown area, percentage of area sown more than once to net sown area, percentage of villages electrified and length of surfaced road per 1000 Sq. Km.

It is of surprising, therefore, that the largest proportion of Santal population exist below poverty line. The proportion of Santhal Parganas is more than 78 per cent against 56.9 per cent in South Bihar and 77.01 per cent in North Bihar.

Plain Life of Newly Settled Santals

Santals have got unique behaviour regarding their settlement ability. They have partial nomadic character, because they are frequently in search of vacant land either in jungle or in plain. It seems that particularly due to this very character they crossed the river Ganges and settled in plain of eastern belt or North Bihar in the district of present Purnea and Saharsa. Geographical position and revenue administration of these districts of Bihar are important points hence to be mentioned. Saharsa and Purnea districts are situated in the basin of Kosi and Mahananda rivers. The region is unlike the plain having jungle hinterland, rather a lower land having flood havoc. From the land tenure point of view these districts have big landlords. The density of population of this area is comparatively lower. Therefore, semi-nomadic settlement attitude of this tribe inspired them to cross the Ganges and to settle themselves there.

From the economic point of view their movement from the jungle region to plain region was comparatively profitable. They were engaged there as slave croppers or as agriculture labours. By this their standard of living started to improve. But they gradually lost their old way of living and became accustomed of new way of living. But some of their old traits remained intact; for example the tribal way of community living, religious outlook, etc.

Though the newly settled Santals are also guided by their tradition and culture, but with a little bit adjusting attitude. The Santals have generally the habit of drinking whether they are on the hill top or in the jungle or even in the plain land of Purnea and Saharsa. Many other habits of the newly settled Santals of North Eastern Bihar are similar to those that live in the plateau of South Bihar.

The economic behaviours of the newly settled Santals too, does not have any significant change to be noticed. The Santals who have settled in the urban areas as new service holder, very often look to be changed people, but when they are back to their village home they again adopt their traditional way of living.

SANTAL AND OTHER TRIBES

The Scheduled Tribes order issued by the President lists as many as 30 tribal communities as in Bihar. However, the Santals the Oraons, the Munda and the Hos are the most numerous and they together constitute almost four-fifth, i.e. 80 per cent of the total tribal population of the State shown in Tables 3.6 and 3.7.

TABLE 3.6

Population of Santals. Munda, Oraons and Hos in Bihar

Tribes	*1941*	*1961*	*1971*	*1981*
Santals	13,92,744	15,41,345	18,01,304	NA
Munda	5,27,116	6,28,931	8,76,218	NA
Oraons	6,37,296	7,35,025	7,23,166	NA
Hos	3,83,737	4,54,745	5,08,172	
Total tribal population of Bihar State	35,70,274	41,87,840	49,32,767	58,10,867

Source: Statistical Hand book of Tribal Welfare and Development.

The comparative study of the principal tribes of Bihar, i.e., Santal, Munda, Oraon and Ho regarding their population, reveals the following facts:

(a) While the population growth rate in Bihar during 1971-81 was 24.06, in the tribal population the growth rate was only 17.8 per cent.

(b) There was a decreasing trend in the tribal population of Bihar during 1971-81 because while the growth rate of tribal population in Bihar during 1961-71 was 17.79, it was 17.08 during 1971-81. Though the rate of decrease is only 0.71 per cent but it is, of course, a very important phenomenon specially for the social scientists.

TABLE 3.7

Percentage of Growth in Santals, Mundas, Oraons and Hos in Populations

Tribes	*From 1941 to 1961*	*From 1961 to 1971*	*From 1971 to 1981*
Santal	10.69%	16.87%	
Munda	19.32%	39.32%	
Oraon	15.33%	(-) 1.95%	
Ho	18.50%	11.18%	
Total Tribals in Bihar	17.30%	17.79%	17.80%
Percentage of increase in total population in Bihar	19.8%	21. 3%	23.09%

Source: Statistical Hand Book of Tribal Welfare and Development.

(c) Among the four principal tribes of Bihar, the Oraon population shows a decreasing trend. The growth rate of population of other three tribes, i.e., Santal, Munda and Ho is comparatively better than the former one. The growth rate in Munda population occupies the highest place among principal tribes of Bihar. The Santal occupies the second position in growth rate.

It is of course, worth mentioning that more than one-half of the Santals are found in Santhal Parganas district and about a quarter in Hazaribagh and Singhbhum districts put together. Their population is also significant in Dhanbad, Purnea, Monghyr and Bhagalpur. On the other hand, over three-fourth of the Oraons are confined to Ranchi, and Palamau comes next. Oraons are also found in a few blocks in Shahabad and Champaran districts. Nearly three-fourth of the Mundas are also found in Ranchi district on the bank of the balance in Singhbhum district. The Hos on the other hand, are virtually confined to Singhbhum district.

The distinguishing features of these principal tribes of Bihar are manifestation of certain institutions which are not found in the non-tribal people. These are the 'Akhara' or the dancing ground the 'Sasan' or the bone burial ground, the 'Sasan' or the sacred grove and the youths dormitory.

Among the Munda, Santal, Ho and Oraon a large open space situated in the middle of the village or on the outskirt is set apart as the Akhara. The second place of institutional importance is the 'Sasan'. The Sasan or the bone burial ground is important among the Munda and the Hos. The third important feature is the 'boy and girls' dormitory. But now-a-days except in a few villages this institution has disappeared. The last characteristic of these tribes is the secred grove. It consists of two Sal Trees which are the only relics of the primeval forest left uncut in the village. Nobody can fell these trees. It is known by different names in different trees, e.g. 'Sarna' among the Munda, and Oraon, Jaher or Johiruburu among the Ho and Santhal. It is there that the entire village community offers sacrifice to certain deities for its well being on the occasion of different festivals. The Santhal, the Munda, the Oraon and the Ho, these four tribes are comparatively advance in the sense that they have taken to settled cultivation as their mode of life. They are gradually getting the benefits of the employment available in the mineral and industrial undertakings scattered over the plateau region of South Bihar.

AN EMPHERICAL POST OF PRESENT REVIEW

In the recent times a great many changes have occurred in the Santal region of Bihar which have a direct bearing on the break up of the social solidarity in the Santal village, the Santals are not exception to them. These changes are due to multiplicity of factors the influence of each of which it is difficult to separate. We may however, attempt to portray the impact of missionary activities, the role of present day headmen, the working of the Community Development Programme, the new Panchayats and the migration of Santal labour outside their immediate neighbourhood.

The missions run a number of schools, hospitals and dispensaries. In those areas where the oppression of the zamindars was the greatest and rapacity of the money lenders the most cruel, people were quick to accept Christianity. By conversion they gained not only moral courage, but the active assistance of the missionaries in securing justice for themselves. The influence which the European missionaries carried with the Government in British days, gave a further impetus to conversion. The welfare services which the missionaries provided also prepared the people mentally for the final consummation of the missionary aim, i.e., conversion.

The missionaries have contributed to the destruction of the social unity and communal life of the village, "Christianity has too often brought not peace, but a sword dividing further against son and a household against itself."

In social relations, there is an estrangement between the Christians and the non-Christians. Their dress, standard of living, method of greeting and the other behaviour patterns are different. A non-Christian cannot accept food at the hands of a convert. Thus a village having both non-Christians and converts is divided into two factions standing not shoulder to shoulder but face to face. When the village is faced with any problem or presented with a programme for development there are always two divergent points of view. In a village consisting of both these groups, no decisions can be made or social actions to follow them up at the village level. The convert regard themselves as being outside the pale of the village headman's authority and consider the missionary as their sole guide not only in the realm of religion, but in that of secular activities as well.

In the recent years a great deal of dissatisfaction has been noticed against the traditional tribal officers in villages. This is specially the case with headman. They come into close contact with petty Government officers, learn urban ways and try to live up to their new experience. They have learnt all the chicanery of alien touts and litigants. There have been many cases of embazzlement, bribery and corruption. They suppress crimes for a consideration. "Local disputes or family dissension are made the subject of vindictive reprisals or private gain and private grudges are satisfied by deliverately manipulating evidence."[16] Consequently, many of the village headmen and elders are no longer dependent for their position on the goodwill of their villagers. They cater to the caprice of Government officers who must be kept in good humour if the village officers are to retain their places. In imitation of other Government servants and conscious of their social and political status, they have adopted a standard of living for beyond their legitimate means."

In the Community Development areas, the approach to the villagers is initially made through the traditional leader, as the headman. These leaders by virtue of the office they hold and by temperament are conservative and tradition-bound. They look askance at the non-development taking place in and around their villages. In such cases the Community Development authorities pick up some young men with progressive ideas and encourage and train them at the village leaders training camp. It is these youngmen who are expected to take up the functional leadership in the village in all developmental activities e.g., promotion of innovations in agriculture, adoption of new ideas in public health and sanitation, organisation of co-operative etc. When these people go to the Block head-quarters, they are more cordially received than the traditional headman. Thus, the growth of a new development leadership has undermined the influence of the traditional headman. People in the village find former influential with the officials and in consequence flock round the new leaders. Not only in development matter but in other matters too, the education and training which the functional leaders acquire enables them to have their say. Thus, the leadership is divided and weakened. The traditional leaders with wounded prestige and denuded respect are always on the look out for finding fault with the ways of the new leaders and their opportunity comes when a particular project or experiment fails for one reason or the other or the Government introduces some measures which they do not like.

Inspite of all, the community development has done a lot to enlarge the people's horizon. By holding village leader's training camp, encouraging sports and other cultural competitions in different villages and by sending Santals on sight-seeing-*cum*-educational tours it has created an urge among people to move about and know more things. This has an effect on the social solidarity of the village as people have to make a choice between tradition and progress. Everything that is old is sought to be discarded for the new. The respect shown to the traditional leaders and the regard for the village panchayat have greatly diminished.

The number of schools in tribal villages of the Santals have been growing and people's interest in educating their children has been aroused. The kind of education, however, that they receive in these schools alienates them from their home and culture. Their teachers are, by and large, non-tribals who look down upon tribal ways and decry tribal culture. Brought up in this atmosphere, the tribal child gradually ceases to listen to his parents. He feels encouraged to give up village life and seek his fortune in some nearby town. He prefers to be a peon in an office rather to remain an agriculturist on his own fields. In the circumstances it is but natural for him to give up his own ways and adopt those of his teachers who are scarcely the best representatives of non-tribal culture.

> The effect of Christian education in mission schools is far worse. The tribal begins to emulate the European missionaries in dress and talk and draws inspiration not from India's past but from European culture. Coming back to his village he begins to look down upon non-Christians at backward and ignorant folk.

In the field of agriculture, the use of chemical fertilizers like ammonium sulphate and super phosphate has resulted in people's increasing dependence on outside supply. If the supply is not available in time, the yield suffers. The same is the case with improved seeds. Formerly tribal people depended upon their own resources in agricultural operations. This increasing dependence on supplies makes the people feel that their world has expanded and that they are parts of the bigger socio-economic system of the region.

It is an irony that community development in some villages has led to the growth of factions and bed blood between the tribals and non-tribals and in general resulted in a decline of the community spirit. This has been brought about by a number of factors. In most of the blocks the workers were non-tribals. They were new to tribal life, ways and thought. They did not understand the tribal language. They were shunned by the tribals who suspected them of some evil design. These workers had to accomplish a number of targets in the different programmes within a limited time. Hence the influential non-tribals living in a tribal village took advantage of the different schemes. They ingratiated themselves into the favour of officers with the result that the erstwhile exploiters of the tribal became the greatest beneficiaries of those programmes. They used their prosperity and increased opportunities to tighten their hold on ignorant tribal people who began to look upon Block authorities as friends and patrons of the exploiters. The extension personnel became suspects in their eyes. The general complaint was that the money meant for the tribal was being spent lavishly on the non-tribals.

In the Santal belt the non-Santals were the only solvent people as they had some surplus. For petty construction works they became contractors and made money much to the charge in of the tribals. These petty contractors inevitably sprang up from the rank of the ex-landlords. Thus in such village two factions, one comprising the tribals and the other the non-tribals come into being. This animosity was reflected in weakening authority of village panchayat, in social affairs.

One of the institutions that foster communal consciousness in the village is the Panchayat. Recent developments in this regard are continuous tale of disruption and decay. In the traditional Panchayat there is no provision for election of members. Formerly people had respect for age and tradition. Now this has come to be questioned. Education and knowledge of the world outside through travel and better passports to influence the membership of the Panchayat. Educated young men and women have shown their impatience with this institution; more so, if there is a miscarriage of justice. Tribal of a case at the village level has the advantage of tribunal in which everyone is acquainted with full details of it. But the risk of personal prejudices and family dissensions coming into the picture and affecting verdict is always there. Hence a tendency is growing to take a case, as soon as it occurs, to the police and the courts. This tendency has been fostred by the police who are none too happy at the case being patched up at the village level or in the statutory panchayat.

With the establishment of statutory Panchayats in the tribal areas, there is a conflict of jurisdiction between the traditional and the new Panchayats. The same kind of cases may be taken at both these bodies as also to the police and courts of law. Strictly social offences may only be dealt with by the informal village Panchayat.

In the new Panchayats the Mukhia is elected by adult franchise and he nominates the members of his executive committee and of the Gram Katchery. The introduction of election in the Panchayat has led to the growth of factions and parties in the village. The tribals uptill now have not been able to understand the technique or the utility of such elections. The result is that in the majority of new Panchayats in the tribal areas, the Mukhias are non-tribals, generally the ex-landlords. The Mukhias as members of the Block Development Committee sanction development schemes and it is no wonder that they appropriate most of the schemes themselves leaving the poor tribals high and dry.

With weakening of the Panchayat organization, traditional social sanctions have been losing weight. The growth of individual land ownership, as against communal control, the development of the means of communication in the region and the opening up of new avenues of employment in distant plantations, mines and factories have been changing the environment of the Santal areas.

It is also interesting to note that forced by circumstances a number of Santal men and women go out to seek employment in road construction, tea gardens, mines and factories. Some of this migration is seasonal, i.e., for months only when there is no agricultural work at home, some may be periodical and some permanent. Most people return just before the outset of the rains. Only such people migrate for long periods who do not have enough land in the village for their sustenance. The scope for employment outside the village has brought the dissenters, the adventures and the needy out of their mob rings and they no longer look to the village authorities for assistance or even for the redressal of their woes and hardships. Labour for the tea gardens is recruited on long-term contracts, the minimum being three years. An organisation called the Tea District Labour Association recruits labour and sends them on to Assam. The tea gardens in Assam are worked chiefly by tribals from Bihar and at present six hundred thousand tribal labourers are working there. The number of the Santal labour has not yet been specified, but it must be thought to be considerable. Some of these labourers return after long intervals, other get settled there, marry and raise family. If both husbands and wife go there they get ready employment. Lovers whose marriage cannot be sanctioned by society at home always flee to Assam or some other towns. Industrial workers returning from the tea gardens, jute mills, mines or factories are received by their co-villagers with an approbation which is largely due to the wealth they bring back and their knowledge of the outside world.

Industrialisation of tribal areas is proceeding at a slow pace. It has become a source of easy employment for the tribals. But it has increased fresh needs too. To satisfy these needs and means is handy. Crime is on the increase in these areas any village elders are powerless to deal with the situation. To escape punishment one has only to join a labour camp. The enormity of the crime is lost in the atmosphere of anonymity in the town. But all these instances are not common because they have not touched the many. They are still confined to the few.

It now remains to give a picture of the present position of the Santal people living in Bihar. The average Santal village situated in Bihar still functions as a social and ritual unit. The structure and organisation remain at least outwardly more or less unchanged. The headman (Manjhi) and the Panchayat are still the recognised authorities but this recognition is likely to mislead us for it is a recognition only for the externals. Prestige and power have now shifted from the hereditory Santal elders to those who have acquired rudimentary education and are in control of the economic resources. They are now the leaders of the Santal people, though many of them are detribalized in spirit. The standard of living of the average Santal home has not appreciably increased though individual families have gone out and come back with money. Customary needs and requirements of the families is based more on mutuality than on communal considerations. The old village economy which catered to the needs of destitute families by subscribing to the village fund maintained by the headman, usually in kind, for meeting the expense of marriage and social ceremonies of those who could not provide the means, has ceased to exist.

The history of the Santal people residing in Bihar has been one of disintegration. The ties uniting the people have weakened. Communal life is not much in evidence. Men have tended more and more to work separately and own separately. As common work has decreased, the common sentiment that held the people together has weakened. The authority of the old over the young has slackened considerably. People have begun to move away from the community. Thus, the Santal village is commonly changing from a relatively integrated and self-sufficient rural community to one dependent cosmopolitan society.

NOTES AND REFERENCES

1. District Gazetteer of Santhal Pargana, 1938, p. 120.
2. *Ibid.*, p. 96.
3. Bengal District Gazetters, Santhal Pargana, 1910, p. 96.
4. *Ibid.*, pp. 96-97
5. Bengal District Gazetters, Santhal Pargana, pp. 97-98.
6. Rishy, H.H., "The People of India", p. 441.
7. Shastri, Mangaidev, "Tulnatmak Bhasha Shastra", p. 290.
8. Gazetteers of the Santhal Pargana, p. 120.
9. *Ibid.*
10. Hihadi Majenom Heẻto, Pipadima Gahilo. Madho Singh no Pipadali ja jo, Jep Chaya Champa Guda. Umda Shankar Santhal Sanskar Ki Ruprekha, p. 141.
11. Datta, Mazumdar, "The Santhal: A Study in Cultural Change", p. 23.
12. Nicolas, R.W., "Rules, Resources and Political Activity", p. 68.
13. Dutta, Kalikinkar, "The Santhal Insurrection of 1855-57", pp. 15-16.
14. Mac Phail, J.M., "The Story of the Santal," p. 63.
15. Datta, Majumdar N., "The Santal: A study in Cultural Change,' p. 37.
16. Majumdar, D.N., 'Affairs of a Tribe', p. 287.

Voluntary Agencies for Development of Scheduled Castes and Scheduled Tribes—Their Role and Function

The Scheduled Tribes are at the lowest strata of the Indian Society. For generations, most of these communities were neglected by the rest of the nation. The British Government isolated the Scheduled Tribes from the rest of the nation. The Scheduled Tribes population in the country has risen to 5.38 crore as per 1981 census. It can be reasonably assumed that over 85 per cent of the total Scheduled Tribe families belong to the category below the poverty-line.[1] They are likely to cover a population of over 4.25 crore.

The tribals, who have remained somewhat aloof, have to be integrated in the mainstream of national life. Thus, to break the vicious circle and isolation, the crying need for these communities is development. In fact, how there seems to be a genuine desire in the country to atone for the mistakes of the past. The general population has now realised what President Kennedy observed, "if a Government cannot help the many who are poor, it cannot save the few who are rich."

It goes without saying that it is too difficult a task for Government agencies to rectify the mistakes of the past centuries and to develop them at par with other sections of the Indian society. For development of these vulnerable sections we need both the society and the state.

ROLE OF VOLUNTARY AGENCIES

Democracy allows scope for the individual to undertake action in a national society, independent of the state. The "Private action, that is to say, action not under direction of any authority wielding power of the state, therefore, is called voluntary action."[2]

On Voluntary action for public purposes, Lord Beveridge has observed as follows: "A Voluntary Organisation, properly speaking, is an organisation which, whether its workers are paid or unpaid, is initiated and governed by its own members without external control."[3]

Definitions given by Mary Morris and Modeline Roof are also similar. Modeline Roof emphasises in addition that these Voluntary Organisations should depend, in part at least, upon funding support from Voluntary sources. On motivation for Voluntary work, Mary Morris observes: "To lead a full life, most people need more than they can find in their work or home. They need to live as members of groups doing things for themselves and their fellow members or for the benefit of others outside the group. The urge to act in groups is fundamental to man".[4]

Thus, voluntary action is a form of organising activities, supporting, strengthening and helping to develop work to meet all types of legitimate needs of individuals and groups in a society.

Voluntary agencies are supposed to be potentially superior to official agencies in three respects: (1) their workers can be more sincerely devoted to the task of reducing the suffering of the poor than Government staff; (2) they can have a better rapport with the rural poor than Government employees; and (3) Since they are not bound by rigid bureaucratic rules and procedures, they can operate with greater flexibility, they can read just their activities quickly and continuously as they learn from experience.[5]

We can add two more points: (1) Voluntary agencies efforts are more economical than the Government departments; and

(2) they can motivate more public participation in development efforts than the Government departments.

VOLUNTARY AGENCIES AND TRIBAL DEVELOPMENT BEFORE INDEPENDENCE

Voluntary action has a long tradition in India. The great forests of India have, for thousands of years, attracted men who desired to retire from the world and devote themselves to spiritual thinking. They were, we are told, kind and gentle to the animals and we may be sure that they were equally kind and gentle to the ancestors of the tribal people and today amongst whom they lived. In fact, when societies of the world were riven with tribes and groups, India had her Manu, Yagnavalkya, Kautilya and Vyas. Their approach to social problems was undoubtedly different. They through of social security on a decentralised basis. The time, however, was not yet ripe for an organised system of education and health services.[6]

Coming to the British period, we find that they isolated the Scheduled Tribes to keep them away from the national movement. Development of the Scheduled Tribes, to enable them to take advantage of the technological order of the modern civilisation, was never a matter of concern for the colonial administration. During that time it was the exclusive burden of the non-official agencies to look after the welfare of the economically, socially and politically backward tribal communities. Among the tribal communities, mention may be made of the humanitarian missionaries of various denominations. The missionaries were the pioneers in education. They opened the first hospital in the tribal areas. Some of them set a shining example by their care of lepers. Their devotion and self-sacrifice in the remotest hills and forests are cited even today as examples of ideal social workers. When we study regarding the formation of a voluntry agency in pre- and post-independence period in India, we find a great difference between former and the latter situations. In the pre-independence period a voluntary agency was almost completely dedicated to its aim and object with enthusiasm and trust in its principle.

In present situation, the formation of a voluntary agency circumscribes so many other elements excluding its aim and object. It does not only concern that after formation of an institution, it starts functioning, rather it requires registration and recognition, is indeed, a long process which takes nearly a year.

On the basis of registration a working committee of the association is formed and a secretariate is established. It has yet to decide the area of operation not according to its aim and object "lone, but in accordance with the availability of fund too.

An area of operation is primarily concerned with geographical and demographic area. A voluntary agency relating to tribal development has its area of operation either inside the jungle or on the edge of jungle and hilly track which is often inaccessible from the point of view of communication and transportation.

The nature of the people for whom they want to work is far from modernity and they have their own way of living. They are either settled or nomadic in nature. There may be either patriarchal or materiarchal type of society. Under such adverse situation they have to prepare their plan according to their aim and object and translate it into action. Thus, the difficulties that arise in the way a voluntary agency is functioning for tribal welfare can be enumerated as follows:

(i) Difficulty in getting devoted workers,
(ii) Scarcity of fund,
(iii) Problem of food, shelter and co-operation from the people for whom they intend to work,
(iv) Lack of Public contribution.

It can therefore, be concluded here that no voluntary agency can be successful in implementing its scheme without Government aid in present circumstances.

The field of getting financial aid from the Government is also not easily accessible. A voluntary agency desirous for financial aid from the Government has to apply before the concerned department according to its nature of work through proper channel with the scheme of expenditure for the financial year in which it is applied. The application has to pass through bureaucratic channel for sanction or rejection of the scheme. It is significant to mention here that procedure of the Central Government in this regard is more liberal, and work-oriented than that of the State Government. Central Government dealing in this regard is direct with the agencies concerned while that of the State

Government is both direct and indirect. To be more clear direct dealing means a voluntary agency is directly related with the Government concerned in all respect including financial aspect. Indirect dealing signifies here that the Government deals with a voluntary agency either through an autonomous or semi-autonomous body in all respects including financial aspect.

But, whatever the route may be, it is, indeed, very difficult to get financial aid either from the Government or through an autonomous body, because in any case, it has to struggle with 'red tapism' as well as many other obstructions. The agency must be careful always and every where otherwise, all its endeavours in this regard can go in vain. Moreover in any case if an agency is successful in getting allocation, it has again to face the treasury and Accountant General's office.

The story does not end here. A voluntary agency which requires Government aid has to submit an audit certificate from a Chartered Accountant alongwith its application and after getting the first instalment it has to report again to the authority of the concerned department with an audit report. Thus a particular scheme of an agency is tested several times in bureaucratic acid. These acid tests kills the normal courage of an agency and increases establishment cost. Finally, the proper function of the agency is hampered and the target aim is left un-finished.

It is almost explicit from the above mentioned facts that the procedure of getting granting Financial aid to a voluntary agency is very difficult, rather very complex. It can, therefore, be suggested that this zigzag path of granting aid to an agency should be made linear. Moreover, the subject of test should be the area and target of the particular scheme. It would be better to test the fruit than to examine the root.

Undoubtedly, the missionaries led the way in certain matters which all workers, officials and non-officials, would do well to follow. In many cases, by their translations of the Bible, they first gave form to the tribal dialects, by the mastery of which they gained much influence on them. Secondly, once they went to a place they usually stayed there for a very long time and some of them actually took vows never to return to their own land. Thirdly, they were always accessible and friendly. They were among the first to inspire the tribal people with the idea of progress and to awaken them to a sense of their rights.[7]

Historically speaking, the American missionaries started schools in Naga villages as early as 1830. They also taught villagers the technique of cultivating tea. Coming to Chotanagpur (Bihar), we find that the advent of Christianity dates back to 1845 when four Lutheren missionaries sent by one father J.E. Gossner of Berlin reached Ranchi. Between 1895 and 1914 the Lutheren Church expanded considerably and alongwith the conversion work, they opened High Schools for both the boys and girls. Dispensaries were also opened at Ranchi, which rendered great service to the Christian as well as the non-Christian public.[8]

The Roman Catholic Missionaries are comparatively latecomers to Ranchi and the first organised mass conversion began with the advent of Fr. Constant LIevens in 1885. In the beginning, Christian Missionaries confined their activities to purely evengelical work but they got little success. It was, therefore, realised later that the only way to attract the tribals was to defend their interests, specially regarding their rights of land tenure and land services. Mass conversion by the Roman Catholic Missionaries began with the advent of Fr. Constant LIevens in 1885. In the beginning, Christian Missionaries confined their activities to purely evangelical work but they got little success. It was, therefore, realised later that the only way to attract the tribals was to defend their interests, specially regarding their rights of land tenure and land services. This news of their help in temporal affairs spread among the poor natives, who began coming to them in large numbers for consultation and for redressal of their grievances. After the missionaries took a few cases at Ranchi and won them, they established their reputation. S.C. Roy has rightly pointed out that in addition to helping the tribal peasants against the land grabbing devices of non-tribal landlords, the Christian missionaries also provided them shield against the exploitation by the money lenders.[9] The initial credit goes to a prominent Catholic Missionary, Father Hoffman, for taking concrete steps to establish Chotanagpur Catholic Mission Co-operative Society in 1909. It had Central Co-operative Bank at Ranchi but it converted the whole of Chotanagpur into several circles in different mission stations which were again sub-divided into several units as working centres.

The Christian missionaries also took active interest in spreading education among the tribals and improving their health and living conditions. In the tribal belts of Orissa, Madhya Pradesh, Andhra Pradesh and other parts of India also, they carried on humanitarian activities on a considerable scale.

When the freedom struggle launched by the national leaders, became stronger, they realised their concern for involving the tribals in their efforts in order to integrate them in the mainstream of the national life.

Under the impact of the Gandhian age a very prominent member of the Servants of India Society, late Thakkar Bapa laid the foundation of another service agency. Like other pioneering projects, this also had a small beginning. He established in 1921, an Ashram at Mirakhedi in Panchmahal District and the Bhil Seva Mandal at Dohad in Gujarat then a part of the old Bombay Presidency. By single minded devotion and hard work, he established 21 institutions in various parts of the country, three each in Andhra and what is now the Madhya Pradesh, two each in Assam, Bihar, Gujarat, Maharashtra, Orissa and Uttar Pradesh, and one each in Kerala, Madras and Rajasthan. There was a magic in his personality. He could create workers, attract workers and hold on to the workers which is the secret of retaining the workers. Shri Dhebar rightly opined that the history of the quarter of a century of dogged endeavour on the part of this singularly quiet and dedicated yet principled personality is a romance of social work in India.[10]

Activities of Thakkar Bapa and his band, prior to Independence, were mostly concentrated in the field of education and in some places in the field of public health. A noteworthy beginning was also made in the field of co-operation in Bombay Presidency.

The first fruitful effort for voluntary action was made in the tribal belt of Bihar with the establishment of a service centre named Seva Kendra in the year 1940. The immediate incentive for improving the socio-economic conditions of the tribes of Chotanagpur is linked with the holding of the All India Congress at Ramgarh, 28 miles from Ranchi in 1939. The important national leaders like Mahatma Gandhi, Dr. Rajendra Prasad, Pandit Jawahar Lal Nehru, Sardar Ballabhbhai Patel and many others, who met in the tribal setting, were deeply impressed to undertake the cause of development of the primitive and backward communities not only of Bihar but also of the whole country. As a part of the programme of freedom fight, it was emphasised to take up the cause of socio-economic development of tribals. The work was immediately started in Chotanagpur by Dr. Rajendra Prasad and his young collaborator Sri Narayanjee. In the thick tribal belt at Gumla at a distance of 40 miles south-west of Ranchi, they started a centre named Seva Kendra. Originally, they mobilised persons to take lessons in literacy in the night and to work in the Khadi Production Centre. In order to run these two programmes, financial help was made available from the savings of the Reception Committee of Ramgarh Congress."

In Madhya Pradesh, the Banabasi Seva Mandal was registered in 1945-46. At present, its head office, situated at Maharajpur in the Mandla District and from the very inception it has laid a great emphasis on the spread of education among the tribals. In addition to the educational programmes, the organisation was managing one agricultural farm, three co-operative societies, one mobile dispensary, one Gram Ikai Kendra, one Lok Karya Kshetra, and one Panchayati Raj Prashikshan Kendra.

Voluntary action, thus, in the beginning was motivated by religious consideration. People used to serve fellowmen in order to please God and acquire *punya*. Voluntary action also took place outside the religious channels, especially during calamities like floods and famines. This system of mitigating problem of indigency by the particular rooms of mutuality of obligations (as manifested through individual philanthropy and religious charity) had been continuing in India right through the 18th century. The growth of residential institutions, as instruments of organised and sustained care, is a 19th century phenomenon in the field of voluntary action in India. Likewise, development of the realistic humanistic tradition in this field is attributed to the early decades of the present century. Organisations like Nai Talim Sangh and Leper Society were later manifestations of this trend.[12]

POLICY ON VOLUNTARY ACTION IN POST-INDEPENDENCE PERIOD

It was only after 1947 that voluntary organisations had anything to do with the Government. The Government, on its part, not only started operating some programmes of social welfare directly but also started a programme of financial assistance to voluntary agencies. In the First Five Year Plan, a provision of Rs. four crore was made for assistance to voluntary organisations as these were found to be capable of "dealing with social problems for which the State cannot provide in sufficient measures" (First Five Year Plan).[13]

In 1953, the Central Social Welfare Board was created with an allocation of 40 million rupees for grants-in-aid to voluntary organisations. This was a pioneering institutional arrangement for mobilising voluntary effort by the Government. In 1954, Welfare Advisory Boards were created in States, With this, the concept of mobilising voluntary effort was decentralised and further decentralisation took place in the community development and panchayati raj institutions.[14]

Even before the Government had come into the picture, the Andhra Mahila Sabha, first in Madras and later in Hyderabad, demonstrated the immense potentialities for mobilising voluntary effort through the zeal, devotion and sincerity of thousands of workers who were not at all career minded but dedicated to service.[15]

In the Third Five Year Plan, importance of the role of voluntary agencies for the successful implementation of our plans was reiterated as follows:

> "For a developing country which cherishes its democratic value, the people's part in the attainment of these objectives is of supreme importance. The peaceful struggle for freedom and tradition of constructive work associated with it had marked out for the people a decisive role in the tasks of planned development indicated 10 years ago. It is evident, however, that the possibilities of full involvement of the people in the process of change and growth are not being realised to a sufficient degree".[16]

Discussing people's participation on an ideological level, the plan document found it necessary to give it a concrete shape and observed:

> "In the activities in which official agencies are engaged, there is a large sphere in which the cooperation of the people can

be sought and secured to achieve a degree of success which would otherwise not be possible. These tasks should be identified, precisely and the obligations and responsibilities of the people in relation thereto made known clearly. The concept of public cooperation is related in its wider aspect to the much larger sphere of voluntary action in which the initiative and organisational responsibility rest completely with the people and their leaders. So vast are the unsatisfied needs of the people that all the investments in the public and private sectors together can, at this stage, only make a limited provision for them."[17]

Thus, Government, in the first two decades after Independence, adopted policy of working with voluntary organisations for promoting welfare of the people.

The Government also initiated the services provided by voluntary agencies so that the programmes undertaken by the Government should be effectively supplemented. The grants-in-aid programmes were evolved for providing certain measure of stability to voluntary organisations for maintaining certain functional level of organisational and financial efficiency. It is, therefore, not at all amazing that voluntary organisations have, over the years, expanded in terms of absolute number as well as the number of services covered by them, of course, with the financial assistance provided by the Government. This made the situation somewhat complex. While in some fields certain services are being rendered by official agencies, in some other fields the same services are rendered by voluntary organisations. Even in the same field, both official and non-official agencies have been found to be working. This raised the problems of uniform financial reporting and accounting by voluntary organisations, and creation of a central intelligence service to keep track of funds received and spent by them. The other problem was regarding coordination of work done by voluntary agencies and the work done by the Government and the local authorities. Related closely to the latter is the need for coordination amongst the voluntary organisation themselves.

Keeping these problems in view, Renuka Ray Study Team on Social Welfare and Welfare of Backward classes recommended in 1959 that coordination councils should be set up at the district, state and national level. About a decade later, in the year 1967, another study team wondered as to where the voluntary organisations stood and what was their role in relation to the State (or the Government) ? An attempt was also made to trace the ideological or conceptual basis of Government funding of voluntary organisations, failing which, it was observed that the prevailing situation does not give any clear-cut picture "whether the State wants these (voluntary agencies to act as an assistant or helper to the Government in its plan efforts or as a catalyst to bring about changes in society by strengthening voluntary action".[18]

Taking a broad review of the efforts during the earlier plan periods, the Sixth Plan observed:

> "During the last three decades social welfare services have grown both in volume and in ranges and the outlays have also increased. . . . The administrative machinery has also expanded and there is better awareness of the developmental concept of social welfare. . . . A large number of voluntary organisations are now being assisted to undertake social welfare programmes in different parts of the country. Inspite of these achievements, deficiencies in the programmes, planning and implementation need to be remedied in order that effectiveness of social welfare schemes can be enhanced. There has been a tendency to depend on schematic patterns in the implementation of the schemes by Government or voluntary organisations leaving little room for flexibility or ability to respond to the requirements and variations in local situations."[19]

A study has been made about the unevenness of the growth of voluntary organisations in different parts of the country. The study has come to the conclusion that: (1) insofar as the grants-in-aid programmes are concerned, the Central funds have flowed more to the areas already having strong administrative machinery and infrastructure for utilisation of funds and the remote and backward areas have been left out more or less untouched; (2) another lacuna that has been identified is the non-materialisation of the linkage of social welfare programmes with economic programmes. Many economic development projects have been launched, particularly in rural areas, without proper consideration of the social impact or the social service, and needs of women and children; and (3) monitoring of programme performance of even important schemes continues to be in terms of financial achievements rather than physical performance related to the objectives of these schemes.

VOLUNTARY ACTION FOR DEVELOPMENT OF ST IN POST-INDEPENDENCE PERIOD

After Independence, several such organisations have been formed in the tribal areas of different states which are working for the tribal development with the financial assistance of the Government and public donations.

Among these organisations, the most important is Bhartiya Adimjati Sevak Sangh which was set up in 1948 on the initiative of Thakar Bapa and was registered in 1949. Its objectives were:

> "The development of the tribal communities of India, socially, economically, culturally and educationally, with a view to enable them to take their legitimate place in national life of the country as equal citizens."[20]

Dhebar report has rightly opined that it has played no small part in helping Government shape its tribal welfare policy at the stage of preparation of the Constitution and thereafter the plans of development. Dhebar report mentions that apex institution had behind it, as affiliated or recognised institutions, 62 bodies; 10 in Maharashtra; 9 in Madhya Pradesh; 6 each in Andhra Pradesh, Bihar, Orissa; 5 in Assam, 4 each in Gujarat and Madras; 3 in Kerala; 2 each in Rajasthan and Uttar Pradesh; and one each in Mysore, West Bengal and Himachal Pradesh; 2 are directly run by it—one in Assam and one in Manipur.[21]

Work done by various Christian Missions has already been discussed. The Ramakrishna Missions are also doing commendable work, which we intend to discuss later on. The Central Social Welfare Board had also done good work in the Community Development Blocks in the fiftees.

Other important non-official agencies, covering tribal welfare in their programmes, area: (1) The Servants of India Society, (2) Sarv Seva Sangh, (3) Gandhi Smarak Nidhi, (4) Kasturba

Smarak Nidhi, (5) The Tata Institute of Social Sciences, Bombay, (6) The Indian Council of Child Welfare, Chhindwara, and (7) Sharatiya Lok Kala Mandir, Udaipur.

The non-official agencies, including the missionary societies concentrated on education, provision of medical facilities, and, in western India, on Forest Labourers' Cooperative Societies till sixties.

Various voluntary agencies in recent years are playing a significant role in advancing the social and economic progress of Scheduled Castes and Scheduled Tribes and other Backward Classes. Some of these agencies are working on all-India basis with grants from the Central Government while a few others, whose activities are confined to one or two states, are assisted by the respective State Governments. Table 4.1 indicates the amount given by the Government of India to the various non-official agencies working for the welfare of the Scheduled Castes, Scheduled Tribes and other Backward Classes during the year 1977-78; 1978-79; 1979-80 and 1980-81.

During 1978-79, the Harijan Sevak Sangh took up the scheme of 'Intensive Area Work' for removal of untouchability in 31 blocks selected in Andhra Pradesh, Bihar, Gujarat, Haryana, Himachal Pradesh, Karnataka, Kerala, Maharashtra, Madhya Pradesh, Orissa, Punjab, Rajasthan, Tamil Nadu and Uttar Pradesh. Fifty villages in each Block were taken up. The 'Intensive Area Scheme' has been chalked out for conducting programme of removal of untouchability within a specified area a definite time-frame. Plans for this purpose are drawn up on the basis of prior surveys conducted from time to time.

Workers of the Sangh have surveyed more than 15,000 villages and gathered information regarding rampant social disabilities of various types, population of Harijan and Landless families and the number of their school-going children, etc. For removal of untouchability, Sangh launched intensive programme, including propaganda through its Pracharaks, publication of literature, film shows, arranging of Padyatras by its workers, holding of meetings and goodwill conferences, etc., which are generally addressed by religious leaders, teachers and intellectuals. At such gatherings, various aspects of the problems of Scheduled Castes were discussed and brought to the notice of the Government for redress. According to the 27th Report of the

TABLE 4.1

Grants Given by Government of India to Some of the Non-official Voluntary Agencies

Sl. No.	Name of Organisation	*Grants-in-aid released during the year (Amount in lakh)*			
		1977-78	*1978-79*	*1979-80*	*1980-81*
	For Scheduled Tribes				
1.	Bhartiya Adimjati Sevak Sangh, New Delhi	2.81	7.36	9.99	8.74
2.	Andhra Rashtra Adimjati Sevak Sangh Nellore, Andhra Pradesh	0.67	0.43	0.50	—
3.	Ramakrishna Mission Ashram, Ranchi	1.69	1.97	1.79	2.78
4.	Ramakrishna Mission Ashram, Cherrapunji	10.16	9.73	4.08	9.33
5.	Ramakrishna Mission, Shillong	0.83	1.57	0.94	3.47
6.	Shri Ramakrishna Advaita Ashram Kalady (Kerala)	0.86	1.11	1.36	1.13
7.	Ramakrishna Mission Sevashram, Silchar	0.99	1.00	N.A.	—
8.	Nagaland Gandhi Ashram, Mokochung	0.30	0.49	0.41	1.33
9.	Sri Ramakrishna Society, Dimapur	0.25	0.25	0.31	2.27
10.	Ashok Ashram, Kalsi (Dehradun)	1.50	1.92	2.71	2.77
11.	Banasthali Vidyapith, Rajasthan	—	2.00	—	—
12.	Nilgiris Adivasi Welfare Association, Nilgiris (Tamil Nadu)	—	0.37	1.25	1.33
13.	Sri Girivanvasi Pragati Mandal, New Delhi	—	2.50	—	—
14.	Sri Ramakrishna Seva Kendra, Calcutta	0.07	0.22	—	—
15.	Akhil Bhartiya Dayanand Sevashram Sangh, New Delhi	1.24	1.58	—	—

16.	Ramakrishna Mission, Nuration Nagar (Arunachal Pradesh)	—	—	1.83	—
17.	Ramakrishna Mission, Anglong (Arunachal Pradesh)	—	—	2.69	4.57
18.	Sri Ramakrishna Seva Kendra, Tripura	—	—	9.24	—
19	Nikhil Bharat Banabasi Panchyat, Jhargram, Midnapur	—	—	2.26	—
20.	Dayanand Sewashram Sangh, North-East India, Bokajam, Karbi-Agglong, Assam	—	—	0.32	—
21.	Gharmora Model Satra Hill and Plains Cultural Institution, North Lakhimpur (Assam)	—	—	0.37	1.72
22.	Himalaya Seva Sangh, New Delhi	—	—	—	0.80
23.	Servants of India Society, Allahabad	—	—	N.A.	0.04

Source: The 26th and the 27th Reports of the Commissioner for Scheduled Castes and Scheduled Tribes, Delhi, Controller of Publications, 1978-81, pp. 197 and 230-31 respectively.

Commissioner for Scheduled Castes and Scheduled Tribes, during 1979-80, the sevaks conducted 4,265 goodwill conferences, meetings and social gatherings and organised 17 mela meetings. The Sangh resumed publication of Hindi-*cum*-English bi-monthly magazine *Harijan Seva Sevaks Guide* and *Anmol Vachan* in Hindi were also published for the guidance of the field workers of the Sangh. The workers of the Sangh succeeded in getting free access of Harijans to 222 temples, 371 wells, 347 restaurants and services of 169 barbers and 40 washerman in the States of Andhra Pradesh, Gujarat, Himachal Pradesh, Karnataka, Kerala, Madhya Pradesh, Maharashtra, Orissa, Rajasthan, Tamil Nadu and Uttar Pradesh in the year 1979-80.

Under the Bhangi Kashi Mukti Scheme, which aims at abolition of scavenging, the workers got 3,737 dry latrines converted into water-borne and 4,209 water borne (sweeper-free) latrines were constructed.

The Safai Vidyalaya at Ahmedabad run by the Sangh, which provides training to a large number of workers in urban sanitation and systematic and hygienic disposal of nightsoil, organised a number of training camps in the districts of Ahmedabad, Broach, Amreti, Mehsana and Valsad in which about 325 workers participated. The Vidyalaya, with the help of Government of Gujarat, arranged 100 exhibitions highlighting rural sanitation, primary care, handflush urinals, etc. The intensive area workers, regional sevaks and mahila pracharaks who concentrate mainly on the rural and semi-urban areas, because of the prevalence of untouchability and unhygienic conditions, visited 7,766 villages in 15 States during 1979-80.

In Delhi, the Sangh is running since 1944 a residential institution for girls, namely, Kasturba Balika Ashram for imparting education to Harijan girls to improve their social status. The Ashram provides education up to 10th class and is affiliated to the Central Board of Secondary Education. During 1979-80, it had 573 girl students on its rolls out of which 190 were resident students. The total number of Scheduled Castes students was 220 and out of 190 resident students, 173 belonged to Scheduled Castes.

Another residential institution, known as 'Bapa Ashram School', exclusively run for children of sweepers and scavengers, though some other deserving students belonging to other

Scheduled Caste Communities are also admitted. The resident students are given free boarding, lodging, clothing and some other facilities. Besides educational development, the students are provided training in other activities, such as chalk-making, ink-making, clay modelling, crafts, etc.

BHARTIYA DEPRESSED CLASSES LEAGUE

The League also works for removal of untouchability. Their main schemes are: (i) appointment of pracharaks for propaganda for removal of the practice of untouchability, (ii) publicity through publishing of posters, pamphlets, etc., (iii) holding of conferences., meals, meetings, seminars, etc., and (iv) attending to complaints from the aggrieved Scheduled Castes and to supervise the work of the Pracharaks. Seventy Pracharaks, including Lady Pracharaks, conducted meetings and arranged meals in various localities to impress upon caste Hindus the desirability of eradicating the unsocial practice of untouchability. During 1979-80, 4,591 public meetings and social gatherings were arranged and 51 temples for Harijans, 89 water-taps/wells, 73 hotels, were got opened and 122 community dinners and 20 cultural programmes were organised for this purpose. In addition, 99 villages were cleaned, 5 night schools were maintained, and 28 Bhajan Mandalis were arranged in the States of Andhra Pradesh, Bihar, Gujarat, Haryana, Himachal Pradesh, Jammu and Kashmir, Karnataka, Madhya Pradesh, Maharashtra, Orissa, Punjab, Rajasthan, Tamil Nadu, Uttar Pradesh, West Bengal and the Union Territories of Pondicherry, Chandigarh, and Delhi. These Pracharaks also assisted Harijan students in getting admission to various educational institutions and helped the aggrieved in registering their complaints of harassment with a police.

HIND SWEEPER'S SEVAK SAMAJ

During 1979-80, the Hind Sweeper's Sevak Samaj continued to run nine Social Welfare and Education Centres at Allahabad, Lucknow, Shahjahanpur, Varanasi, Fatehpur, Katni and Ranaghat in Uttar Pradesh; Gurgaon in Haryana; and Patiala in Punjab, to cater to the needs of the children and women belonging to the Scheduled Castes. The Samaj also maintained one hostel for

Scheduled Caste post-matric students at Allahabad where special coaching was provided to the 35 inmates, in addition to free board and lodging facilities. The Samaj also maintained an Ashram school for sweepers at Allahabad. Poor Scheduled Caste children of school-going age of the surrounding rural areas, particularly the ones belonging to sweeper community, were accommodated and provided free board and lodging. In addition, the Samaj also maintained one short-hand and type-writing centre at Lucknow.

BHARTIYA ADIM JATI SEVAK SANGH

The Bhartiya Adim Jati Sevak Sangh, founded by late Sri Thakkar Bapa, undertakes works for the welfare of Scheduled Tribes through its central office in New Delhi as well as through its affiliated branches in various states. During 1979-80, Government of India reviewed the scheme of 'Life Membership' and agreed to give grants-in-aid of Rs. 6.42 lakh for Scheme. Under this scheme a cadre of 56 Life Members (20 senior, 12 junior and 24 volunteers) was evolved in organisation, in addition to 13 Life members already borne on the Sangh's cadre. The Life Members were reported to have been posted in the remote tribal areas located in the States of Andhra Pradesh, Assam, Bihar, Gujarat Himachal Pradesh, Karnataka, Kerala, Madhya Pradesh, Maharashtra, Nagaland, Orissa, Rajasthan, Uttar Pradesh, West Bengal, and Arunachal Pradesh. During 1980-81, the Life Members have made very significant contribution towards the welfare of tribals by living in their environments, surveying their areas of abode and activities, to have first-hand knowledge about the problems of the tribals and to find out remedial solutions to these problems. These Life Members work in close collaboration with the district authorities and are well aware about the day-to-day instructions of the Government. They keep themselves up-to-date in the sphere of their activities.

In addition, during 1980-81, the Sangh continued their schemes of Training Centre at Rupa (Arunachal Pradesh), concentrated efforts were made to cultivate the sentiments of national and emotional integration amongst the local tribals through various welfare programmes. At Jhalod (Gujarat) the Sangh is running Gujarat Tribal Women's Training Centre to train women workers to undertake and implement child welfare programmes and to do extensive work amongst rural and tribal women. At Srikakulam (Andhra Pradesh), the Sangh is maintaining a Tribal Kanya Ashram School, where tribal girls from Srikakulam district and its interior areas come for studies up to college stage.

NAGALAND GANDHI ASHRAM, CHUCHUGIMLONG (NAGALAND)

Nagaland Gandhi Ashram, Chuchugimlong was established in 1955. The first activity taken up by the Ashram was a small medical aid centre. In 1977, a multipurpose medical relief camp was organised. Encouraged with the success, the Gandhi Ashram, in October, 1979 started a Health Centre. Later on, a health service scheme on the lines of health insurance was designed. Under the provisions of the scheme, patients desirous to have treatment at the centre, have to pay a nominal fee of Rs. 6 per patient per year. After the payment, a patient is entitled to Till obtain facilities at the centre throughout the year. March, 1980 a total number of 224 members were registered under the scheme. Almost all the members belonged to the Scheduled Tribes of the State. A total number of 2,700 patients were provided medicines till the end of March 1980. Sri Natwar Thakkar, the Secretary of the Ashram and his team of dedicated workers have done excellent work for the upliftment of rural inhabitants of Nagaland and Chuchugimlong in particular. Commissioner of Scheduled Castes and Scheduled Tribes has rightly opined that judging from the success which the Ashram had achieved, it was desirable that the influence of good work started by Sri Natwar Thakkar and his Ashram should be extended and more and more such Gandhi Ashrams should be started in Nagaland and its surrounding regions.

RAMAKRISHNA MISSON ASHRAM, PURI

Taking the cue from Sri Ramakrishna's message "To serve Jiva it to serve Shiva", Swami Vivekananda, after his return from the West, formed on May 1, 1897 an association—'Ramakrishna Mission' which was got registered on May 4, 1909 under the Societies' Registration Act XXI of 1960. It has 139 branch centres all over the world with the head quarters at Belur (near Calcutta), which are engaged in worship of God in man through various activities—relief and rehabilitation, medical services, educational work, work in rural and tribal areas, etc. Ramakrishna Mission Ashram, Puri is conducting a Students' Home for the students belonging to Scheduled Castes/Tribe, During 1979-80 the total strength of she Students' Home stood at 65 out of whom 13 belonged to Scheduled Castes, 46 to Scheduled Tribe and the remaining 6 to the economically backward and other backward classes. The Ashram under the "Type-Writing Training Scheme" imparted training to a group of 15 trainees under the guidance of a part-time instructor. Special coaching was also given to the students regularly with the help of the teachers appointed for the purpose. In addition two other projects of Dairy and Bakery were also taken up. The dairy farm maintained by the Ashram provided practical demonstration in cattle rearing to the students and also provided milk to inmates. The Bakery imparted training to students in making biscuits, etc.

RAMAKRISHNA MISSION ASHRAM, RANCHI

The Ramakrishna Mission Ashram, Ranchi is running Divyayan (meaning the Divine Way) which was started in 1969 with threefold objectives; economic, social and spiritual. Divyayan concept is one of total approach for the rehabilitation of man and the endeavour is to work at the grassroots level. With a humble beginning, it has now grown into a full-fledged training institute with a poultry (about 6,000 birds), a dairy (about 45 cattle heads), a 3-storeyed hostel, a workshop with modern equipment and machinery with a separate carpentary section, a mobile audiovisual unit with film projectors, slide projectors, films, slides, VCR, TV, etc., and demonstration farms of nine acres at the centre plus 144 acres in the villages of Getalsud and Mahespur (P. S. Angara, District Ranchi) about 35 Km. away from the Centre, being developed for demonstration, seed multiplication, research, social forestry, etc.

In all, 3,776 farmers have been trained under on-campus programme (till 1987) and 11,877 under off-campus programmes, most of whom belong to backward communities of Chhotanagpur. Impressed with the success achieved by Divyayan in imparting skill-oriented training to the grassroots level farmers. Indian

Council of Agricultural Research has recognised it as a Krishi Vigyan Kendra since 1977.

RAMAKRISHNA MISSION ASHRAM, CHERRAPUNJI

The Government of India assisted the Ashram for maintenance of technical, middle, primary and J.B. Schools for uplift of the tribals living in remote areas of Meghalaya. Under the scheme, the Ashram maintained 46 schools. During 1980-81, there were more than 3,000 students on the rolls of these schools. Under the Dairy and Poultry Farming scheme started during the year 1980-84 for the first time, the Ashram is imparting training in mordern dairy and poultry farming to the tribal youth. It also enables the inmates of Cherra and Shohbar Students Hostels to get fresh milk and eggs which are very difficult to procure from the local market.[22]

ROLE OF VOLUNTARY AGENCIES IN PLANNING, IMPLEMENTATION AND EVALUATION

Voluntary agencies can play a useful role in planning, implementation and evaluation of various development plans which has been endorsed by various commissions. To begin with, Dhebar Commission opined as early as in 1961:

> "The *raison detre* for successful functioning of a participating democracy is direct, active and purposeful participation of the people at all levels, in planning and implementation of welfare activities. This principle can be best served by assigning an important role to non-official organisations. It is necessary in any democratic framework that a measure of the constructive activity of the nation should be done under non-official Auspices."[23]

Sivaraman Committee, in its report on the role of voluntary agencies, opines that voluntary agencies which are engaged in social and developmental work, especially in rural areas, can be profitably involved in planning and/or implementation of the integrated rural development programme. The committee has recommended that, to begin with, voluntary agencies may be involved in planning and implementation of about 100 block plans. It has further recommended that a high-powered committee should be set up at the centre which would select voluntary agencies and the areas where they will work in cases where comprehensive block planning and or implementation is to be undertaken by the voluntary agencies. Coordination committees are also to be set up at the state level for selecting voluntary agencies and the area of operation in case where part of the block plan is involved. It is understood that recommendations of the committee are under the consideration of the Government.[24]

It is thus clear that voluntary agencies could be used to plan the programme on the basis of real local needs and resources at the village and block level and be entrusted with execution of programmes, which is urgently required for Harijan and Tribal development. Thus, for instance, the Dantwala working group on block level planning calls attention to the fact that the village level, the unemployed or underemployed prefer to remain so, if employment is offered to them in locations far away from their houses (this is more true about the Scheduled Tribes). This is the kind of situation which a voluntary agency takes into account in both planning employment programmes and executing them in the village(s) concerned. Similar gaps exist in Training of Rural Youth for Self-employment (TRYSEM) programme and the recently started RLEGP, which through voluntary agencies, can be set right, to an extent.[25]

A study of the history of Harijan and Tribal development indicates that these two communities are mere passive spectators of the drama of development. However, development cannot be achieved unless beneficiaries themselves become conscious of their own rights, of the conditions and the circumstances which made them socially and economically disadvantages and have an urge to alter the situation with proper understanding of the correlations of social-economic forces. The voluntary agencies can make them active participants in the change process.[26]

Group action and exogenous support is essential in IRDP for making correct selection of beneficiaries, choice of investment, getting the loans sanctioned in time and making a reasonable income by overcoming the unfavourable market forces. A dedicated voluntary organisation could educate, conscientise and prepare the ground for collective action of the beneficiaries by making suitable intervention at all these points.[27]

Voluntary agencies at national, state or local levels down, could be asked to do evaluation of programmes. According to studies made by some research institutions and even some official agencies, only 10 per cent of Rs. 500 crore funds allocated to the programme in the three years 1980-81 to 1982-83, actually reached the poor families for whom it was intended.[28]

Under these conditions, voluntary agencies can help in monitoring IRDP programmes executed by Government functionaries to ensure that the benefits reach the beneficiary for whom they are intended to the maximum extent possible.

Thus, there cannot be two opinions on active role of voluntary agencies. It has many advantages; the plans are conceived and formulated on the basis of the felt-needs of the people, there is sizable saving in expenditure; implementation becomes easier; and finally peoples' aspirations are largely met. Dhebar has rightly said that they can also become the training-ground of social service workers on a mass scale.

NEW FIELDS FOR VOLUNTARY AGENCIES IN TRIBAL DEVELOPMENT

No doubt, voluntary agencies are doing appreciable work for Harijan and Tribal Development, yet there are still certain areas of Tribal Development where even greater involvement of these is needed. They are as follows:

1. Ignorance about tribal customs and traditions about land-holdings in certain areas has resulted in wrong recording in surveys by settlement authorities resulting in transfer of title of their land. It is giving rise to tribal discontent. Voluntary organisation should take this matter in their hand.
2. An estimation places the total number of bonded labour, both tribal and non-tribal, in the country at about 32 lakh. Attempts were made to identify tribal bonded labourers during the first four years of the Sixth Five Year Plan, in the large tribal States of Bihar and Madhya Pradesh, identification was noticeably poor. It would be of interest, therefore, to see the contribution of voluntary organisations in identification of bonded-labour. The

Programme Evaluation Organisation study included this aspect.

3. The battle has acted as an important conduit through which the wily forces of exploitation have long been entering tribal areas. Sanskar Kendras to prevent the tribals from drinking on the pattern organised in the State of Gujarat should be introduced in the tribal areas in good number through voluntary agencies, who may be assisted cent per cent by special Central assistance.
4. There are 72 primitive tribal groups in the country with an estimated population of 14 lakh. There is a need to carry out ecological study of each one of these primitive tribes highlighting their pattern of distribution in space, adaptive process in their social organisation, economic activities, their world-view *vis-a-vis* physical and social environment, social organisation or labour, time budgeting, etc. Each of these aspects requires to be studied in detail for preparing a blue-print for their future. There has been an emphasis, since the Fifth Plan period, on preparation of a project report for each of these groups relative to its situation. Nevertheless, there has been considerable neglect in this regard. Apart from continued misery conditions in which they live, risk of extinction of some of those tribes is not unreal. The extremely onerous and delicate dimensions of the problem of primitive tribal groups inclines us to the belief that public and voluntary agencies should share the responsibility of the care and nursing of primitive tribal groups along with Governmental agencies. The voluntary organisations should come forward to accept the challenge in this regard.
5. It has been estimated by the Task Force on Shifting Cultivation, set up by Ministry of Agriculture, that approximately 9.95 million hectares in the tribal and hilly areas of the country are under shifting cultivation. The problem cannot be lightly brushed aside as over six lakh tribal families depend on this source for their living. This Problem could be tackled easily if the voluntary agencies adopt a programme of educating the shifting cultivators on advantages of settled cultivation, which

should be taken up along with implementation of the settlement/resettlement scheme.

6. There is a concentration of industrial and mining activity in the tribal belt of the country. The abrupt juxtaposition has produced traumatic results for the tribals. Instead of having benefited from the new ferment, the tribals have suffered loss of land and forest. Some of the cottage, village and small industries commonly in operation in the tribal areas, which need encouragement, include: (a) forest-based small industries, and (b) mineral-based cottage and village industries, weaving, sericulture and others. Arrangements for marketing could be done through various voluntary agencies.
7. Various studies have revealed that developmental efforts have not reached tribal women. The tribal women should be encouraged to set up 'Mahila Mandals' and 'Mahila Samities' and such organisations should be taken into confidence during planning and implementation of their welfare/development programmes. On an experimental basis, reputed voluntary women's organisations will have to be identified and entrusted with selected programmes.

AN EVALUATION OF THE VOLUNTARY AGENCIES

When we try to evaluate the role of voluntary agencies we had faced with a lot of controversies about their performance. There are two diametrically opposed views about them. For example, Mohit Sen views, 'It is wrong and even harmful to rely on voluntary agencies even partially for the implementation of plan projects, especially directed at poor millions."[29] Kamal Narayan Kabra opines, "like so many false alternatives being propagate to so many genuine issues, the officially recognised, financed and co-opted voluntary agencies will prove another anarchonism and false alternative."[30] On the other hand, we have a long list of politicians, academics and social workers who have landed their role for development of the weaker sections. For example, the Prime Minister's directive to Chief Ministers in October, 1982 to involve voluntary organisations in development by forming consultative Groups[31], and the current move by the government to set up a National Council of Rural Voluntary Agencies are all signs of change for better in the official attitude towards voluntary organisations. Planning Commission members, C.H. Hanumantha Rao,[32] and Raj Krishna[33] and social workers, like Mahasveta Devi[34] and many others have made some praise in favour of voluntary agencies. No doubt, there are good and bad voluntary agencies.

For example, we may visit Narendrapur in Calcutta and Coimbatore, amongst others, doing silent work of training, with echo around, under Ramakrishna Mission, Nilokheri, situated on the National Highway, 150 kilometers north of Delhi, with its rural-*cum*-urban township and the quest therein soon after 1947 for a "road to new India" is another example of voluntary action by many a volunteer totally committed to the cause and supported strongly by Nehru despite opposition from within Government and without.[35] What SEWA has done in Ahmedabad is something that a Government agency has not have been able to do. What the Tagore Society for Rural Development is doing in 27 villages in five islands of the Sunderban area in West Bengal is an unlikely proposition for a bureaucratic and hierarchical state agency.[36] The examples, but a few, cited in the foregoing, are illustrative of what can follow when the 'cause is honest' and there is integrity, inspiration and fire from within.

We have another example too. S.K. Dev has mentioned about some of the activities of Sarva Seva Sangh. He writes:

> "It was decided to have a pilot project under the Sangh in the backward district of Koraput in Orissa, where eight tribal blocks had already been covered by 'Gram Dan' to 'Block Dan'. One of the Blocks was taken under the unfettered change of the Sangh with full resources, but staff appointed exclusively by them. A year passed, the entire resources had been spent out. All that happened was that the Block Development Officer selected and appointed exclusively by them out of their own youth group, had established an Ashram for himself immeasurably better fitted and equipped than Gandhiji's own at Sevagram. . . . A vital young Adibasi girl of rare beauty found her place to look after the Ashram and its occupant. . . . There came also a big store house for

jungle produce with hardly 5 per cent of space occupied. When the doings were reported to the Sangh, the young man was removed. The joint programme also came virtually to an end.[37]

The works of the foreign Christian Missions are also not an unmixed evil. One may see a village which at one time worked and lived as a single unit now split into a Christian hamlet and a Non-Christian hamlet. Dhebar report mentioned about a village where no fewer than five Missions were carrying on propaganda, opening separate schools and teaching different forms of Christianity.[38]

These days, Government is facing some difficulties from foreign voluntary agencies, particularly in scheduled areas. It would be desirable to subject the foreign assistance received by such organisations to strict check before permitting its utilisation in tribal area programmes.[39] Chief Editor of *Yojana* has also opined, "My sterious, they say, are the ways of the unseen hand that backs them.[40] We should be careful not to encourage development rackets in the name of people's participation and involvement of voluntary agencies.

After assessing the role of voluntary agencies for Tribal and Harijan development, we come to the conclusion that they have come to stay. The United Nations Children's Fund reports opines, "All over the world, non-governmental organisations (NGOs), both national and international, are active partners of communities and Governments in their efforts to protect the health and normal growth of their children. . . . World-wise, it has been estimated that more than 3,000 international NGOs are at work, and they mobilise more than 2.3 billion every year for assistance to the developing world."[41] A devoted Governmental agency can certainly do the work of development to some extent, but if it had the support of the voluntary organisations, it could do the job much better. We have seen from experience during the last three decades that Rashtra Shakti or government action by itself could not achieve much unless it was supported by 'Lok Shakti' or 'Jan Shakti'.

The State's agency bureaucracy would require sensitisation, which could come through very largely, if it were made to work along with voluntary organisations. Beyond doubt, the experience all over the world is that non-officials could communicate to people with greater understanding and conviction than officials.

There are people who charge that there has been misuse of funds by voluntary agencies. There is some truth in it. But the amount misused is likely to be much smaller in the aggregate than the vast amounts wasted by Government agencies.

With the adoption of new strategies for the economic and educational development of Scheduled Castes and Scheduled Tribes during the Sixth Plan, it has now become more important to involve voluntary organisations fully in this gigantic task. Voluntary Organisations are now gradually coming forward to take up various developmental programmes for the Scheduled Castes and Scheduled Tribes. The decision has to be taken about the type of programmes to be entrusted to such organisations during the Seventh Plan so that there may be a clear-cut demarcation of areas of operation between the programmes undertaken by the State Governments and those entrusted to the Voluntary Organisations to avoid duplication.

It cannot be denied that the entire backward rural areas of the country cannot be covered by the voluntary organisations. But at the same time, it has also to be accepted that the Government organisations could not reach these areas completely. There is, thus, no other alternative to the Government-voluntary agency partnership for the crusade against poverty.

Notes and References

1. S. Narayanaswamy, Report of the Working Group on Development of Scheduled Tribes during Seventh Five Year Plan, New Delhi, Ministry of Home Affairs, 1984, p. 13.
2. V.M. Kulkarni, Voluntary Action in a Developing Society, New Delhi, Indian Institute of Public Administration, 1969.
3. *Ibid.*, p. 8.
4. *Ibid.*
5. Raj Krishna, "It would Just be a Futile Exercise", *Yojana*, Vol. 28, Nos. 20 & 21, November 1984, p. 7.
6. U.N.Dhebar, Report of the Scheduled Areas and Scheduled Tribes Commission, New Delhi, Government of India Press, 1961, p. 301.
7. *Ibid.*
8. L.P. Vidyarthi, The Peasant Organisation in India (Case study of Voluntary Organisation in Tribal Bihar), Ranchi, Council of Social and Cultural Research, 1977, p. 40.

9. S.C. Roy, "The Effects on the Aborigins of Chotanagpur and their Contracts with Westerns Civilisation", *Journal of Bihar and Orissa Research Society*, Vol. 17, Part IV, 1931.
10. U.N. Dhebar, *op. cit.*, p. 303.
11. L.P. Vidyarthi, *op. cit.*, p. 39.
12. Jai Mangal Deo, "Voluntary Agencies *vis-a-vis* Government", *Yojana*, Vol. 31, No. 4, March 1-15, 1987, p. 12.
13. *Ibid.*
14. Durgabai Deshmukh, "Leadership Role of Voluntary Organisations in Social Development and Social Welfare" in T.H. Chaturvedi and Shanta Kohli Chandra (ed.), Social Administration: Development and Change, New Delhi, Indian Institute of Public Administration, 1980, p. 280.
15. *Ibid.*
16. Bikram Sarkar, "They Do Have a Role to play", *Yojana*, Vol. 28, Nos. 20 and 21, November 1984, p. 49.
17. *Ibid.*
18. CIRT Voluntary Services in India: A Study, New Delhi, CIRT, 1967.
19. Bikram Sarkar, *op. cit.*
20. U.N. Dhebar, *op. cit.*, p. 303.
21. *Ibid.*
22. The author has relied heavily on the 26th and the 27th Reports of the Commissioner for Scheduled Castes and Scheduled Tribes in this portion.
23. U.N. Dhebar, *op. cit.*, p. 307.
24. Quoted by Shishir Kumar in 26th Report of the Commissioner for Scheduled Castes and Scheduled Tribes.
25. Malcolm S. Adiseshiah, "No Good for this High Task," *Yojana*, Vol. 28, Nos. 20-21, November, 1984, p. 17.
26. D. Bandyopadhyay, "An Escape or a Commitment", *Yojana*, Vol. 28, Nos. 20 and 21, Nov. 1984, p. 28.
27. *Ibid.*, p. 29.
28. Quoted by Malcolm S. Adiseshiah, *op. cit.*, p. 16.
29. Mohit Sen, "No, No, Nothing Doing with Them", *Yojana*, Vol. 28, Nos. 20 and 21, November, 1984, p. 23.
30. Kamal Nayan Kabra, "Why Go for a False Alternative, *Yojana*, Vol. 28, Nos. 20 and 21, p. 30.
31. J.B. Singh, "Lets First Understand Them", *Yojana*, Vol. 28, Nos. 20 and 21, p. 45.
32. C.H. Hanumantha Rao, "As Planning Commission Views the Concept", *Yojana*, Vol. 28, Nos. 20 and 21, pp. 5-6.
33. Raj Krishna, *op. cit.*, pp. 7-8.
34. Mahasveta, Devi, "You just Can't Do Without Them", 1. *Yojana*, Vol. 23, Nos. 20 and 21, pp. 52-54.
35. S.K. Dev, Why Don't We Learn from the Past ?" *Yojana*, Vol. 28, Nos. 20 and 21, p. 10.

36. Krishna Dev Diwan, "Shall We not be Running a Risk", *Yojana*, Vol. 28, Nos. 20 and 21, p. 42.
37. S.K. Dev, *op. cit.*, p. 11.
38. U.N. Dhebar, *op. cit.*, p. 301.
39. S. Narayanaswamy, *op. cit.* p. 188.
40. Chief Editor *(Yojana)*, "Wanted Good Guys", *Yojana*, Vol. 28, Nos. 20 and 21, p. 4.
41. James P. Grant, The State of the World's Children, 1987 (UNICEF), Oxford University Press, UK, p. 58.

Role of Government in Tribal Development and Social Change

It is of course, very difficult to find out data and references regarding the development of measures for the Bihari Santhal before the sub-plan period, i.e., Fifth Five Year Plan (1974-79). It was only in the Draft Sub-Plan of the Tribal Region of Bihar that the detailed figures of the development measures for the Santhals came into light and we could find out that more than one-half of the Santhals in Bihar are found in Santhal Parganas and about a quarter in the Hazaribagh and Singhbhum put together. Their numbers are also significant in Dhanbad, Purnea, Monghyr and Bhagalpur. However, these four districts and also Hazaribagh, except Pirtard Block were outside the sub-plan in Fifth Plan period.

According to the guideline of the Planning Commission, the Blocks having 50 per cent tribal concentration should be identified as scheduled areas to be covered by the sub-plan, the following sub-divisions of Santhal concentration can be identified:

(a) Sadar (Dumka), Jȧmtara, Pakur and Rajmahal Sub-Divisions of Santhal Parganas.

(b) Sadar (Chaibasa) and Saraikela Sub-divisions of Singhbhum district.

The level of development of the Santhal before the commencement of the sub-plan can be noticed from the statement given in Tables 5.1 to 5.6.

TABLE 5.1

Percentage of Literate Santhals to Total Population

Person	*1961*		*1971*		
	Male	*Female*	*Person*	*Male*	*Female*
60.08	10.77	1.34	7.51	13.02	2.01

Source: Draft Sub-Plan for Tribal Region, Bihar (1974-79), p. 22.

TABLE 5.2

Percentage of Cultivators and Agricultural Labourers

Name of Micro Area	*Percentage to total rural workers (1961)*			*Percentage to total rural workers (1971)*		
	Cultivators	*Agril. labourers*	*Total*	*Cultivators*	*Agril. labourers*	*Total*
Dumka	76.8	7.8	34.6	62.5	23.8	86.3
Chaibasa	67.3	14.2	81.5	50.2	35.1	85.3
Bihar	57.2	24.4	81.6	46.9	41.8	88.7

Source: Draft Sub-Plan for Tribal Region, Bihar (1974-79), pp, 24.

TABLE 5.3

Area Irrigated by Different Sources

(In thousand acres)

Name of District	*Canal*	*Tanks*	*Tube-wells*	*Other wells*	*Other Sources*	*Grand Total*
Santhal Parganas	14.6	82.8	0.5	7.7	22.78	128.3
Singhbhum	28.4	18.6	0.1	0.7	9.2	58.9

Source: Draft Sub-Plan for Tribal Region, Bihar (1974-79), pp. 26-27.

TABLE 5.4

Number of Villages Electrified

Name of Micro Area	*Total number of villages*	*Number of villages electrified*	*Percentage*
Dumka	3375	402	4.8
Chaibasa	4673	147	3.1

Source: Draft Sub-Plan for Tribal Region, Bihar (1974-79), p. 28.

TABLE 5.5

Length of Surfaced Road Per 1000 Sq. Km.

Name of District	*Length in Km. as on 31.3.1968*	*Length in Km as on 31.3.1972*
Santhal Parganas	64.6	33.2
Singhbhum	39.8	63.4
Bihar State	67.6	94.4

Source: Draft Sub-Plan for Tribal Region, Bihar (1974-79), p. 29.

TABLE 5.6

Number of Primary, Middle and High Schools (Anticipated 1973-74)

Name of District	*Primary*	*Middle*	*High*
Santhal Parganas	3329	540	188
Singhbhum	2049	473	104

Source: Draft Sub-Plan for Tribal Region, Bihar (1974-79), p. 32.

The Tribal sub-plan area of Bihar (1974-79), consists of the districts of Ranchi (43 Blocks) and Singhbhum (32 Blocks), 31 Blocks of Santhal Parganas district, 9 Blocks of Palamau district, 1 Block of Giridih (Part of old Hazaribagh) and Dhanbad districts and 2 Blocks of Rohtas (Part of old Shahabad) district. The area covers 119 Blocks out of a total of 587 in the State.[1] In them 117 Blocks are in the Chhotanagpur and Santhal Parganas region which has a total of 193 Blocks in all. The sub-plan area has been divided into four Micro areas divided into 15 Meso areas.[2] Four Blocks in the district of Giridih, Dhanbad and Rohtas functioned as independent Micro areas, which were not included in any Meso area. The total tribal population covered by the above-mentioned sub-plan was 33.32 lakhs according to 1961 census. The Scheduled Tribes population which was in that Sub-Plan covered formed 81.4 per cent of the rural Scheduled Tribes population of the State.

The Sub-Plan (1974-79) was drawn up for a total outlay of Rs. 420.42 crores. The share of the State Plan outlay allocable to sub-plan area come to Rs. 217.50 crores and hence an additional outlay of Rs. 102.92 crores was sought for the Tribal region.

It is almost obvious that we are chiefly concerned here specially with Dumka Macro area which is a special area of Santhal concentration. This Micro area includes five Meso areas, namely, Dumka, Pakur, Jamtara," Godda and Rajmahal. The total area of this micro area is about four thousand square miles having total population of about two millions out of which tribal population is about one million and they are mostly Santhals.

The tribal sub-plan area in Bihar has already been delineated during the Fifth Plan period and the same is being continued in the Sixth Plan also which includes: (i) Ranchi, Gumla, Lohardaga and Singhbhum districts, (ii) whole of Latehar Sub-Division plus Bhandaria Block of Garhwa sub-division of Palamau district, and (iii) Dumka and Sahebganj district in their entirely, and the whole of Pakur and Jamtara Sub-division plus Sundar Pahari and Baarijore Blocks of Godda district. The area mentioned above are distributed in the two divisions, i.e., the South Chhotanagpur and the Santhal Pargana Divisions. The Tribal sub-plan in Bihar covers 112 Blocks and has an area of 43604 Sq. Kms. According to 1981 census, the sub-plan covered a population of 8756 lakhs, the area which was covered by the sub-Plan was 15 per cent. The total area of the state is 173877 Sq. Kms. and the total population of the State is (699 lakhs). The tribal population is 43.29 lakhs in the sub-plan area according to the 1981 census which are 74.5 per cent of the total tribal population of the State (58.11 lakhs) living in the sub-plan area. The entire sub-plan area has been divided into 14 Integrated Tribal Development Projects each of which has respective administrative Sub-divisions except in Latehar. Pakur and Rajmahal in all of which, besides the subdivision bearing that name, some adjoining Blocks are also added. For example,

TABLE 5.7

Abstracts of Meso and Micro Area of Bihar

Sl. No.	Name of Meso Area	Area in Sq. Mile	Population		Tribal Population		Percentage	
			Total	Rural	Total	Rural	Total	Rural
1	2	3	4	5	6	7	8	9
I.	**Ranchi Micro Area**							
1.	Ranchi Meso Area	1463.0	586.295	575.862	314.705	312.429	53.7	54.3
2.	Khunti Meso Area	1463.07	438.924	421.433	279.219	275.485	63.6	65.4
	Total	2931.7	1025.219	997.345	593.924	537.914	57.9	58.9
II.	**Gumla Micro Area**							
1.	Gumla Meso Area	2059.9	464.924	474.214	354.976	350.664	73.2	73.9
2.	Lohardaga Meso Area	576.9	172.363	159.160	110.795	108.780	64.3	68.3
3.	Simdega Meso Area	1452.2	315.306	305.368	251.801	226.408	73.4	74.4
4.	Latehar Meso Area	2929.6	310.332	300.553	150.897	143.035	48.6	49.6
	Total	6113.0	1263.425	1239.300	848.360	834.887	66.1	67.4
III.	**Chaibasa Micro Area**							
1.	Chaibasa Meso Area	1188.0	460.435	410,127	323,298	309,028	78.2	75.4

(Contd.)

TABLE 5.7 (*Contd.*)

1	2	3	4	5	6	7	8	9
2.	Chakardharpur Meso Area	822.1	304.693	273,787	192,863	109,835	68.2	69.2
3.	Dalbhum	8327.9	543.551	521,622	207,038	258,393	47.8	49.5
4.	Saraikela Meso Area	1050.4	413.188	403,724	175,001	173,247	42.4	43.2
	Total	4388.4	1721.867	1609,260	951,000	932,503	55.2	57.9
IV.	**Dumka Meso Area**							
1.	Dumka Meso Area	1435.4	809,182	549.092	315,718	314,954	51.8	53.3
2.	Pakur Meso Area	695.6	347,012	335.267	196,496	195,129	56.6	58.2
3.	Jamtara Meso Area	697.4	324,145	312.592	126,606	125,532	39.0	40.2
4.	Godda Meso Area	577.1	271,177	263.677	114,961	114,406	42.4	43.4
5.	Rajmahal Meso Area	619.4	414,277	376,067	163,439	162,906	39.4	43.4
	Total	4024.9	1967,023	1898,695	917,220	913,020	46.6	48.6
	Total (A)	17463.0	5997,534	2624,600	3310,513	3268,324	55.2	58.1
(B)	**Tribal Development Blocks not included in** Meso Areas							
1.	Adhaura (Rohtas)	335.5	16,985	16,985	9,737	9,737	67.3	57.3
2.	Nauhatta (Rohtas)	125.5	34,672	34,672	4,269	4,269	12.3	12.3
3.	Pirtand (Giridih)	151.7	41,307	41,307	19,835	19,835	48.0	48.0
4.	Tudi (Dhanbad)	152.5	59,548	59,548	29,763	29,763	50.0	50.0
	Total (B)	813.2	152,512	152,512	63,104	63,604	41.7	41.7
	Grand Total	18277.2	6160,646	5877,112	3374,117	3331,920	54.9	56.9

Source: Draft Sub-Plan for Tribal Region of Bihar (1974-79). pp. 266-76 (Based on 1961 census).

Bhandaria Block of Latehar, Sundar Pahari Block of Pakur, and Boarinjore Block of Rajmahal. Ranchi, Khunti, Lohardaga, Gumla, Siradega, Chaibasa, Dhalbhum, Saraikela, Chakradharpur, Latehar Dumka, Jamtara, Pakur, and Rajmahal are the ITDPs or Meso Project areas.

Out of the fourteen ITDPs the Santhal Parganas includes four, namely, Dumka, Pakur, Jamtara and Rajmahal (Table 5.8).

The four Integrated Tribal Development Projects of the Santhal Parganas include 29 Blocks out of which 13 are Tribal Development Blocks. A detailed figure of all the 29 Blocks are given in the Table 5.9.

The growth rate among S.T. during the decade ending 1981 is 14.3 per cent in the Sub-Plan area whereas it is 17.8 per cent in the State as a whole. In the previous decade, i.e., the one ending 1971, the corresponding are 15.2 per cent and 17.3 per cent. This means that decreasing trend in growth rate of Tribals of Sub-Plan as against more area has not been arrested. The situation calls for increased spread of health facilities and infrastructural growth in the sub-plan area. Living under poorer and inhospitable land conditions, the tribals in sub-plan area seen to require more assistance than has been available so far. The higher growth rate in area outside the sub-plan indicates the better nature of land and facilities in those areas.

The comparative figures for 1971 and 1981 census in the growth rate of the total and tribal population in the four districts of the sub-plan area are given in Table 5.10. The table also reveals the position of the Santhals who are inhabited mostly in the Santhal Parganas.[13]

Block-wise number of literate persons for 1981 census is not available. Literacy of sub-plan area was 21.3 in 1971. According to 1981 census the State tribal literacy percentage is 26.2 per cent but in Ranchi and Singhbhum districts the literacy percentage as per 1981 census is as high as 31.4 and 34.6 respectively whereas in Palamau and Santhal Parganas it is 20.4 and 22.3 respectively. It reveals that literacy percentage is higher in Ranchi and Singhbhum but lower in Santhal Parganas and Palamau.

A REVIEW OF THE PROTECTIVE PLAN LIFE

Development of Scheduled Tribes and the tribal area was

TABLE 5.8

Integrated Tribal Development Projects in the Santhal Parganas

Sl. No.	ITDPs	No. of Blocks covered		Area (sq.kms.)	Population (1971 Census)		
		Fully	Partly		Total	S.T.	%age
1.	Dumka	10	—	3716	713444	357287	50.8
2.	Pakur	7	—	2132	443295	256535	57.87
3.	Jamtara	4	—	1802	377711	135807	35.96
4.	Rajmahal	8	—	1944	576847	232397	40.29
	Total	29	—				

Source: Tribal Sub-Plan Areas, 1983, p. 53.

TABLE 5.9

Detailed Figure of ITDPs in Santhal Parganas

Sl. No.	Sub-division covered by ITDP	Partly	Blocks covered under TTDPs		TD or CD	Area Sq. Kms.	Total	S.T.	%age	Village
			Fully	Partly						
1	2	3	4	5	6	7	8	9	10	11
1.	Dumka	—	Mukka	—	CD	378.80	100256	43062	43.0	276
			Ramshwar	—	CD	346.60	65017	29537	45.4	217
			Masalia	—	TD	460.20	75944	48488	63.8	317
			Jama	—	CD	385.90	78112	44023	56.4	320
			Jarumundi	—	CD	399.20	90189	26385	27.3	526
			Saraiyahat	—	CD	298.10	68401	14608	21.4	352
			Ramgarh	—	CD	481.40	90320	49903	55.3	347
			Gopi Kandar	—	TD	220.60	26885	23256	86.5	129
			Kathikund	—	TD	306.20	43149	28137	65.2	197
			Shikaripara	—	TD	439.20	75171	49888	64.4	261
2.	Pakur		Pakur	—	CD	221.70	98913	27387	27.7	189
			Maheshpur	—	CD	448.90	105638	58207	55.0	345
			Hiranpur	—	CD	169.60	40451	18310	45.3	133
			Lithipara	—	CD	413.60	60455	46169	76.4	304
			Amarapara	—	TD	273.30	36571	31998	87.5	123

(Contd.)

TABLE 5.9 *(Contd.)*

1	*2*	3	*4*	*5*	*6*	*7*	*8*	*9*	*10*	*11*
		—	Pakuria	—	TD	299.80	61050	41047	67.2	156
			SundarPahari	—	TD	326.80	40217	33417	83.1	NA
3.	Jamtara		Jamtara	—	CD	471.80	117526	44546	37.9	252
			Narayanpur	—	CD	338.80	78800	21846	27.7	302
			Nala	—	CD	540.00	102443	40806	39.8	344
			Kunadhit	—	TD	451.40	78942	28609	36.2	268
4.	Rajmahal		Rajmahal	—	CD	220.10	130290	10281	7.9	255
			Barharwa	—	CD	187.20	69903	8312	11.9	239
			Sahebganj	—	CD	173.30	64800	4057	6.3	32
			Barhait	—	TD	308.80	66167	41937	68.4	275
			Pathana	—	TD	163.20	41546	28502	68.6	150
			Taljhari	—	TD	158.30	41192	30087	73.0	273
			Borio	—	TD	389.20	93282	64018	68.6	580
		Godda	Boarjore	—	TD	343.60	69667	45203	64.9	NA

Source: Tribal Sub-Plan Area, 1983, pp. 34-37.

TABLE 5.10

Comparative Growth Rate of Tribal Population

Sl. No.	*District*	*Total Population*		*Increase in the decade*	*Tribal Population*		*Increase*
		1971	*1981*		*1971*	*1981*	
1.	Ranchi	26.11	30.70	17.6	15.17	1732	14.2
2.	Singhbhum	24.38	28.62	17.4	11.24	12.62	12.3
3.	Palamau (Sub-Plan area)	3.32	4.02	21.1	1.63	1.91	17.2
4.	Santhal Parganas (Sub-Plan area)	21.11	24.21	14.7	9.82	11.84	16.5
	Total Sub-Plan Area	74.92	87.56	16.9	37.86	43.29	14.3
	Bihar State	563.53	699.15	24.06	49.33	58.11	17.8

envisaged from the beginning of the plan era. Since, these groups were distinct and suffered from Socio-economic handicaps which placed them in a disadvantageous position, supplementary programmes for their development were taken up under a separate sector known as 'Backward Classes Sector'. For a long time tribal development programme remained confined to with the four corners of one sector of a State's budget (the backward classes welfare sector) or in the rigid schematic framework of a development Block. At other time, the two were simultaneously in operation more or less, compartmentalised. It was only with the beginning of the Fifth Five Year Plan, that the sectoral barriers could be transcended and it started acquiring broad inter-sectoral integrated approach.

It is well known that the strategy for integrated development led to the launching of tribal sub-plan concept in the Fifth Plan period. Three basic parameters of tribal situation in the country were recognised in the formulation of the concept. First, that there is variation in the social, political, economic and cultural milieu among the different Scheduled Tribe Communities in the country, second, that their demographic distribution reveals their concentration in parts of some States. Further, that the primitive tribal communities live in secluded regions. Hence, the broad approach to tribal development has to be related to their level of development and patter of distribution. In predominant tribal regions, area approach with focus on development of tribal communities has been favour while for primitive groups community-oriented programmes have been preferred. For dispersed tribals, their participation in activities of rural development has been thought to be the apt development mechanism. For execution of programmes having the integrated thrust, pooling of finances from all sources has been regarded as an essential requisite.

From the statement mentioned in Table 5.11 it can be seen that in absolute terms the Tribal sub-plan strategy has led to increasing investment. In percentage terms also, it shows an ascending order. Increasing investments in tribal areas of the country should lead to worthwhile and concrete results for population, particularly the target group.

In accordance with the target set in the Sixth Plan period of raising fifty per cent of families in the TPS area from below the poverty-line to above the poverty-line, 23 lakh families will be assisted economically over a period of time to enable them to cross the poverty-line. Reports monitored at the national level show that by the end of financial year 1982-83, about 23 lakh families have already been economically assisted. But a precise idea of the economic assistance rendred and the capacity of the families to cross the poverty barrier have not been formulated.

TABLE 5.11

Plan Provisions for Tribal Development

(Rs. in crores)

Plan	*Total Provision*	*Tribal Development Programme*	*Percentage*
First Plan*	1950	19.93	1.00
Second Plan*	4972	42.92	0.9
Third Plan*	8577	50.53	0.6
Annual Plans	6756	32.32	0.6
Fifth Plan**	3932	1182.00	3.1
Annual Plan (1979-80)**	12176.5	855.17	7.00
Sixth Plan (1980-85)**	97500	7460.47	7.6

Note: *Expenditure.
**Outlay.

The success of family benefiting programme is vitally dependent on the support and supplementation of some infrastructure and some human resources development sectors. Finally balanced planning formulations of family development, human resources development and infrastructure development sector has been called for each State, depending on the parameters of the situation there.

Operation of Tribal sub-plan and emphasis on family benefiting programmes has led to higher flows from the State Plans. The Central Plan also should ensure adequate flow. Not only the funds of Centrally sponsored and Central schemes, but also the role of Central Ministries in providing leadership and guidance for tribal development should become more significant.

Insistence on monitoring and systems in States, particularly in the context of the 20-Point Programme, has at least, borne some fruit inasmuch as there is presently some information trickle. But the monitoring machinery has to be improved qualitatively and strengthened physically. The data flow has to be more authentic and meaningful.

It appears from the Table 5.11 that plan outlay for Tribal Development has gone up maximum of 17.6 per cent in the Sixth Plan average which is more than seven times higher than the First Plan expenditure. From the table it also appears than the Tribal sub-plan has given much stress on tribal areas development and their welfare projects. Therefore, in the First Sub-Plan period the outlay becomes 3.1 per cent and then after 7.6 per cent. Against the huge investment made during the sub-plans period, it is difficult to make a fair assessment of the quality of impact on the Socio-economic conditions of the tribal committees. Both total and sectoral evaluation are necessary.

Notes and References

1. A Macro Plan at the national state or regional level, attempts at providing a frame at the respective level within which various facets of the economy can be balanced so that they move in unison. The macro plan also provides a broad direction for development and defines the internal structure of the economy.
2. The State's Tribal Sub-Plan is expected to provide a broad policy frame at the macro-level covering the total administrative effort in these areas including development, regulation, general administration, etc. The existing Block or smaller units depending on the demographic situation in each area, is taken as the micro-unit for planning. These micro-units serve as the building, Block or a messo-level structure which serves as the primary unit for planning and implementation.
3. Annual Sub-plan for Tribal Areas to Bihar, 1984-85, p. 7.

Voluntary Organisations and Tribal Development—A Case Study

(A) CASE STUDY THROUGH SAMPLE SURVEY

The Rhetoric— Development targets are high sounding, achievements are but less high sounding, so its grass-root functioning position should be examined.

The Reality— Government work is not so fruitful and people's own efforts in participation with growth are also not encouraging.

As per synopsis to conduct empirical test of one thousand beneficiaries dwelling in twenty different villages scattered in the four districts of Santhal Pargana division are all tribals. 1000 tribals including Santhal and Paharias viz. Surya and Mai Paharia. All the samples were selected by applying random number on voter lists available in the election offices. Questionnaires relating to general socio-economic condition, production consumption, education and literacy, other welfare aspects (Government Projects in above aspects) were included in the questionnaire schedules preparation.

The survey was conducted in targeted families of the universe and their opinion has been sought. Tabulated figures will speak the achievement made by the Government and the voluntary agencies. Efforts had been made to give more emphasis on projects or scattered work done by Government and voluntary agencies simultaneously. Further attempt has been made to measure efficiency of schemes directly implemented by the Central Government. Central Government schemes implemented by the State Government. State Government's own schemes implemented by its own machinery or by some agencies as Panchayat Schemes and works. It has been tried to find out whether the schemes and projects have achieved its target in relation to benefit envisaged if not fully, then whether the benefit lies between 0 to 99.

Again an attempt has been made to search a few islands in the Ocean of vast Government work. These islands are voluntary organisations, developmental efforts either financed by one ministry or more from the Govt. of India or through State Government or through local bodies or through own resources or contribution of Philanthropic societies and by internal and foreign agencies.

Voluntary organisations undertake projects or schemes mostly of socio-welfare orientation. Productive efforts done by them cover only 13 per cent of the total work. For example, the work of Santhal Paharia Seva Mandal can be judged from its budget. Its major coverage is health, child care, pregnant mother and delivery schemes. Then comes the welfare and educational schemes. Lastly, the productive schemes include production of Khadi cloth, cotton, Tasar silk, Katya, etc. Its budgets are similar in different year. Budget samples are shown in Appendix. There is one voluntary organisation which is newly formed and functioning in Mihijam situated on the boarder of Bihar and Bengal. The work of this agency is totally production-oriented in the field of sericulture relating to raring of edi and tasar silk yarn, cocoon processing, spinning, weaving and marketing. It gives 80 per cent tribal employment to male and female both, chiefly Santhal. The following table will reveal the reality.

Badlao Foundation, Mihijam Welfare Activities (1985-89)

Welfare activities	1985-86		1986-87		1987-88		1988-89	
	No.of benefi-ciaries	*Total income in Rs.*	*No. of benefi-ciaries*	*Total income in Rs.*	*No. of benefi-ciaries*	*Total income in Rs.*	*No. of benefi-ciaries*	*Total income in Rs.*
Sericulture	253	553027	265	567466	276	577810	297	630915
Animals and husbandry	67	1056603	91	124506	94	127764	98	131076
Fisheries	71	123365	74	126753	77	128432	78	129934
Cane-bamboo industry	16	64305	19	76588	21	84974	23	93405

In this context work of one more prestigious voluntary agency Ramakrishna Math, Jamtara is worth mentionable. They have taken up whole village comprising only Santal. Their work is commendable and they are doing for village reconstruction in the field of agricultural production details of which are as follows.

(B) REPORT OF THE TRIBAL WELFARE PROJECT TILL THE YEAR 1989

The Ramakrishna Math at Jamtara is a very old Ashram. It was established in the year 1921 by the Second President of this Holy Order Revered Srimat Swami Shivanandaji Maharaj. Its inception was basically as a retreat centre for the monks of this order.

But times have changed and keeping pace alongwith the growth of science and technology they too have kept their horizons wider. Even then it was realised that though the world is growing fast Jamtara lying in a remote corner of Bihar was still to see the daylight of advancement made elsewhere. It was decided to convert this centre into a bustling place where people come for knowledge. It has now become a bastion of revolution, the revolution carried on the Ideals land down by Sri Ramakrishna and Swami Vivekananda. The immortal ideals being 'service to man is service to God."

We therefore started in the year 1988 our Tribal Welfare Project. We took up four villages comprising only of Santhals. With meagre and limited resources but with the full co-operation of the Ramakrishana Mission Lakashiksha Parishad, Narendrapur we started the work regardless of the obstacles. Lying in the Santhal Parganas of Bengal and Bihar this place has a lot of inherent problems. The soil is hard and rocky. The slopes uneven and water is a very precious commodity. Trees are scarce and the climate is extreme. Being in a corner it has always been neglected and transport is still poor.

The first problem we faced was the distrust of the villagers, which is an inherent trait of every closed community alongwith their being an oppressed lot from times immemorial. That some one could come for their welfare was beyond their comprehension. They first thought that we were politically motivated, then later on that we were trying to sweet talk them into giving up their lands. Poor souls they did not even know that according to the Santhal Parganas law no land can be given away as gift or debt. Then was the language. But all those paled away when accosted by the natural conditions prevailing there.

But sorrow seeks its own companions and slowly we could gain their guarded confidence. We started learning their language also.

We began with four programmes:

1. Non-Formal School.
2. Agriculture.
3. Medical Aid.
4. Bamboo and Cane products straining.

Along with the above other programmes were also taken up and will be detailed below as and when necessary.

A. Non-Formal School

Each village has a non-formal School. Formerly the young boys did not go to school because it was too far and their natural spirit of freedom was hampered. So we brought education to their doorsteps. We selected the most educated person of the village who often turned out to be Class VIII pass and made them the teacher. Wide parameters were given as to the syllabus and they taught according to their capacity. They were paid the wages prevailing at the time that is, Government wages prescribed for non-formal school teachers. Each school was given a petromax lantern. The boys and girls were given slates and books. A blackboard was also supplied. In each village a house was provided by the people themselves for this purpose. The four schools and their strength are listed below.

Village name	*First year*		*Second year*	
	Boys	*Girls*	*Boys*	*Girls*
Baghdhara	15	10	20	10
Rampur	8	8	8	10
Kanchanbera	24	10	20	10
Amlabani	17	10	20	15

Before the project started there was not a single girl student but now due to the opening of the schools in the village itself girls are attending and this is bound to increase with time.

Today the villagers are aware of the need of education and so are taking care to see that their ward receives education. The medium being Santhali they feel very easy and have picked up a lot of Hindi, Bengali and English as well.

B. Medical Aid

When this was first started we had to face opposition from the people that these were spurious drugs and better to throw then). Later on they began to doubt the motive and said that we were out to fleece money from the authorities. But slowly we overcame the initial problems. Formally after dispensing the medicines we had to go to the village and check up on the patients as to whether they were taking dosage or not and many a time advice them to take it. Today the scene has changed and the people have become more aware of the need of preventive and curative aspects of medical aid. They regularly take the medicines and do not wait till its worse.

The dispensary runs only one day a week, i.e., Saturday from 4 p.m. to 6 p.m. Medicines are dispensed free. This programme was started in the year 1987 and from 2 to 3 patients in a week in 1987 it has now increased to 50 to 55 patients in a week in 1989. This year we treated 1,525 patients. Since T.B. was rampant in the four villages we undertook to eradicate it completely, 25 cases were identified and treated. Today there is not a single case of T.B. in the four villages under us. We are at present treating 17 patients who are tribals but from other villages.

In the year 1990 we plan to take up immunisation programme. The child mortality percentage is high about 4 dying in every 10 born. Out of the remaining six, two succumb to polio and thus the need for immunisation. We are taking it up late because of the fear of the people of sickness which appear on taking the dose. We have also been able to convince the people of the need of family planning and five couples have agreed to utilise the facility given.

The Eastern Coalfields Limited, Ladies Club donate milk powder for the nutrition purpose of the children. Each child is given 150 ml. of milk three days a week, in the village itself. Their ages range from 1 year to 6 years. The beneficiaries number up to 250.

Besides the above the Math also runs a Homeopathy Clinic 6 days a week in the morning from 9 A.M. to 12 noon. This is open for all. This year it treated 9,720 patients.

A free Cataract Operation Camp was organised on and from 3rd November to 10th November. The number of patients was 74. The operation was performed by Dr. Sunil C. Bagchi, FRCS and his team of doctors. All the cases were successful. The Gujarati Relief Society of Calcutta donated the medicines for the camp and each patient was given a blanket on being discharged,

C. Bamboo and Cane Products Training

Economic independence is what is the main cause of poverty and dependency on money lenders. With this point in view, the bamboo and cane products training programmes were started. Since bamboo is found in abundance here and along with cane from outside the products are worth their name. Primarily to preserve their cultural heritage of handicrafts and also to add to their income as a side occupation. There are 7 boys at present who work here. Five are in production having acquired the necessary skill and two have just recently joined as trainees. There are 4 tribals and 3 non-tribals. Local markets like Chittaranjan and Assansol are present and this year the sale crossed over Rs. 10,000.

The reason as to why this has not caught on is because it is a time consuming and skillful art and they have not the patience to learn it. Also the day's pay is Rs. 10 at par with the market price, but the people rather work as daily labour then be skilled. But slowly we are making inroads.

D. Agriculture

Though the land is hard and rocky and water scarce, the main source of livelihood for these people is agriculture. This was one of the main thrust areas. The tribals by nature are very lazy people. They take life as it comes. Scanty rainfall due to denudation of forest has led to lot of people becoming daily labours in the Jamtara town which is 5 km. away. We took it up as a challenge to change all this.

Land Under Cultivation	*Low lands*	*Uplands*	*Total*
Before Project	253.75 acr	—	253.75 acr
First year	259.50 acr	7.00 acr	266.50 acr
Second year	275.00 acr	20.00 acr	295.00 acr

Details of the Crops and their Respective Yields

Crops	*Before Project*		*First Year*		*Second Year*	
	Area	*Yield*	*Area*	*Yield*	*Area*	*Yield*
Rice	250.00 acr	1500.00 q.	255.00 acr	1785.00 q.	258 acr	1815.00 q.
Wheat	@ 6 q/acres	@ 7 q/acres	@ 10 q/acrs (HYV)			
	1.00 acr	6.00 q.	5.00 acr	32.50 q.	20 acr	130.00 q.
Maize	@ 6 q/acr		@ 6.5 q/acr		@ 6.5 q/acr	
	1.98 acr	1.50 q.	2.00 acr	6.00 q.	8 acr	24.00 q.
Bakra	@ 3 q/acr		@ 3 q/acr		@ 3 q/acr	
	0.25 acr	0.625 q.	1.00 acr	2.50 q.	2 acr	5.G0 q.
Potato	@ 2.5 q/acr		@ 2.5 q/acr		@ 2.5 q/acr	
	1.00 acr	10.00 q.	1.50 acr	18.00 q.	2 acr	30.00 q.
Arhar	@ 10 q/acr		@ 12 q/acr		@ 15 q/acr	
	1.00 acr	5.00 q.	2.00 acr	11.00 q.	5 acr	30.00 q.
	@ 5 q/acr		@ 5.5 q/acr		@ 6 q/acr	

The mandays were calculated and found as below:

	Days	*Productivity*
Before Project	11 days	Rs. 600
First year	37 days	Rs. 1,950
Second year	69 days	Rs. 4,756

@ 1 bigha one person and prevailing market price of yield (1 q.) Agricultural loans which were given have shown a high percentage of return. The first year Rs. 5,400 given to 31 beneficiaries—80 per cent return. The second year Rs. 10,800 given to 137 beneficiaries—60 per cent return. The reason being irregular rainfall and crops failing. Many of the cultivation done now is by cooperative. The HYV paddy I.T.E. 1444 Rassi was used as demonstration but yield was poor due to lack of rainfall. However winter crops and a few summer crops are being intended.

Firstly their methods were age old. We taught them better methods of farming. They used old low yielding seeds and we substituted them with the high yielding variety. Along side we supplied them with fertilizers and pesticides which they had never used before. Pumps were made available for their use. Since rice is their main food they used to grow only paddy during the rainy season. Other crops like wheat, maize, arhar, bajra and potato were virtually unknown. They were slowly introduced by us and now have gained acceptance amongst them. Formerly only the lowlands used to be cultivated but now uplands have also been included. There is a small rivulet flowing past the villages which gathers water from the sub-soil seeping through. Four chock bandhs have been built and where the level used to be only a feet, has an accumulation of nearly seven feet. This is used for winter cultivation. We have thus increased the number of mandays of these people. They have now begun to show an interest in agriculture. The foregoing table will give an idea of the development in this field, along with the above programmes we are also trying to inculcate the orbit of animal husbandry but it will take a long time. Non-formal adult education in the form of weekly meetings are held to teach the elders the importance of health and hygine. Three plantations have been taken up in earnest and will now be given a major thrust in the year 1990. One of the villages—Amlabani 250 people (Population) have built a club and the entire village has decided to do cooperative farming. The Eastern Coalfields Limited. Ladies Club has donated a small protable B/W T.V. which is taken to the villages and thus the people are made aware of the world. Four boys have gone to Narendrapur for training in pump repairing for the session 1989-90 for three months and will work in the village on the completion of their course. Fourteen persons were taken to Ranchi on an educational tour. For the winter season we have distributed amongst the poorer villagers 76 pcs, of saries, 25 pcs. dhotis, 176 pcs. old pants and shirts.

One of the most fascinating developments was the initiative taken by four tribals desirous of initiation from this Holy Order. Some of them even came and attended the prayer which is held daily.

But a lot still remains to be done for development work is always on unfinished agendá.

Now developmental activities being done by Government including voluntary agencies and cooperative activities (LAMBS) are presented on the basis of conducted socio-economic sample survey of 500 families. Tables are presents here after. Similarly, working of Santhal Paharia Seva Mandal in the field of rural upliftment and more particularly agricultural development on the scientific line of action is as follows:

The villages taken for working are in the Deoghar district of Santhal division. It has been found out that the Santhal Paharia Seva Mandal is also doing miraculous work in setting Paharias and nursing in them attitude of regular settled cultivation in place of sifting cultivation, but uptil now progress made in this regard is that Nomadic Paharias have settlements partially where Government had failed.

Here in the subsequent paragraph achievements of Santhal Paharia Seva Mandal in the field of modern agriculture in the Santhal villages are described below.

(C) REPORT OF HOME SCIENCE ACTIVITIES FROM JUNE 1985 TO JULY 1987

Chanda Prasad, Training Associate

Home Science Unit of Seva Mandal Krishi Vigyan Kendra, Sujani, Deoghar has been started on June 1985. The objective was to plan and conduct the need-based skill-oriented training programmes for the farm ladies, school drop outs, village level community workers, etc

Extension programme in the village helped the farm ladies in adopting the new techniques in the field of Home Science, Crop Production, Horticulture and Animal Husbandary time-to-time.

The simple and suitable skills such as the latest technology has been developed and passed on the women folk. The main emphasis was given to the need of the local people and the priority have been fixed to Smokeless Chullah, fruit and vegetable preservation, health and child care and nutrition. In addition, Tailoring and Embroidary, knitting, Handicrafts, use of waste materials, etc. were also covered in the training programme. The details are given on next page.

Sl. No.	Title of the Programme	Duration	No. of Candi-dates	No. of pro-gramme
1.	Nutrition	14 days	125	5
2.	Tailoring and Embroidery	220 days	103	15
3.	Knitting	26 days	21	4
4.	Nutrition garden	14 days	47	3
5.	Health, Hygiene & Sanitation	15 days	59	5
6.	Child and mother care	20 days	73	6
7.	Fruit and vegetable preservation	36 days	136	15
8.	Handicrafts	41 days	38	4
9.	Use of waste material	4 days	38	3
10.	Smokeless Chullah	16 days	169	9
11.	Low cost nutritive recipe	1 day	15	1
	Total		824	70

1. Nutrition, Health and Child Care

Course on Nutrition, health and child care was organised for rural women. Main emphasis was laid upon to improve the nutritional status of the whole family by encouraging village women to consume more and more nutritions inexpensive foods, i.e., green leafy vegetables (Amar nath, cabbage, phoolgobhi, sag, colocacia leaves) (Arbi) drum stick leaves, corriander leaves, radish leaves and spinach, tomatoes, papaya, sprouted (green gram whole) etc., which are locally available. They were also highlightened with the proper cooking methods, weaning mixtures and improved weaning practices.

Observation

The programme started with balanced diet and its importance. Some of the ladies expressed that all the items mentioned under food groups are consumed by them daily. But at the end they were convinced that they were not consuming in enough quantities. According to them the cereal is the dominating item in the diet. Hence, they were made to understand that the available items can be consumed properly to keep away the malnutrition and deficiency diseases.

The deficiency diseases commonly present are night

blindness, leanbody, crack in the corner of the mouth and pale body. For which the remedy was given to use available green leafy vegetables, sprouted pulses, papayas, amla and milk daily to the possible extent.

The cooking methods were also found to be deficient and the correct ways were shown through chart and demonstration.

The concerned families started using the vegetable, sprouted pulses, papaya, etc. in their diet due to the availability of vegetable and fruit in their back yards.

2. *Tailoring, Embroidery and Knitting*

As a part of self-employment activity on campus training programme activity in tailoring Embroidery and Knitting were conducted for about 230 days duration. The trainees were selected from those families, where there is an immense urge to raise their family income. Course content was divided into various steps and the time to complete each skill was adjusted according to their individual efficiency of learning technique.

Observation

60 per cent of the trainees are totally illiterate, hence they had to learn numericals and Hindi alphabets. First they were taught the numericals and in the next steps they were asked to identify the numbers on the measuring tape for taking 1/3rd or 1/4th of the total measurements. They were also taught to fold the tape three times or four times with the measured length of tape to get required measurement.

There was a competitive spirit among trainees which resulted in fast and accurate learning. Infact this helped some trainees to learn Hindi alphabets and numericals to be at par with others which reduced the problems while drafting. Since the programme was started with simple garments like Jangias, underwear, petticoat, later on there was no problem in stitching garments like shirts, blouse, half pant, etc.

Besides, these programme nutrition, child and mother care, preparation of pickles, squash, jelly and Murrabba, demonstration of smokeless chullah, use of waste materials were also conducted to these trainees.

3. Fruit and Vegetable Preservation

On campus as well as off campus training programme was conducted on fruit and vegetable preservation, keeping in view the available materials in the villages. The main objective of this programme is to preserve the fruit and vegetables when they are surplus for off seasons.

Observation

Jackfruit, mango, tomatoes are abundant during season. Very few are in the habit of making preserves. Hence, items like jackfruit pickles, mango squash, tomatoes sauce, guava. jelly, etc. were demonstrated by involving trainees.

In addition, training programme on smokeless chullahs were given and as respect so far 69 families have adopted this new technology which in turn, reduced the drudgery of rural women. The entire village of Govindpur was converted to a smokeless village.

The training course both integrated and specific were designed and imparted to the beneficiaries of the programme as well as other families of the adopted villages. In addition, a number of extension activities such as farmer's fairs, field days, preparation and distribution of leaflets were also taken up for giving support to the programme and for having multiplier effect of the programme.

Mahila Mandal (Women clubs) were organised which helped in improving the skills of the farm women for better living.

By learning about nutrition and child-care they have improved their living habits and started paying more attention to the proper development of their children.

Some of the rural women have learnt a few food crafts such as papad-making, badi-making. They can also make beautiful dolls and other useful articles such as plastic wire bag, sutti bag, and tokri.

Extension Publication

For wide dissemination of 'Transfer of Technology' publication of extension literature was considered indispensable. In course of two year (1985-87) the following publication either in leaflets and other literature form have been brought out for distribution among the literate farm women and others interested in home-science.

Subject	*Title of the Publication*
Home Science	1. Dhuma Rahit Chullah.
	2. Ahar men Dudh Ka Paustic Mahtwa.
	3. Kupushan Ek Am Samashaya.
	4. Paustik Bayanjan.

Training Programme

Before starting the training programme visits were made for surveying in the present condition and to assorted needs of the village people. Then the selection of the training takes place according to the norms of the ICAR.

Keeping in view of this different type of the short and long term courses organised by this unit, emphasising specially in food and nutrition child care and mother care, Health and Hygiene, some scientific practices in cooking of foods. New technique adopted in agriculture development and in kitchen garden, fruit preservation practices, tailoring, knitting and in allied crafts etc.

The programme for the year, 1985 to 1987, were planned with the help of our past experience. There are certain farming operations which are left entirely to women, these include seeding, transplanting of seedlings, weeding, fertilizer application and processing and storage of food grains, pig management, goat management are included in the future programme.

List of the Villages from where Trainees Come for Home-Science Training Programme

Sl. No.	*Name of the Village*	*Block*	*District*
1	*2*	*3*	*4*
1.	Rakudih	Deoghar	Deoghar
2.	Jamuni	"	"
3.	Konkribank	"	"
4.	Kaduatilha	"	"

(*Contd.*)

1	2	3	4
5.	Sujani	,,	,,
6.	Govindpur	,,	,,
7.	Baghori	,,	,,
8.	Lerwa	,,	,,
9.	Bangberia	,,	,,
10.	Ghoriash	,,	,,
11.	Dharawadih	,,	,,
12.	Sirsia	Madhupur	,,
13.	Banoga	Deoghar	,,
14.	Madhuban	Mohanpur	,,
15.	Muridih	Kundohit	Dumka
16.	Khijuria	,,	,,
17.	Suiapara	,,	,,
18.	Maheshpur	Kundshit	,,
19.	Badahit	Sariyahat	,,
20.	Garh Simla	Sundar Pahari Godda	,,
21.	Angwali	-do-	,,
22.	Gandey	Gandey Giridih	,,
23.	Vijaydih	Jamua	,,

The study will select five tribal dominated villages from the four districts of Santhal Pargana division, viz., Godda, Deoghar, Dumka and Sahebganj, From each district 5 villages are being made the target of study. From each village 50 respondent including male and female have been chosen. How they have experienced from the welfare-oriented and developmental schemes? Average 10 independent exclusive schemes practiced 20 different areas have been examined. Thus, total 1000 respondent surveyed through a well trained team of investigators on the basis of empirical-oriented questionnaires as far as practicable exactness has been brought in qualification. On this basis table has been drawn and analysed and in conclusion result has been drawn regarding comparative efficiency of Government and voluntary organisation.

TABLE 6.1

Important Statistics of Santhal Pargana Division

			Bihar State	*Santhal Pargana District*
1		*2*	*3*	*4*
Population	Total	Persons	69,914,734	3,717,528
		Males	35,930,560	1,899,410
		Females	33,984,174	1,818,118
	Rural	Persons	61,195,744	3,461,435
		Males	31,170,556	1,760,678
		Females	30,025,188	1,700,757
	Urban	Persons	8,718,990	256,093
		Males	4,760,004	138,732
		Females	3,958,986	117,361
Decennial Population Growth Rate 1971-81			+ 24.06	+ 16.65
Area (sq. kms.)			173,877.0	14,206.0
Density of Population (per sq. km.)			402	262
Sex Ratio (Number of Females per 1,000 Males)			946	957
Literacy Rate		Persons	26.20	22.26
		Males	38.11	33.49
		Females	13.62	10.52
Percentage of Urban Population to Total Population			12.47	6.89
Percentage to Total Population				
(i) Main Workers		Persons	29.68	33.03
		Males	49.20	53.12
		Females	9.06	12.05
(ii) Marginal Workers		Persons	2.67	7.67
		Males	0.98	2.18
		Females	4.44	13.40
(iii) Non-workers		Persons	67.65	59.30
		Males	49.82	44.70
		Females	86.50	74.55

(Contd.)

1	2	3	4
Break-up of Main Workers: Percentage Among Main Workers—			
(i) Cultivators	Persons	43.57	59.62
	Males	46.71	62.23
	Females	25.54	47.60
(ii) Agricultural Labourers	Person	35.50	20.86
	Males	30.65	17.51
	Females	63.33	36.28
(iii) Household Industry	Persons	2.38	3.78
	Males	2.32	3.49
	Females	2.76	5.12
(iv) Other Workers	Persons	18.55	15.74
	Males	20.32	16.77
	Females	8.37	11.00
Percentage of Scheduled Castes Population to Total Population	Persons	14.51	8.39
	Males	14.36	8.36
	Females	14.67	8.42
Percentage of Scheduled Tribes Population toTotal Population	Persons	8.31	36.80
	Males	8.11	36.34
	Females	8.52	37.27
Number of Occupied Residential Houses		9,891,123	616,245
Number of Villages	Total	79,208	12,250
	Inhabited	67,546	10,015
	Uninhabited	10,302	2,142
	Constituents of Towns	1,360	93
Number of Towns		220	12

TABLE 6.2

Details of Operational Holding in Santhal Pargana Division

Category	*Size Class in Heals*		*Operational Holdings*	
			Number	*percentage*
	Below	0.5	145.5	29.1
Marginal	0.5	1.0	92.0	18.4
Small	Below	1.0	237.5	47.5
	1.0	2.0	97.5	19.5
	2.0	3.0	66.0	13.2
	3.0	4.0	33.5	6.7
Semi-	2.0	4.0	99.5	19.9
Medium	4.0	5.0	26.0	5.2
	5.0	7.5	21.5	4.3
	7.5	10.0	10.5	2.1
Medium	4.0	10.0	58.0	11.6
	10.0	20.0	6.0	1.2
	20.0	30.0	1.0	0.2
	30.0	40.0	0.5	0.1
	40.0	50.0	6.0	0.0
	50.0 and above		—	—
Large	10.0 and above		7.5	1.5
Total			500.0	100.0

TABLE 6.3

Comparative Tribal Demography of Santhal Pargana Division

		Bihar State	*Santhal Pargana District*	*Percentage*
Rural	Persons	61135744	3461435	
	Males	31170556	1760678	
	Females	30025188	1700757	
Urban	Persons	8718990	056093	
	Males	4760004	138732	
	Females	3938994	117361	
Total	Persons	69914734	3717528	
	Males	35930560	1899410	
	Females	33984174	1818118	

TABLE 6.4

Development of Irrigation Facilities in the Santhal Pargana Division

Year	*Govt. Canal*	*Private*	*Tank*	*Tubewell*	*Ordinary*	*Others*	*Total*
1946-47	—	3625	55023	—	1977	26910	329740
1950-51	—	35440	202710	—	14468	77594	350212
1954-55	—	517	155557	—	3236	53690	213000
1960-61	8197	1105	95376	500	2540	18175	149606
1961-70	13543	3174	75877	1393	5719	26002	125708
1977-78	29810	—	39677	4690	22644	24354	121175
1981-83	57000	—	16160	12240	8160	16320	11016
1989-90	63572	—	25380	17363	10300	27203	16789

TABLE 6.5

Yield of Main Agriculture Crops in the District of Santhal Pargana During the Plan Period

Year	*Rice*	*Wheat*	*Maize*	*Mahua*	*Sugarcane*	*Arhar*	*Sugarcane*	*Potato*	*Mustard*
1947-48	355	3.2	55	—	3.6	—	5.0	—	11.8
1950-51	264	0.8	13.8	—	1.2	—	0.2	—	1.1
1953-54	503	1.2	24.8	7.0	4.7	4.1	0.5	—	3.3
1960-61	503	3.3	84.09	—	11.1	4.5	5.4	4.7	4.6
1970-71	395	19.8	10.8	0.4	2.6	1.9	13.1	19.9	4.8
1978-79	543	43	44	1.4	5.0	1.0	12	14.0	2.2
1981-83	459	34	72	—	6.0	5.0	16	52.0	—
1989-90	532	39	97	1.4	5.7	2.2	21	60.0	—

TABLE 6.6

Socio-Economic Position of Sample Villages of Dumka District

Name of the Villages	*Area of villages (in km²)*	*Total Population*			*Scheduled Tribes*		*Literates*		*Total Main Workers*	
		P	*M*	*F*	*M*	*F*	*M*	*F*	*M*	*F*
1	*2*	*3*	*4*	*5*	*6*	*7*	*8*	*9*	*10*	*11*
Masalia	229.35	515	280	235	85	92	174	52	156	18
Jamtara	313.83	13888	7555	6333	280	181	5090	2572	3564	259
Narayanpur	221.55	1395	726	669	10	7	392	127	388	45
Nala	232.57	1516	793	723	31	26	458	204	330	17
Kundahit	285.38	2022	1053	969	24	21	667	252	558	74

(Contd.)

TABLE 6.6 (*Contd.*)

Name of the Villages	*Cultivators*		*Agricultural Labour*		*Household Industry*		*Other Workers*		*National Workers*		*Non-Workers*	
	M	*F*	*M*	*F*	*M*	*F*	*M*	*F*	*M*	*F*	*M*	*F*
1	*12*	*13*	*14*	*15*	*16*	*17*	*18*	*19*	*20*	*21*	*22*	*23*
Masalia	56	2	7	13	13	1	80	2	—	—	124	217
Jamtara	534	71	103	21	68	26	2859	241	91	28	3900	5946
Narayanpur	119	6	54	21	14	2	201	16	—	35	338	589
Nala	331	—	23	7	1	—	173	10	133	96	330	610
Kundahit	158	15	98	32	7	4	295	23	27	15	468	880

TABLE 6.7

Socio-Economic Position of the Sample Villages of Deoghar District

Name of the Villages	*Area of Villages (in km²)*	*Total Population*			*Scheduled Tribes*		*Literates*		*Total Main Workers*	
		P	*M*	*F*	*M*	*F*	*M*	*F*	*M*	*F*
1	*2*	*3*	*4*	*5*	*6*	*7*	*8*	*9*	*10*	*11*
Dharwadih	488.09	830	418	412	216	220	104	19	221	1
Siktia Jogiya	480.90	701	383	318	265	246	140	45	190	20
Kanali	91.23	316	168	148	163	141	38	7	89	6
Dubjora	236.67	294	167	127	57	43	32	5	93	22
Palojori	197.77	467	223	244	152	171	101	10	138	—

(*Contd.*)

TABLE 6.7 (*Contd.*)

Name of the Villages	*Cultivators*		*Agricultural Labour*		*Household Industry*		*Other Workers*		*Marginal Workers*		*Non-Workers*	
	M	*F*	*M*	*F*	*M*	*F*	*M*	*F*	*M*	*F*	*M*	*F*
1	*12*	*13*	*14*	*15*	*16*	*17*	*18*	*19*	20	21	22	23
Dharwadih	216	—	—	—	—	—	5	1	—	—	197	411
Siktia Jogiya	61	7	18	4	8	7	103	2	35	94	158	204
Kanali	83	2	2	1	—	—	4	3	—	24	79	118
Dubjora	54	10	21	11	3	1	15	—	—	—	74	105
Palojori	118	—	10	—	2	—	8	—	15	162	70	82

TABLE 6.8

Socio-Economic Position of Sample Villages of Godda District

Name of the Villages	*Area of Villages (in km²)*	*Total Population*			*Scheduled Tribes*		*Literates*		*Total Main Workers*	
		P	*M*	*F*	*M*	*F*	*M*	*F*	*M*	*F*
1	*2*	*3*	*4*	*5*	*6*	*7*	*8*	*9*	*10*	*11*
Tuka	146.35	329	160	169	169	169	20	—	87	6
Balua	131.37	351	182	169	182	169	23	—	109	92
Basbhita	69.13	373	185	188	185	188	17	—	126	29
Diara	77.15	215	110	105	110	105	32	1	56	38
Tilabad	390.89	692	353	339	312	306	110	34	199	44

(Contd.)

TABLE 6.8 (*Contd.*)

Name of the Villages	*Cultivators*		*Agricultural Labour*		*Household Industry*		*Other Workers*		*Marginal Workers*		*Non-Workers*	
	M	*F*	*M*	*F*	*M*	*F*	*M*	*F*	*M*	*F*	*M*	*F*
1	*12*	*13*	*14*	*15*	*16*	*17*	*18*	*19*	*20*	*21*	*22*	*23*
Tuka	82	5	—	1	5	—	—	—	—	79	73	84
Balua	51	—	—	55	91	—	1	3	—	—	73	77
Basbhita	83	8	43	21	—	—	—	—	—	—	59	159
Diara	47	34	8	4	—	—	1	—	—	5	24	62
Tilabad	178	—	15	43	2	—	4	1	—	7	153	289

TABLE 6.9

Socio-Economic Position of Sample Villages of Sahebganj District

Name of the Villages	Area (in sq. km²)	Total Population			Scheduled Tribes		Literates		Total Main Workers	
		P	M	F	M	F	M	F	M	F
1	2	3	4	5	6	7	8	9	10	11
Talihari	149.42	918	460	458	245	262	155	88	219	70
Lakhanpur	103.59	157	81	76	81	76	—	—	44	19
Telo	428.61	1432	726	706	321	337	173	18	371	132
Litipara	460.72	214	641	573	474	471	318	112	373	43
Hiranpur	132.95	514	261	253	46	47	126	65	125	50

(*Contd.*)

TABLE 6.9 (*Contd.*)

Name of the villages	*Cultivators*		*Agricultural Labour*		*Household Industry*		*Other Workers*		*Marginal Workers*		*Non-Workers*	
	M	*F*	*M*	*F*	*M*	*F*	*M*	*F*	*M*	*F*	*M*	*F*
1	*12*	*13*	*14*	*15*	*16*	*17*	*18*	*19*	*20*	*21*	*22*	*23*
Talihari	89	6	16	18	11	1	103	45	6	26	235	362
Lakhanpur	38	17	—	—	—	—	6	2	—	30	37	27
Telo	264	101	75	25	23	4	9	2	9	154	346	420
Litipara •	161	10	45	20	13	—	154	13	88	202	180	338
Hiranpur	26	—	33	2	10	48	56	—	8	8	133	195

TABLE 6.10

Amenities Available in the Sample Villages: District—Dumka

Name of the Village	*Area (in Km.^{2})*	*Total Population*	*Educational*	*Literates*	*Medical*	*Drinking Water (Potable)*
1	2	3	4	5	6	7
Masalia	229.35	515	PMH	226	(—5)	WR
Jamtara	313.83	13888	PMCC	7662	HRP	WRO
Narayanpur	221.55	1395	PM	519	–(5-10)	W
Nala	232.57	1516	PM	662	–(5-10)	W
Kundahit	285.38	2022	PM	919	–(—5)	W

(Contd.)

TABLE 6.10 (*Contd.*)

Name of the Village	*Post and Telegraph*	*Day or Days of Market*	*Communications: Bus Stop, Railway Station Waterways*	*Approach to Village*	*Power Supply*	*Staple, Food*
1	*8*	*9*	*10*	*11*	*12*	*13*
Masalia	Phone	—	B.S.	KR	—	Rice, Maize
Jamtara	Phone	—	B.S.	PR, KR	—	Rice, Maize, Wheat
Narayanpur	–(—5)	–(—5)	B.S.	KR	—	Rice
Nala	–(—5)	–(—5)	B.S.	KR	—	Rice
Kundahit	–(—5)	–(—5)	B.S.	KR	—	Rice

TABLE 6.11

Amenities Available in the Sample Villages: District—Deoghar

Name of the Village	*Area (in Km.^{2})*	*Total Population*	*Educational*	*Literates*	*Medical*	*Drinking Water (Potable)*
1	*2*	*3*	*4*	*5*	*6*	*7*
Dharawadih	488.09	830	-(—5)	123	-(—5)	W
Siktia	480.90	701	P	185	-(—5)	W
Yogiya Kanali	91.23	316	-(—5)	45	-(—5)	W
Dubjora	236.67	294	-(—5)	37	-(—5)	W
Palojori	197.77	467	P	111	-(—5)	W

(Contd.)

TABLE 6.11 (*Contd.*)

Name of the Village	*Post and Telegraph*	*Day or Days of Market*	*Communications: Bus Stop, Railway Station Waterways*	*Approach to Village*	*Power Supply*	*Staple Food*
1	*8*	*9*	*10*	*11*	*12*	*13*
Dharawadih	–(—5)	(—5)	–(—5)	KR	—	Rice
Siktia	–(—5)	–(—5)	–(—5)	KR	—	Rice
Yogiya Kanali	–(—5)	–(—5)	–(—5)	KR	—	Rice
Dubjora	–(—5)	–(—5)	–(—5)	KR	—	Rice
Palojori	PO. Phone	–(—10)	B.S.	KR PR	—	Rice, Wheat

TABLE 6.12

Amenities Available in the Sample Villages: District—Godda

Name of the Village	*Area (in Km?)*	*Total Population*	*Educational*	*Literates*	*Medical*	*Drinking Water (Potable)*
1	2	3	4	5	6	7
Tuka	146.35	329	-(—5)	20	-(5—10)	W, TK
Balua	131.37	351	-(—5)	23	-(5—10)	W
Basbhita	69.13	373	-(—5)	17	-(5—10)	W
Diara	77.15	215	-(—5)	33	-(—5)	W
Tilabad	390.89	692	P.M.	144	-(—5)	W, TK

(Contd.)

TABLE 6.12 (*Contd.*)

Name of the Village	*Post and Telegraph*	*Day or Days of Market*	*Communications: Bus Stop Railway Stn., Waterways*	*Approach to Village*	*Power Supply*	*Staple Food*
1	*8*	*9*	*10*	*11*	*12*	*13*
Tuka	–(-5)	–(5—0)	–(5—10)	KR	—	Rice
Balua	–(—5)	–(5—10)	–(—5)	KR	—	Rice
Basbhita	—(—5)	–(—5)	–(—5)	KR	—	Rice
Diara	–(—5)	–(—5)	–(—5)	KR	—	Rice
Tilabad	P.O.	–(5—10)	–(—5)	KR	—	Rice

TABLE 6.13

Amenities Available in the Sample Villages: District—Sahebganj

Name of the Villages	*Area (in Km²)*	*Total Population*	*Educational*	*Literates*	*Medical*	*Drinking Water (Potable)*
1	2	3	4	5	6	7
Talihari	149.42	918	–(—5)	243	–(—5)	W
Lakhanpur	103.59	157	—	—	—	W
Telo	28.61	1432	–(—5)	191	–(—5)	W
Litipata	460.72	1214	–(—5)	430	–(—5)	W
Hiranpur	132.95	514	P, Na	191	–(—5)	W, TK

(Contd.)

TABLE 6.13 (*Contd.*)

Name of the Village	*Post and Telegraph*	*Day or Days of Market*	*Communications: Bus Stop, Railway Station Waterways*	*Approach to Village*	*Power Supply*	*Staple Food*
1	*8*	*9*	*10*	*11*	*12*	*13*
Talihari	–(—5)	–(5—10)	–(—5)	KR	—	Rice
Lakhanpur	—	–(—5)	—	KR	—	Rice
Telo	–(—5)	–(—5)	–(—5)	KR	—	Rice
Litipata	–(—5)	–(—5)	–(—5)	KR	—	Rice
Hiranpur	–(—5)	–(—5)	–(—5)	KR, NR	—	Rice

TABLE 6.14

Land-use of the Sample Villages of Dumka District

Name of the Village	*Area (in Km.[1])*	*Forest*	*Irrigated by Source*	*Unirrigated*	*Culturable Waste*	*Area not Available for Cultivation*
Masalia	229.35	—	W (0.81)	63.99	0.96	38.36
			O (.27)			
Jamtara	313.83	—	W (.61) TK			
			(6.07)	93.89	5.50	81.16
			O (.93)			
Narayanpur	221.55	—	(.81)	20.81	4.50	55.65
			TK (0.81)			
Nala	232.57	—	R (0.61)	33.28	0.83	15.15
Kundahit	285.38	—	W (0.32)	10.84	4.93	11.36
			(1.78)			

TABLE 6.15

Land-use of the Sample Villages of Deoghar District

Name of the Village	*Area (in Km.^{2})*	*Forest*	*Irrigated by Source*	*Unirrigated*	*Culturable Waste*	*Area not Available for Cultivation*
Dharwadih	488.09	6.19	W (0.41)	53.24	15.49	0.77
Siktia	480.90	8.09	O (8.09)	21.31	7.74	2.07
Jogiya Kanali	91.23	—	R (1.85)	9.11	4.94	1.32
Dubjora	236.67	—	W (1.21)	28.00	—	2.88
			O (0.91)			
Palojori	197.77	—	TK (0.89)	39.38	2.54	3.14

TABLE 6.16

Land-use of the Sample Villages of Godda Districts

Name of the Village	*Area (in Km.^{2})*	*Forest*	*Irrigated by Source*	*Unirrigated*	*Culturable Waste*	*Area not Available for Cultivation*
Tuka	146.35	—	TK (1.05)	22.41	1.30	1.67
Balua	131.37	—	TK (0.45)	23.90	2.56	8.68
Babhita	69.13	—	TK (0.86)	52.13	6.68	9.66
Diara	77.15	—	TK (1.28)	23.63	3.95	7.40
Tilabad	390.89	—	TK (1.67)	31.85	3.55	1.40

TABLE 6.17

Land-use of the Sample Villages of Sahebganj District

Name of the Village	*Area (in Km.^{2})*	*Forest*	*Irrigated by Source*	*Unirrigated*	*Culturable Waste*	*Area not Available for Cultivation*
Talihari	149.42	—	R (3.24)	56.95	—	7.61
Lakhanpur	103.95	—	R (4.05) O (2.02)	15.27	—	1.38
Telo	428.61	—	R (1.21) O (0.81)	1.57	—	0.50
Litipara	460.62	—	R (2.02) O (2.02)	51.07	—	6.06
Hiranpur	132.95	—	W (0.61)	45.66	15.07	1.23

TABLE 6.18

Comparative Picture of Beneficiaries from the Government and Voluntary Agencies in the Sample Villages of Dumka District

Name of the Village	*No. of Persons*	*SCHEMES*									
		Literacy		*Health Care*		*Agriculture Development*		*Livestock*		*Forestry*	
		Govt.	*Vol.*	*Govt.*	*Vol.*	*Govt.*	*Vol.*	*Govt.*	*Vol.*	*Govt.*	*Vol.*
1	2	3	4	5	6	7	8	9	10	11	12
Masalia	105	8	12	10	21	44	6	40	—	105	—
Jamtara	125	11	23	12	25	51	11	71	—	125	—
Narayanpur	85	15	35	9	17	41	9	35	—	85	—
Nala	95	13	33	10	19	49	7	46	—	95	—
Kundahit	90	19	48	9	18	63	12	37	—	90	—
Total	500	66	151	50	100	245	45				

(Contd.)

TABLE 6.18 (*Contd.*)

Name of the Village	*Fishing*		*Mining and Quarring*		*Trade and Commerce*		*Household Industry*		*Other than Household Industry*	
	Govt.	*Vol.*	*Govt.*	*Vol.*	*Govt.*	*Vol.*	*Govt.*	*Vol.*	*Govt.*	*Vol.*
1	*13*	*14*	*15*	*16*	*17*	*18*	*19*	*20*	*21*	*22*
Masalia	10	—	3	—	2	—	3	2	1	—
Jamtara	12	—	5	—	3	—	2	2	1	—
Narayanpur	8	—	1	—	1	—	5	—	1	—
Nala	9	—	2	—	—	—	—	—	1	—
Kundahit	9	—	1	—	—	—	1	—	—	—
Total							11	4		

TABLE 6.19

Comparative Picture of Beneficiaries from the Government and Voluntary Agencies in the Sample Villages of Deoghar District

Name of the Village	*No. of Persons*	*SCHEMES*									
		Literacy		*Health Care*		*Agriculture Development*		*Livestock*		*Forestry*	
		Govt.	*Vol.*	*Govt.*	*Vol.*	*Govt.*	*Vol.*	*Govt.*	*Vol.*	*Govt.*	*Vol.*
1	*2*	*3*	*4*	*5*	*6*	*7*	*8*	*9*	*10*	*11*	*12*
Dharwadih	110	19	65	11	22	51	7	45	—	110	—
Jogiya Kanali	107	21	49	10	21	69	12	39	—	107	—
Dubjora	65	14	31	6	13	31	3	29	—	65	—
Palojori	123	12	22	12	25	79	13	59	—	123	—
Siktia	95	9	23	9	18	35	8	30	—	95	—
Total		75	190	48	99	265	33	202			

(Contd.)

TABLE 6.19 (*Contd.*)

Name of the Village	*Fishing*		*Mining and Quarring*		*Trade and Commerce*		*Household Industry*		*Other than household Industry*	
	Govt.	*Vol.*	*Govt.*	*Vol.*	*Govt.*	*Vol.*	*Govt.*	*Vol.*	*Govt.*	*Vol.*
1	*13*	*14*	*15*	*16*	*17*	*18*	*19*	*20*	*21*	*22*
Dharwadih	11	—	4	—	—	—	2	1	1	—
Jogiya Kanali	10	—	3	—	2	—	—	1	1	1
Dubjora	6	—	2	—	—	—	3	—	1	—
Palojori	12	—	5	—	1	—	—	1	—	—
Siktia	9	—	1	—	1	—	—	1	1	—
Total							5	4		

TABLE 6.20

Comparative Picture of Beneficiaries from Government and Voluntary Agencies in the Sample Villages of Godda District

Name of the Village	*No. of Persons*	*SCHEMES*									
		Literacy		*Health Care*		*Agriculture Development*		*Livestock*		*Forestry*	
		Govt.	*Vol.*	*Govt.*	*Vol.*	*Govt.*	*Vol.*	*Govt.*	*Vol.*	*Govt.*	*Vol.*
1	2	3	4	5	6	7	8	9	10	11	12
Tuka	66	5	8	6	13	26	13	47	—	66	—
Balua	107	6	9	10	21	47	12	59	—	107	—
Babhita	105	3	5	10	21	51	9	47	—	105	—
Diara	97	9	12	9	19	32	3	52	—	97	—
Tilabad	125	25	42	12	25	66	17	74	—	125	—
Total		48	75	48	99	222	54				

(Contd.)

TABLE 6.20 (*Contd.*)

Name of the Village	*Fishing*		*Mining and Quarring*		*Trade and Commerce*		*Household Industry*		*Other than household Industry*	
	Govt.	*Vol.*	*Govt.*	*Vol.*	*Govt.*	*Vol.*	*Govt.*	*Vol.*	*Govt.*	*Vol.*
1	*13*	*14*	*15*	*16*	*17*	*18*	*19*	*20*	*21*	*22*
Tuka	6	—	2	—	—	—	2	1	—	—
Balua	10	—	3	—	—	—	3	—	1	1
Babhita	10	—	4	—	1	—	2	—	—	—
Diara	9	—	3	—	—	—	1	1	1	—
Tilabad	12	—	2	—	2	—	—	1	2	1
Total							8	3		

TABLE 6.21

Comparative Picture of Beneficiaries from Government and Voluntary Agencies in the Sample Villages of Sahebganj District

Name of the Village	*No. of Persons*	*SCHEMES*									
		Literacy		*Health Care*		*Agriculture Development*		*Livestock*		*Forestry*	
		Govt.	*Vol.*	*Govt.*	*Vol.*	*Govt.*	*Vol.*	*Govt.*	*Vol.*	*Govt.*	*Vol.*
1	2	3	4	5	6	7	8	9	10	11	12
Talihari	98	25	48	9	18	15	2	42	—	98	—
Lakhanpur	78	—	—	7	14	45	3	38	—	78	—
Telo	107	13	36	10	21	52	8	45	--	107	—
Litipara	109	29	65	10	21	63	21	72	—	109	—
Hiranpur	108	16	25	10	19	36	15	59	—	108	—
Total		83	174	45	93	211	49				

TABLE 6.21 (*Contd.*)

Name of the Village	*Fishing*		*Mining and Quarring*		*Trade and Commerce*		*Household Industry*		*Other than household Industry*	
	Govt.	*Vol.*	*Govt.*	*Vol.*	*Govt.*	*Vol.*	*Govt.*	*Vol.*	*Govt.*	*Vol.*
1	*13*	*14*	*15*	*16*	*17*	*18*	*19*	*20*	*21*	*22*
Talihari	9	—	—	—	—	—	—	1	—	1
Lakhanpur	7	—	1	—	—	—	2	1	2	1
Telo	10	—	1	—	1	—	1	—	—	1
Litipara	10	—	2	—	1	—	—	—	2	—
Hiranpur	11	—	3	—	2	—	—	1	—	1
Total							3	3		

TABLE 6.22

Per Capita Annual Expenditure in the Sample Villages by Government and Voluntary Institutions of District Dumka

Name of the Sample Village	*Name of the Block*	*Development*		*Welfare*		*Infrastructure*	
		Govt.	*Vol.*	*Govt.*	*Vol.*	*Govt.*	*Vol.*
Masalia	Masalia	11	3	13	6	7	—
Jamtara	Jamtara	15	4	20	8	11	—
Narayanpur	Narayanpur	12	2	10	4	4	—
Nala	Nala	10	1	7	3	3	—
Kundahit	Kundahit	9	1	10	2	1	—
Total		56	11	60	23	26	—

TABLE 6.23

Per Capita Annual Expenditure in the Sample Villages by Government and Voluntary Institutions of District Deoghar

Name of the Sample Village	*Name of the Block*	*Development*		*Welfare*		*Infrastructure*	
		Govt.	*Vol.*	*Govt.*	*Vol.*	*Govt.*	*Vol.*
Dharwadih	Madhupur	7	2	7	1	6	—
Siktia	Deoghar	15	5	5	2	8	—
Jogiya Kanali	Mohanpur	8	1	8	—	5	—
Dubijora	Sarwan	6	—	9	2	2	—
Palojori	Palojori	11	2	12	1	1	—

TABLE 6.24

Per Capita Annual Expenditure in the Sample Villages by Government and Voluntary Institutions of District Godda

Name of the Sample Village	*Name of the Block*	*Development*		*Welfare*		*Infrastructure*	
		Govt.	*Vol.*	*Govt.*	*Vol.*	*Govt.*	*Vol.*
Tuka	Poreyahat	13	3	10	1	9	—
Balua	Pathargama	12	1	8	2	3	—
Basbhita	Mahagama	16	—	11	3	4	—
Diara	Meherma	9	1	9	—	2	—
Tilabad	Sundar Pahari	15	2	15	1	1	—

TABLE 6.25

Per Capita Annual Expenditure in the Sample Villages by Government and Voluntary Institutions of District Sahebganj

Name of the Sample Village	*Name of the Block*	*Development*		*Welfare*		*Infrastructure*	
		Govt.	*Vol.*	*Govt.*	*Vol.*	*Govt.*	*Vol.*
Taljhari	Taljhari	16	4	16	1	3	—
Lakhanpur	Pathna	15	3	12	2	7	—
Telo	Borio	12	2	15		1	—
Litipara	Litipara	11	1	9	1	2	—
Hiranpur	Hiranpur	13	—	11	3	1	—

TABLE 6.26

Ramakrishna Mission
Income and Expenditure A/c of the year 1990

Expenditure	*Amount Rs.*	*Income Rs.*	*Amount Rs.*
Establishment Expenditure	11,67,98,227	Donations	2,14,54,160
Boarding Expenditure	3,89,09,959	Grants from Government	10,05,98,743
Education and Cultural Expenditure	1,60,60,944		
Medical Expenditure	1,08,79,267	Public bodies	65,78,112
Relief and Rehabilitation Expenditure	60,62,393	Fees and charges	6,83,80,724
Rural Development Expenditure	23,82,344	Income from investment	2,48,38,720
Purchases and Production Expenditure	2,23,84,280	Income from sales	2,77,47,346
Puja and Celebration Expenditure	30,69,549	Other Income	59,67,253
Other Expenditure	1,85,54,489	Closing stock	1,03,12,680
Opening stock	93,66,079		
Surplus carried down	2,69,90,207		26,58,77,738
	26,58,77,738		

TABLE 6.27

Santal Pahariya Seva Mandal
Income and Expenditure A/c of the year 1988

Expenditure	*Amount Rs.*	*Income Rs.*	*Amount Rs.*
Establishment Expenditure	1,99,332	Donation and subscription	11,17,407
Expenditure on Welfare activities	23,73,471	Government receipts	6,20,243
Expenditure on Rural Development	14,80,809	Grant from Welfare Department of Bihar	9,00,000
Expenditure in Rehabilitation	4,15,919	Received from Government of India	10,80,125
Expenditure on other Welfare work	2,83,334	Grant from Health Department of India	1,80,920
		Received from Government of India under Rehabilitation of handicapped schemes	1,40,350
		Others	7,13,820
	47,52,865		40,39,045

TABLE 6.28

Adim Jati Seva Mandal
Income and Expenditure A/c of the year 1988

Expenditure	*Amount Rs.*	*Income Rs.*	*Amounts Rs.*
Supplementary food	93619.50	Grants from	
Contingencies	10027.30	Bhartiya Adimjati	
Wages and Salaries	1,24,800.00	Sevak Sangh	1,21,401
Doctor's fees	22,000.00	Central Social	2,47,117.90
Medicines	11,692.17	Welfare Board	
Expenditure on Audit	400.00	Donation	13,733
Depreciation	1,844.23	Bank Interest	13,738.40
Excess of Income over expenditure	1,17,875.00		
	3,82,258.30		3,82,258.30

Socio-economic position of the sample villages indicates that tribals are poorer in comparison to total population. After having a consideration of the samples taken from the targeted area, it is now relevant to present the position of beneficiaries from Government and voluntary organisations from twenty sample villages of Santhal Pargana in the concerned four tables from 6.18 to 6.21. In the five villages from Dumka district the number of adult literates is 66 due to the efforts of voluntary agencies. It means that the achievement of the Government in the field of adult literacy in the sample area of Dumka district is about 1178 while that of voluntary agencies it is about 308. Similarly in the field of health care performance of the Government is about 108 while that of voluntary agencies it is 208. In the field of agriculture the contribution of the Government is almost 508 while that of voluntary agencies it is only 98. In case of live stock raring achievement of voluntary agencies is nil while Government's contribution in this field is about 408. It has also been found out that in forestry, fishing, mining, and quarring. trade and commerce household industry and others achievement of voluntary agencies is nil or negligible, while the role of Government in these fields is undoubtedly positive, but the performance is very poor. Similar is the position in the Deoghar, Godda and Sahebganj districts.

In Tables 6.22 to 6.25 per capita expenditure in the sample

villages by Government and voluntary institutions has been presented in the targeted villages of the four districts. From the expenditure point of view three heads have been indicated, i.e., development, welfare and infrastructure. Per capita annual expenditure has been taken into consideration. With regard to development head, Government expenditure is almost more than five times that of voluntary agencies in Dumka district while in Godda district it is more than seven times and Deoghar it is 4.7 times. In Sahebganj it is 6.7 times. In the field of welfare Government's expense is 2.6 times more than voluntary agencies while in Deoghar it is 6.9 times and in Godda it is 7.5 times and in Sahebganj it is 5.3 times. In the field of infrastructure the position of voluntary agencies is nil. Therefore, the question of comparison does not arise.

The above analysis indicates that capacity of voluntary agencies in relation to Government is much below average. But they are committed workers. On them expenditure is average one-fourth. Their offices are either in a rental houses or in free houses. But in the case of Government it is much more. The total establishment expenditure of the Government is 200 times more than that of voluntary agencies. While on workers it is 10.1 and on salary it is 4:1. Thus, total Government expenditure is much more than that of voluntary organisations.

From the above quantitative analysis in the context of four districts of Santhal Pargana, it also appears that voluntary agencies are avoiding inaccessible areas while Government has no way out than to work in a comprehensive and cohesive area at least in principle.

On the basis of figures of income and expenditure available from the Government and voluntary agencies, socio-economic indicators have been prepared from the targeted areas as well as from the 20 villages in consideration of Government and voluntary agencies. The indicators are presented in the Table 6.29. The indicators speak of the work done by the effort of the Government. According to the indicators, the sample area has its position much below in the division in the field of agricultural production. As has been indicated by the value of output of major crops it is Rs. 1498 per hectare in the division, but it is Rs. 1256 in the sample area. It indicates the difference of two hundred forty-two points. It means in the term of percentage there is a difference

TABLE 6.29

Santhal Pargana's Some Selected Indicators

	All India	*Bihar*	*Santhal Pargana*	*20 Sample villages in Santhal Division*
Index of level of economic development 1990 (All India 100)	100	61	47	37
Area and Population				
Area ('000 sq. kms.)				
Population (Lakhs)	17	23	37	3
Growth of population (%) (1981-90)	25	24	16	1.5
Density (persons/sq. kms.)	216	402	261	60
Urbanisation (%)	23	13	7	Nil
Literacy (%)	36	26	22	4
ST Population (%)	8	8	39	27
Labour Force (%)	33	30	33	28
Labour Force Employed in (%):				
Cultivators (%)	42	44	59	11
Agriculture Labourers (%)	25	35	21	22
Household Industry (%)	3	2	4	1
Others (%)	30	19	16	4
Forest area as % of geographical area	20	16	5	.01
Average size of operational holdings (hectares)	1.0	1.1	2.0	2.4

Per hectare of cropped area (kg.)	45	3	7	6.3
P/H Value of output of major crops (Rs.)	1468	1590	1498	1256
Industry:				
Workers employed in mining and quarrying per lakh persons	109	622	765	745
Workers employed in factories per lakh persons	1057	507	184	103
Employment in household industries per lakh persons	1125	708	1243	1285

of 13.5 per cent. It reveals that the sample survey report has significant position and it has reliability. Similarly in the case of employment, it is almost the same as in the case of the division. Now the question is that the work done by the Government and similar work done as the voluntary agencies which of these two is more efficient. Figures regarding cost and achievement have been presented in the tables. It appears tint on the whole voluntary agencies are comparatively more efficient. According to the tables entitled comparative picture of benefit it appears that in the field of adult literacy the achievement of voluntary agencies is 2.3 times more than that of Government performance. In respect of health voluntary agencies contribution it is just double. The efficiency of the Government is 4.4 times more in the field of agricultural development. Again in the field of live stock raring the contribution of voluntary agencies is nil.

In this context it seems pertinent to say that voluntary agencies are efficient only in limited fields. In the present context, it is impossible that total work maybe done by them, although they are comparatively more efficient than the Government organisation.

It appear by analysing the figures and field observation that they have higher efficiency in limited field and in a limited area. Therefore, it is impossible to entrust the major projects that covers a large region. Thus in the vast ocean of development, they should be entrusted with small field of working and specific project to set examples to inspire Government Organisation. In this way it seems pertinent that they should be allowed to continue only on the basis of specific projects prepared by them and they should be entrusted full autonomy in implementation of such projects. In this regard it is also necessary to suggest that Government should appoint at a given time interval a team of experts dominated by non-Government people to enquire into their working pattern and achievement. The practical aspect of their experience can be utilised in the implementation of Government plan.

Present Comparative Picture

Economic development means change from present status to a higher status both in the macro and micro sense. But from a point where rigidity reigns supreme the level of the socio-economic condition is not static. To generate momentum is not an ordinary task. In a democratic planning set up through its bureaucratic developmental agents the Government enters in a big way to add developmental life blood and to make the society dynamic. In this context in the tribal areas the developmental efforts had different phases in its four decades. The first phase was of general planning efforts which included welfare activities, infrastructure building and development projects. The second phase comprised regional planning era and special regional projects were taken up to suit a particular region, because developmented areas were recognised and for them special projects were allotted for speedy growth, so that these areas could catch the national growth target. But from the Fifth Five Year Plan the present shape of tribal sub-plan takes its birth considering inadequacy of earlier development efforts. But, since the beginning of the developmental efforts voluntary agencies are moving with the governmental efforts in hand and glove.

The plan framers have realised the role of voluntary agencies and they have accepted their role in developmental efforts. The

Government was very keen in helping voluntary agencies in conducting their functions. Therefore, they are given grants and other assistance. On this line government itself organised voluntary agencies with all possible help. The aim behind it was to develop people's co-operative functions between the government and voluntary agencies. No doubt, it is a voluntary organisation, but it guided, and controlled by bureaucrats. Under this circumstance co-operative societies can not be considered as pure voluntary organisations. The story of cooperative movement in the tribal areas which starts from general co-operative societies to LAMP is not related to grand success and our purpose of study which confines between Government and voluntary agencies will not therefore include co-operative movement of the tribal areas.

Now, our study has reached a stage to put forward two vivid pictures, i.e., governmental efforts in welfare and social services as well as infrastructure building and thirdly pure developmental projects. On the other hand, it includes role of voluntary organisations in these fields or beyond them if any.

For this an effort has been made to prepare table on above aspects and deal them in brief. In the end of the Chapter on the basis of analysis of the data collected from the targetted sample villages a conclusion has been drawn.

To collect data in the above context, on the basis of random number and census list five villages from each of the four districts of Santhal Pargana division have been selected. Applying the same principle 500 samples (he or she) have been collected from each of the four districts. Thus altogether 2000 samples have been collected. Direct questions have been prepared in the questionnaire and investigators have been deputed to survey 2000 respondents and data gathered by this were presented in the tables. Tables were framed in a manner so that it can clearly exhibit the achievement of the Government and the voluntary organisations.

Conclusion and Recommendations

In this project an attempt has been made to find out suitable procedure of growth so that it may be smoothly adopted by the population for whom it is meant for. In this context considering the democratic trend of planning and people's participation in tribal life where the plant of growth is not bringing forth suitable fruit, the role of voluntary organisations and government have been explained. The report begins with the presentation of Indian tribal life specially in the socio-economic context. How the growth has changed the tribal life style, has also dealt-with.

In the Second chapter role of voluntary organisations in economic development and social change with special reference to tribal upliftment and more emphatically on Santhals has been dealt-with. Here, an attempt has been made to find out why voluntary organisations are not springing up with full commitment for socio-economic growth. Organisations inside and outside tribals area engaged in socio-economic work are appearing now-a-days but it seems, new life blood is not generated. This has been explained with the help of study of important voluntary organisations like Santhal Paharia Seva Mandal, Adim Jati Sevak Sangh, Ramakrishna Mission, Badlao, Vidyarthi Parished and a few missionary Christian organisations. Their role has been studied in relation to Santhals.

The Fifth Chapter deals with role of Government in tribal development in general and Santhal in particular. Here governments effort in plan has been shown in the context of economic growth. Up-to-date position of recent tribal sub-plan has been taken into account. In the second part of this Chapter how economic development brought social change in the universe of the study has been found out. Santhals are agriculturists. They have tendency to live in permanent settlement. They have their own life style. How they are experiencing development and how they are changing their life style have been presented here.

The Sixth Chapter deals with sample survey for which twenty villages were selected randomly from each of the four districts and by the application of random member 2000 respondents have been selected and surveyed through direct interview. For the purpose of finding out impact of development through government schemes and projects as well as through voluntary organisations.

In the last Chapter the findings of the universe through direct interview has been arranged into tables and on the basis of them a comprehensive assessment has been prepared to expose what has been done by the government and at the same time by voluntary organisations. Again, it has been attempted through primary data to find out the role of voluntary organisations and the mode and area of their working. Why they are inclined to a particular area only or they are true to this thesis that small is beautiful. Considering the points a suitable conclusion has been drawn.

The need for strengthening and suitably equipping the institutional framework can hardly be overemphasised. But no external assistance to the people can become a lasting solution to the problems arising from class of interests and hardening of lines. It is imperative that members of Scheduled Tribes are themselves prepared for facing the challenge. Wherever education has advanced and there is diffusion of knowledge the people have been able to assert for themselves. Nevertheless, the normal processes particularly in tribal areas are so slow that it will be gross in justice to wait for those processes to become strong enough for meeting the challenge. Mobilisation of Scheduled

Castes and Scheduled Tribes, therefore, should be important concerning their welfare and advancement.

The voluntary organisations have played a valuable role wherever they have been able to induct dedicated persons. The State's support for mobilisation of the poor is rather limited notwithstanding the fact that it has been accepted as an integral part of poverty alleviation strategy. Moreover, even, where such support is forthcoming there are inherent limitations in a situation where the concerned people may be struggling against the malfunctioning of the administration itself, as in the case with the tribal people. And in case a voluntary organisation strikes roots and gains confidence of the people it tends to get detracted from its main objective. Its support is coveted by political parties which makes it difficult for them to remain neutral and continue objective espousing of the cause of the poor.

Another serious limitation of State assistance for voluntary work arises from the need for performance appraisal. In mobilisation work the assessment of individual's contribution with reference to certain quantifiable indicators is not possible, which is otherwise so easy, e.g., for institutions engaged in specific social service activities like education, health, etc. Consequently, if the activities of an organisation are limited to mobilisation, there is no real check in a formal system for ensuring that the assistance is being used for the intended purpose. Such organisations may be used just as a ploy for getting funds from the State and may be treated by the administration as a fund giving device to the favourites.

The role of the State aided voluntary agencies with regard to mobilisation can, therefore, be only limited. Some of them are doing commendable work particularly in remote areas where they have established educational and health institutions. But the scope of these activities also cannot be large since the real strength of voluntary organisations is the smallness of their operation. If their work expands beyond a point they are also likely to be begged down with the problems of management as in other bureaucratic organisations. Moreover, the social services are to be provided by the State and what is necessary it that the general quality of those services improves. The small isolated effort, howsoever commendable, cannot be a substitute for an effective and efficient State programme.

The work of mobilisation of the poor needs an informal support structure. Unfortunately, private funds for voluntary social work are almost non-existent notwithstanding the emergence of an outsized class of neo-rich in the country. The experience of inducing industrial houses in philanthropic work has not been a happy one but for a few exceptions. Even in their case the work amongst the Scheduled Tribes did not receive any attention. It is an irony that the major support for voluntary organisations, particularly for those which are presently working in tribal areas, comes from foreign organisations. The voluntary workers in these cases ostensibly enjoy a lot of freedom of operation and can also work for sensitization and mobilisation. But mobilisation through foreign assistance, particularly in sensitive areas of a country, has its own limitations and cannot be allowed to go beyond stringently prescribed limits. Consequently, whatever may be the formal stance of voluntary organisations receiving foreign aid, their role in mobilisation cannot but be limited. Their position is bound to become incongruous when their programme brings them in confrontation with the local administration. Here again is the question of the general national milieu. Much will depend on how the sensitive people in the country respond to these challenges facing the weaker sections of the community.

Having said this, it cannot be conceded that the State can absolve itself of the responsibility of providing the needed support to the people even for their mobilisation against adverse forces, even though they may be emanating from the processes of development or the State's own actions. The State is duty bound to do so, for example, in the case of the Scheduled Castes and Scheduled Tribes, particularly the latter. And this is feasible though within reasonable limitations. The most promising area in this respect will be to channelise the ferment amongst the educated youth some of whom are keen to participate in constructive programmes. A significant number of young men and women are in search of a challenge and a purpose. They are joining voluntary organisations and even extremist groups at considerable risk. But many of them get disillusioned as the scope of work in voluntary organisations cannot sustain their interest for long, particularly because of the problems which they face when basic issues get involved and the struggle against the system through extremist methods proves to be a blind alley. The Government may prepare a plan for involving students, specially those belonging to Scheduled Tribes themselves; for mobilisation work during the course of their educational career, say, after their secondary examinations on a voluntary basis. A student volunteer corps could be organised comprising those students who may agree to work back in the village for one full term and in the processes also organise the people and sensitize them about their rights and responsibilities. It is important that this period should not be less so that non-serious students do not enter. It should not be more either so that it does not degenerate into a job opportunity. Volunteers may be given a subsistence allowance. These students could be given credit for this work if they resume their studies at higher levels and also in the matter of employment by recruiting agencies.

It can, therefore, be suggested that:

(i) Suitable forums may be established at the block, district, state and national levels, for a continuing dialogue with these social activists/voluntary organisations which primarily engaged in the mobilisation of the Scheduled Castes and Scheduled Tribes and resolution of conflict situations which may arise from time to time on various issues with the local officials.

(ii) The Government may consider organising a Student Volunteer Corps, particularly those, belonging to the Scheduled Castes and Scheduled Tribes. Each volunteer may work for a year in the Corps and do mobilisation work through participation in the ordinary economic activities of the people. The student volunteer may be given subsistence allowance equivalent to minimum wage prevalent in the area. This work of volunteers should be accorded academic recognition and should also be given some weightage later in recruitment to services.

In contrast to the situation in the Fifth Schedule areas in middle India, the tribal communities in the North-East are governed by the Sixth Schedule which specifically provides for self-governance with regard to all matters concerning their day-to-day life. This includes management of land and forest resources, adjudication of disputes and criminal acts of individuals. The jurisdiction of the police does not extend to their villages. The tribal people in middle India could not imagine a better place than a State where the Patwari, the Forest Guard, the Police Constable and the Excise Inspector were not present.

Even though the authority of the traditional institutions has been greatly eroded in middle Indian tribal belt, they are still functioning because the civil matters concerning marriage and divorce are still governed by their tradition and managed by the community organisations. Moreover, the people are sacred to approach the administration in other matters as well and prefer settlement within the community because there everyone knows the facts of the case and also the conventions about the settlement. He is spared from the trauma of facing the authorities and the courts where everything is unknown including the procedures and even the convention about making a statement about the facts of the case. The tribal people are facing a tremendous challenge as the authority of their traditional institutions is being increasingly challenged these days in the society. As a community they are facing both the backlash of development and the challenge of individualism. They are destined to face disorganisation of an order unprecedented for any community in the history because of the confluence of forces which they are unable to contend. It is essential that the people are empowered and enabled to respond to the new forces according to their genius.

It can therefore, be suggested that:

At the village level Panchayati Raj institutions in tribal areas should be specially constituted so as to be in consonance with the traditions of the tribal community. This may be done either through a special provision in the concerned Panchayati Raj law or through a Regulation amending the said law to the extent necessary. In particular, it should envisage—

(i) All institutions at the hamlet/village level in tribal areas should be answerable directly to the people in the hamlet/village.

(ii) These institutions should function in the open in accordance with a procedure which may be decided upon by the people in the regard.

(iii) These institutions should have wider responsibilities covering all matters concerning people's day-to-day life and also management of local resources including land and forget.

Taking overall view regarding voluntary agencies and people's participation in plan projects and Government plan implementation which require a suitable balance and which can be achieved by allocating fund of depending on the size and degree of projects, it appears that voluntary agencies prefer work in the fields of adult literacy, village and household industries, health care, child welfare, etc., i.e., mostly welfare-oriented schemes. Again during emergency, due to some natural or man-made havocs, they come forward with various kinds of resques. They are also responsible for creating macro-consciousness, so that people may realise dignity to work as well as their place and involvement in plan. Therefore, it is essential that they should be involved in the matters detailed above.

Clear cut principles regarding the workers and organisers of voluntary agencies should be evolved. Further there should be a code of conduct for state and national organisations. Their fund should be audited annually in a proper way by central team of auditors under the guidance of Controller and Auditor General of India. Further as indicated in the study there should be a special commissioner type office in Delhi or at other central places like the Commissioner of Scheduled Castes and Scheduled Tribes for which suitable constitutional provisions may be made. It is also necessary to have a central body having adequate power and norm to guide inspire and suggest different registered or other type of voluntary agencies, so that they can become efficient.

At present voluntary agencies are inevitable in the context of democracy and mixed economy. It is supposed that it is meant for educating people so that they may become politically and socio-economically conscious as well as dutiful towards national building.

APPENDICES

APPENDIX I

A prospective plan has been prepared for proper development of Santhal Pargana in the context of the project study which is as follows:

Industries for Dumka Sub-Division for the Year 1990-95

Sl. No.	*Name of the units*	*No. of units*	*Location*	*Investment in Lac.*			*Sources of Financed*				*Em-ploy-ment*
				Fixed	*Work-ing*	*Total*	*State Govt.*	*Bank, B.F.C., N.S.I.C.*	*Own*	*Total*	
1	2	3	4	5	6	7	8	9	10	11	12
	Agro-Based										
1.	Modern Rice Mill (250 Kg.)	2	Nonihat & Raneshwar Jame, Ramgarh, Masalia	1.00	2.00	3.00	—	2.25	0.75	3.00	30
2.	Rice & flour Mill (Hull & chakki type)	6	Saraiyahat, Kathikuud & Shikaripara	0.90	0.30	1.20	—	0.90	0.30	1.20	18

3.	Dal Mill	2	Dumka & Jarmundi	1.00	1.50	2.50	—	1.88	0.62	2.50	20
4.	Chura Mill	4	Nonihat Saraiyahat, Jarmundi & Raneshwar	0.80	1.00	1.80	—	1.36	0.44	1.80	20
5.	Oil Mill	1	Dumka	0.55	0.50	1.05	—	0.79	0.26	1.05	5
6.	Bakery	3	Jarmundi, Nonihat & Shikaripara	0.45	0.60	1.05	—	0.79	0.26	1.05	24
7.	Cattle & Poultry feed	1	Dumka	1.00	1.50	2.50	—	1.88	0.62	2.50	16
8.	Fruit Juice & Squashes	1	Dumka	0.35	0.25	0.60	—	0.45	0.15	0.60	10
	Forest-Based										
1.	Sizing of Wood	2	Dumka & Shikaripara	0.60	1.00	1.60	—	1.20	0.40	1.60	10
2.	Wooden furniture & Building Materials	3	Nonihat, Shikaripara & Raneshwar	0.21	0.75	0.96	—	0.72	0.24	0.96	15
3.	Cane & Bamboo Wares	1	Dumka	0.05	0.15	0.20	—	0.15	0.05	0.20	5
4.	Rope-Making	1	Jama	0.15	0.25	0.40	—	0.30	0.10	0.40	6
5.	Tassar Reeling & Spinning	2	Kathikund & Shikaripara	0.40	1.00	1.40	—	1.03	0.37	1.40	20

(*Contd.*)

APPENDIX I *(Contd.)*

1	*2*	*3*	*4*	*5*	*6*	*7*	*8*	*9*	*10*	*11*	*12*
6.	Tassar Silk Weaving	2	Dumka & Shikaripara	0.30	0.90	1.20	—	0.90	0.30	1.20	16
7.	Non-Edible Oil Mill	1	Dumka or Kathikund	0.55	0.50	1.05	—	0.79	0.26	1.05	4
8.	Pickles & Preserves	1	Dumka	0.40	0.25	0.65	—	0.49	0.16	0.65	5
	Mineral-Based										
1.	Stone Chips & Boulders	2	Dumka & Saraiyahat	1.00	1.00	2.00	—	1.50	0.50	2.00	60
2.	L.T. Insulators	1	Kathikund or Dumka	3.00	2.00	5.00	—	3.80	1.20	5.00	38
3.	Crockery & Stone Wares	1	Dumka or Kathikund	2.40	0.55	2.95	—	2.22	0.73	2.95	29
4.	Mosaic Floor Tiles	1	Dumka	4.00	0.60	4.60	—	3.45	1.15	4.60	26
5.	Coal Briquette	1	Jarmundi or Nonihat	0.20	0.15	0.35	—	0.26	0.09	0.35	4
	Live Stock-Based										
1.	Fancy Leather Goods & Novelty Items	1	Dumka	0.47	0.75	1.22	—	0.92	0.30	1.22	16
2.	Brief Case & Bags	1	Dumka	0.07	0.18	0.25	—	019	0.06	0.25	5
3.	Woollen Carpet	1	Saraiyahat	0.07	0.20	0.27	—	0.20	0.07	0.27	4

	Chemical-Based									
1.	Printing Ink	1	Dumka	1.25	2.50	3.75	—	2.81	0.94	3.75	11
2.	Corrogated Papers & Board	1	Jarmundi or Dumka	1.50	3.75	5.25	—	3.94	1.31	5.25	25
3.	Injectables & Vitamins	1	Dumka	2.10	1.78	3.88	—	2.91	0.97	3.88	8
4.	Plastic Buttons	1	Nonihat or Jarmundi	0.22	0.13	0.35	—	0.26	0.09	0.35	9
5.	Glass Amples	1	Dumka	0.12	0.03	0.15	—	0.11	0.04	0.15	7
6.	Ice Cream & Ice Candy	2	Nonihat & Raneshwar	0.70	0.20	0.90	—	0.68	0.22	0.90	22
7.	Agarwatti	1	Dumka	0.07	0.18	0.25	—	0.19	0.06	0.25	13
	Demand-Based										
1.	Agriculture Implements	1	Nonihat	0.15	0.25	0.40	—	0.30	0.10	0.40	4
2.	Steel Trunk & School Boxes	1	Dumka	0.06	0.15	0.21	—	0.16	0.05	0.21	5
3.	Pump & Auto Repairing Works	1	Dumka	0.90	0.15	1.05	—	0.79	0.26	1.05	6
4.	Gate, Grills & Rolling Shutter	1	Dumka	0.15	0.15	0.30	—	0.23	0.07	0.30	4
5.	Wire Nails	1	Dumka	0.67	1.60	2.27	—	1.70	0.57	2.27	7
6.	Transistor & Radio Repairing Works	4	Nonihat, Shikaripara, Raneshwar & Hasdiha	0.06	0.20	0.26	—	0.20	0.06	0.26	4

(*Contd.*)

APPENDIX I *(Contd.)*

1	2	3	4	5	6	7	*8*	*9*	*10*	*11*	12
7.	Transistor & Radio Assembling	1	Dumka	0.40	2.40	2.80	—	2.10	0.70	2.80	8
8.	Bicycle Break Shoe	1	Dumka	0.10	0.30	0.40	—	0.30	0.10	0.40	9
9.	Bicycle Stand	1	Dumka	0.25	0.31	0.56	—	0.42	0.14	0.56	10
10.	Bicycle Carrier	1	Dumka	0.12	0.35	0.47	—	0.35	0.12	0.47	8
11.	Bicycle Bells	1	Dumka	0.43	0.50	0.93	—	0.70	0.23	0.93	9
12.	Gun Metal Bushes	1	Dumka	0.1S	0.60	0.78	—	0.59	0.19	0.78	7
13.	Spectacles Frames	1	Dumka	0.44	0.40	0.84	—	0.63	0.21	0.84	8
14.	Office Gum Paste	1	Dumka	0.05	0.30	0.35	—	0.26	0.09	0.35	4
15.	Sealing Wax	1	Dumka	0.05	0.15	0.20	—	0.15	0.05	0.20	3
16.	Hair Ribbons	1	Dumka	0.04	0.10	0.14	—	0.11	0.03	0.14	3
17.	Electric Horns	1	Dumka	0.20	0.35	0.55	—	0.44	0.11	0.55	14
18.	Bakelite Electrical	1	Dumka								
	Accessories			0.30	0.40	0.70	—	0.52	0.18	0.70	12
	Total	71		30.43	35.11	65.54	—	49.29	16.25	65.54	626

Industries for Deoghar Sub-Division for the Year 1990-95

Sl. No.	Name of the units	No. of units	Location	Investment in Lac.			Sources of Financed				Employment
				Fixed	Working	Total	State Govt.	Bank, B.F.C., N.S.I.C.	Own	Total	
1	2	3	4	5	6	7	8	9	10	11	12
	Agro-Based										
1.	Mini Modern Rice Mill (1.5 ton)	1	Palazori	1.75	3.00	4.75	—	3.55	1.20	4.75	30
2.	Rice and flour mill and (Huller and chakki type)	4	Mohanpur, Sarath, Sarwa, and Karaon	0.60	0.20	0.80	—	0.60	0.20	0.80	8
3.	Oil Mill	2	Deoghar and Madhupur	1.10	1.00	2.10	—	1.60	0.50	2.10	10
4.	Dal Mill	2	Deoghar and Madhupur	1.00	1.50	2.50	—	1.48	0.66	2.50	20
5.	Chura Mill	4	Sarath, Sarwa, Karaon and Palazori	0.80	1.00	1.80	—	1.35	0.45	1.80	20
6.	Bakery	3	Madhupur, Palazori and Deoghar	0.45	0.60	1.05	—	0.80	0.25	1.05	24

(Contd.)

APPENDIX I (*Contd.*)

1	2	3	4	5	6	7	8	9	10	11	12
7.	Ground and Processed Spices	1	Deoghar	0.15	0.12	0.27	—	0.20	0.07	0.27	3
	Forest-Based										
1.	Wooden furniture	6	Deoghar, Mohanpur, Madhupur, Sarath Palazori and Sarwa	0.30	1.20	1.50	—	1.33	0.17	1.50	24
2.	Sizing of Wood	2	Deoghar and Madhupur	0.60	1.00	1.60	—	1.20	0.40	1.60	10
3.	Packing Boxes of Soft Wood	1	Jasidih	0.25	0.30	0.55	—	0.41	0.14	0.55	5
4.	Machia-making (Machanised)	3	Deoghar, Mohanpur and Sarath	0.30	0.30	0.60	—	0.45	0.15	0.60	12
5.	Wooden Toys	1	Deoghar or Madhupur	0.15	0.25	0.40	—	0.30	0.10	0.40	5
6.	Honey Processing and Packing	1	Madhupur	0.15	0.10	0.25	—	0.19	0.06	0.25	10
	Mineral-Based										
1.	Stone Chips and Boulders	4	Mohanpur, Sarath, Palazori and Madhupur	2.00	2.00	4.00	—	3.00	1.00	4.00	120

2.	Emery Stone Chakki	1	Jasidih	0.12	0.15	0.27	—	0.20	0.07	0.27	3
3.	Mosaic Floor Tiles	1	Madhupur	4.00	0.60	4.60	—	3.45	1.15	4.60	26
4.	Stone Ware, Jars, Blows and Kundies	1	Madhupur or Deoghar	1.78	1.20	2.98	—	2.24	0.74	2.98	22
5.	Glass Mirror	1	Deoghar	0.25	0.50	0.75	—	0.56	0.19	0.75	7
6.	Glass Bangles	1	Deoghar	0.85	1.50	2.35	—	1.77	0.58	2.35	125
7.	Brick Kiln	1	Jasidih	0.30	1.25	1.55	—	1.17	0.38	1.55	45
8.	L.T. Insulators	1	Madhupur	3.00	2.00	5.00	—	3.80	1.20	5.00	38
9.	Crockery Wares	1	Madhupur	2.40	0.55	2.95	—	2.22	0.73	2.95	29
10.	Asbestos Pipes and Fittings	1	Deoghar	0.72	0.60	1.32	—	0.99	0.33	1.32	20
	Chemical-Based										
1.	Shoe Polish	1	Sarath	0.31	0.25	0.56	—	0.42	0.14	0.56	12
2.	Nail Polish	1	Mohanpur	0.05	0.12	0.17	—	0.13	0.04	0.17	5
3.	Dry Distempers	1	Madhupur	1.00	1.10	2.10	—	1.58	0.52	2.10	14
4.	Tooth Powder	1	Deoghar	0.40	0.60	1.00	—	0.75	0.25	1.00	10
5.	Plastic Toys	1	Deoghar	0.25	0.40	0.65	—	0.49	0.16	0.65	5
6.	Plastic Comb	1	Deoghar or Madhupur	1.30	0.80	2.10	—	1.58	0.52	2.10	10

(Contd.)

APPENDIX I (*Contd.*)

1	2	3	4	5	6	7	8	9	10	11	12
7.	Rubber Balloons	1	Deoghar	0.20	0.30	0.50	—	0.38	0.12	0.50	8
8.	Plastic Rain Coats	1	Deoghar	0.25	0.60	0.85	—	0.64	0.21	0.85	8
9.	Agarwatti	1	Deoghar	0.07	0.18	0.28	0.25	0.19	0.06	0.25	12
10.	Plastic Bucket, Bags and Film	1	Deoghar	.5.50	5.15	10.65	—	7.99	2.66	10.65	46
11.	Ammonium Chloride	1	Deoghar	0.98	1.58	2.56	—	1.92	0.64	2.56	9
12.	Sulfogunidin Tablets	1	Deoghar	1.10	0.75	1.85	—	1.39	0.46	1.85	10
13.	Ice Cream and Ice Candy	2	Palazori and Sarwa	0.70	0.20	0.90	—	0.68	0.22	0.90	22
	Live Stock Based										
1.	Fancy Leather Goods and Novelty Items	1	Deoghar	0.47	0.75	1.22	—	0.92	0.30	1.22	16
2.	P.V.C., Foot Wear (Chappals and Shoes)	1	Deoghar	1.24	0.80	2.04	—	1.53	0.51	2.04	11
3.	Croam Tanned Leather	1	Jasidih	1.30	2.28	3.58	—	2.69	0.89	3.58	30

4.	Blanket and Woollen Carpet Weaving	1	Madhupur	0.07	0.20	0.27	—	0.20	0.07	0.27	4
	Demand-Based										
1.	Agriculture Implements	1	Mohanpur	0.15	0.25	0.40	—	0 30	0.10	0.40	4
2.	Stainless Steel Utensils	1	Deoghar	1.75	1.25	3.00	—	2.30	0.70	3.00	10
3.	Steel Trunk, Suit Case and School Boxes	1	Deoghar	0.06	0.15	0.21	—	0.16	0.05	0.21	5
4.	Gate, Grills and Rolling Shutter	1	Deoghar or Madhupur	0.15	0.15	0.30	—	0.23	0.07	0.20	4
5.	Mechanical Repairing Works	1	Jasidlh	0.25	0.10	0.35	—	0.26	0.09	0.35	5
6.	Ferrous Casting	2	Deoghar and Madhupur	0.50	0.80	1.30	—	0.98	0.32	1.30	20
7.	Non-Ferrous Casting	1	Jasidih	0.25	2.12	2.37	—	1.78	0.59	2.37	11
8.	Readymade Garment	4	Deoghar, Palazori, Sarath and Mohanpur	0.20	0.40	0.60	—	0.45	0.15	0.60	12
9.	Conduit Pipes	1	Deoghar	0.36	0.80	1.16	—	0.87	0.29	1.16	10

(Contd.)

APPENDIX I (*Contd.*)

1	2	3	4	5	6	7	8	9	10	11	12
10.	Electric Toys	1	Deoghar	0.20	0.60	0.80	—	0.60	0.20	0.80	9
11.	Electric Horns	1	Madhupur	0.20	0.35	0.55	—	0.44	0.11	0.55	14
12.	Bakelite Electrical Accessories	1	Deoghar	0.30	0.40	0.70	—	0.52	0.18	0.70	12
13.	Cattle and Poultry Feed	1	Sarath	1.00	1.50	2.50	—	1.90	0.60	2.50	16
14.	Corgated Paper and Boards	1	Jasidih	1.50	3.75	5.25	—	3.94	1.31	5.25	25
	Total	80		45.78	50.00	95.78	—	72.26	23.52	95.78	1025

Industries for Jamtara Sub-Division for the Year 1990-95

Sl. No.	Name of the units	No. of units	Location	Investment in Lac.			Sources of Financed				Employment
				Fixed	Working	Total	State Govt.	Bank, B.F.C., N.S.I.C.	Own	Total	
1	2	3	4	5	6	7	8	9	10	11	12
	Agro-Based										
1.	Rice and Flour Mill (Huller and chakki)	5	Jamtara, Narainpur, Karmatarh, Kundhit and Nala	0.75	0.25	1.00	—	0.75	0.25	1.00	15
2	Oil Mill	1	Jamtara	0.55	0.50	1.05	—	0.80	0-25	1.05	5
3	Dal Mill	1	Jamtara	0.50	0.75	1.25	—	0.92	0.33	1.25	10
4.	Chura Mill	4	Narainpur, Karmatarh, Kundhit and Nala	0.80	1.00	1.80	—	1.35	0.45	1.80	20
5.	Bakery	2	Mihizam and Nala	0.30	0.40	0.70	—	0.52	0.18	0.70	16
6.	Rice Bran Oil	1	Jamtara	8.00	0.28	8.28	—	6.20	2.08	8.28	7
	Live Stock Based										
1.	Leather Goods (Shoes and Chappals)	2	Jamtara and Mihizam	0.12	0.20	0.32	—	0.24	0.08	0.32	10

(Contd.)

APPENDIX I *(Contd.)*

1	2	3	4	5	6	7	8	9	10	11	12
2.	Fancy Leather Goods and Novelty Items	1	Mihizam	0.47	0.75	1.22	—	0.92	0.30	1.22	16
	Mineral-Based										
1.	Sodium Silicate	1	Jamtara	1.50	0.50	2.00	—	1.50	0.50	2.00	9
2.	Mineral Grinding	1	Jamtara	1.00	1.50	2.50	—	1.85	0.65	2.50	15
3.	Stone Chips and Boulders	3	Jamtara, Mihizam and Karmatarh	1.50	1.50	3.00	—	2.25	0.75	3.00	90
4.	Brick Kiln	2	Mihizam and Jamtara	0.60	2.50	3.10	—	2.30	0.80	3.10	90
5.	Coal Briquette	1	Mihizam	0.0	0.15	0.35	—	0.26	0.09	0.35	40
	Forest-Based										
1.	Sizing of Wood	2	Mihizam and Nala	0.60	1.00	1.60	—	1.20	0.40	1.60	10
2.	Wooden furniture	2	Mihizam and Jamtara	0.10	0.40	0.50	—	0.38	0.12	0.50	8
	Chemicals-Based										
1.	Washing Soap	2	Jamtara and Mihizam	0.20	0.30	0.50	—	0.38	0.12	0.50	10
2.	Writing Ink	1	Jamtara	0.03	0.07	0.10	—	0.08	0.02	0.10	3
3.	Ice Cream and Ice Candy	2	Jamtara and Kundhit	0.70	0.20	0.90	—	0.68	0.20	0.90	22
4.	Nail Polish	1	Jamtara	0.50	0.12	0.17	—	0.13	0.04	0.17	5
5.	Agarwatti	1	Jamtara	0.06	0.18	0.24	—	0.18	0.06	0.24	10
6.	Paper Plate	1	Mihizam	0.30	0.30	0.60	—	0.45	0.15	0.60	10
7.	Corgated Paper and Boards	1	Mihizam	1.50	3.75	5.25	—	3.93	1.32	5.25	30

	Demand-Based										
1.	Photo Framing	1	Jamtara	0.02	0.05	0.07	—	0.05	0.02	0.07	1
2.	Readymade Garment	3	Kundhit, Nala and Narainpur	0.15	0.30	0.45	—	0.34	0.11	0.45	9
3.	Steel Metal Works (Almirah, Trunks, School Box and Furniture)	1	Mihizam or Jamtara	0.35	0.35	0.65	—	0.49	0.16	0.65	6
4.	Gates, Grills and Rolling Shutter	1	Jamtara	0.15	0.15	0.10	—	0.23	0.07	0.30	4
5.	Stainless Steel Utensils	1	Jamtara	1.75	1.25	3.00	—	2.30	0.70	3.00	15
6.	Nuts and Bolts	1	Mihizam	4.50	1.40	5.90	—	4.42	1.48	5.90	24
7.	Agriculture Implements	1	Mihizam	0.15	0.25	0.40	—	0.30	0.10	0.40	4
8.	Paint and Hair Brushes	1	Jamtara	0.20	0.20	0.40	—	0.30	0.10	0.40	9
9.	Radio and Transister Repairing	5	Mihizam, Kundhit, Nala, Narainpur and Karmatarh	0.15	0.25	0.40	—	0.30	0.10	0.40	5
10.	Aluminium Utensils	1	Jamtara	4.00	2.00	6.00	—	4.50	1.50	6.00	39
11.	Hosiery Goods	1	Jamtara	0.11	0.25	0.36	—	0.27	0.09	0.36	6
12.	Nail Cutters	1	Mihizam or Jamtara	0.90	0.60	1.50	—	1.13	0.37	1.50	12
13.	Gul and Guraku Paste	1	Jamtara	0.15	0.25	0.40	—	0.30	0.10	0.40	8
	Total	57		32.36	23.90	56.26	—	42.20	14.06	56.26	593

Industries for Godda Sub-Division for the Year 1990-95

Sl. No.	Name of the units	No. of units	Location	Investment in Lac.			Sources of Finance				Employment
				Fixed	Working	Total	State Govt.	Bank, B.F.C., N.S.I.C.	Own	Total	
1	2	3	4	5	6	7	8	9	10	11	12
	Agro-Based										
1.	Modern Rice Mill (1/2 tone)	1	Godda	1.00	1.50	2.50	—	1.88	0.62	2.50	20
2.	Modern Rice Mill (2.50 Kg.)	2	Meharma and Pathargama	1.00	2.00	3.00	—	2.25	0.75	3.00	30
3.	Chura Mill	1	Poraiyahat	0.20	0.25	0.45	—	0.34	0.11	0.45	5
4.	Dal Mill	1	Godda	0.60	1.00	1.60	—	1.20	0.40	1.60	10
5.	Oil Mill	1	Godda	0.55	0.50	1.05	—	0.79	0.26	1.05	5
6.	Bakery	1	Meharma (Lalmatia)	0.20	0.30	0.50	—	0.38	0.12	0.50	8
	Forest-Based										
1.	Sizing of Wood	1	Meharma (Lalmatia)	0.30	0.50	0.80	—	0.55	0.25	0.80	5
2.	Wooden Furniture and Building Material	2	Lalmatia and Godda	0.14	0.50	0.65	—	0.48	0.16	0.64	10

3.	Tassar Reeling and Spinning	3	Sunderpahari, Boyarizore & Meharma	0.60	0.50	2.10	—	1.58	0.52	2.10	30
4.	Wooden Sports Godda	1	Godda	0.28	0.38	0.66	—	0.49	0.17	0.66	46
5.	Pickles & Preserves	1	Boyarizore	0.08	0.25	0.33	—	0.25	0.08	0.33	4
6.	Honey Processing & Packaging	1	Sunderpahari	0.12	0.25	0.37	—	0.28	0.09	0.37	10
7.	Cane Basket and Bamboo Matting	1	Lalmatia	0.05	0.15	0.20	—	0.15	0.05	0.20	5
	Live Stock Based										
1.	Leather Goods	2	Godda and Poraiyahat	0.15	0.30	0.45	—	0.34	0.11	0.45	10
	Mineral-Based										
1.	Stone Chips and Boulders	3	Poraiyahat, Boyarizore and Meharma (Lalmatia)	1.50	1.50	3.00	—	2.25	0.75	3.00	90
2.	Brick Kiln	3	Godda, Meharma (Lalmatia) and Pathargama	0.90	3.75	4.65	—	3.49	1.16	4.65	135
3.	Lime Stone Dust	1	Lalmatia	1.35	1.50	2.85	—	2.14	0.71	2.85	8

(Contd.)

APPENDIX I (*Contd.*)

1	2	3	4	5	6	7	8	9	10	11	12
	Chemical-Based										
1.	Writing Ink	1	Godda	0.03	0.07	0.10	—	0.08	0.02	0.10	3
2.	Tyre-Retreading & Resoling	1	Lalmatia	0.80	0.50	1.30	—	0.98	0.32	1.30	6
3.	Shoe Polish	1	Godda	0.12	0.48	0.60	—	0.45	0.15	0.60	12
4.	Agarwatti	1	Mahgama	0.07	0.18	0.25	—	0.19	0.06	0.25	13
5.	Sealing Wax	1	Godda	0.05	0.15	0.20	—	0.15	0.05	0.20	3
6.	Ice Cream & Ice Candy	2	Poraiyahat and Meharma	0.75	0.20	0.95	—	0.72	0.23	0.95	22
	Institutional Demand Based on Lalmatia Coal Mines										
1.	Mining Basket (Steel)	1	Lalmatia	0.10	0.80	0.90	—	0.68	0.22	0.90	8
2.	Shovel, Fork and Gaita	1	Do	0.45	0.60	1.05	—	0.79	0.26	1.05	4
3.	Picks	1	Do	0.20	0.40	0.60	—	0.45	0.15	0.60	3
4.	Mining Boots and Belts	1	Do	0.05	0.60	0.65	—	0.49	0.16	0.65	6
5.	Mining Helmet	1	Do	0.75	0.75	1.50	—	1.12	0.38	1.50	5
6.	Mining Trolleys	1	Do	0.55	0.60	1.15	—	0.86	0.29	1.15	9
7.	Electric Repairing Works	1	Do	0.25	0.15	0.40	—	0.30	0.10	0.40	6
8.	Mechanical Repairing Works	1	Lalmatia	0.25	0.10	0.35	—	0.29	0.06	0.35	5

9.	Automobile Repairing Works	1	Do	0.90	0.15	1.05	—	0.78	0.27	1.05	8
10.	Nuts and Bolts	1	Do	4.50	1.40	5.90	—	4.40	1.50	5.90	24
11.	Building Hard Wares	1	Do	0.80	0.25	1.05	—	0.79	0.26	1.05	25
12.	Chain Pully Block	1	Do	2.75	2.20	4.95	—	3.71	1.24	4.95	21
13.	Wheel and Axle	1	Do	3.00	2.30	5.30	—	4.00	1.30	5.30	28
14.	Coal Tub Block	1	Do	1.55	1.20	2.75	—	2.06	0.69	2.75	14
15.	C. Type Tub Cupling Chain	1	Do	1.50	0.50	2.00	—	1.50	0.50	2.00	8
16.	Fish-Plate (30 Lb.)	1	Do								
17.	Dog Nail	1	Do	0.25	0.30	0.55	—	0.41	0.14	0.55	3
18.	M.S. Rivet	1	Do	0.25	0.30	0.55	—	0.41	0.14	0.55	3
	Demand-Based										
1.	Steel Trunk & School Boxes	1	Godda	2.50	2.90	5.40	—	4.00	1.40	5.40	13
2.	Improved Agriculture Implements	1	Pathargama	0.05	0.15	0.20	—	0.15	0.05	0.20	4
3.	Iron Domestic Utensils	1	Paraiyahat	0.10	0.20	0.30	—	0.23	0.07	0.30	5
4.	Aluminium Utensils	1	Godda	4.00	2.00	6.00	—	4.50	1.50	6.00	39
5.	Gates, Grills and Shutters	2	Lalmatia and Godda	0.15	0.20	0.35	—	0.26	0.09	0.35	5
6.	Radio & Transister Repairing Works	3	Poraiyahat, Pathargama and Mahagama	0.09	0.15	0.24	—	0.18	0.06	0.24	3

(Contd.)

APPENDIX I *(Contd.)*

1	2	3	4	5	6	7	8	9	10	11	12
7.	Cycle Repairing Works	4	Poraiyahat, Boyarizore, Pathargama & Sunderpahari	0.04	0.16	0.20	—	0.15	0.05	0.20	8
8.	Readymade Garments	5	Lalmatia, Pathargama, Boyarizore, Sunderpahari & Poraiyahat	0.15	0.35	0.50	—	0.38	0.12	0.50	15
9.	Bakelite Electric Accessories	1	Godda	0.30	0.40	0.70	—	0.52	0.18	0.70	12
	Total	70		36.37	36.52	72.89	—	55.04	17.85	72.89	734

Industries for Sahibganj Sub-Division for the Year 1990-95

Sl. No.	Name of the Units	No. of Units	Location	Investment in Lac.			Sources of Financed				Employment
				Fixed	Working	Total	State Govt.	Bank, B.F.C., N.S.I.C.	Own	Total	
1	2	3	4	5	6	7	8	9	10	11	12
	Agro-Based										
1.	Mini Modern Rice Mill	1	Barharwa	1.75	3.00	4.75	—	3.55	1.20	4.75	30
2.	Rice and Flour Mill (Huller Chakki Type)	5	Borio, Barhati, Taljhari, Pathna and Rajmahal	0.75	0.25	1.00	—	0.75	0.25	1.00	10
3.	Oil Mill	2	Sahibganj and Barharwa	1.10	1.00	2.10	—	1.60	0.50	2.10	10
4.	Dal Mill	1	Sahibganj	0.50	0.75	1.25		0.92	0.33	1.25	10
5.	Bakery	3	Tinpahar, Barhait, and Barharwa	0.45	0.60	1.05	—	0.80	0.25	1.05	24
	Forest-Based										
1.	Non-Edible Oil Mill	1	Borio or Sahibganj	0.55	0.50	1.05	—	0.80	0.25	1.05	4
2.	Sizing of Wood	1	Sahibganj	0.30	0.60	0.80	—	0.60	0.20	0.80	5

(Contd.)

APPENDIX I *(Contd.)*

1	2	3	4	5	6	7	8	9	10	11	12
3.	Wooden furniture	3	Rajmahal, Barharwa and Sahibganj	0.15	0.60	0.75	—	0.56	0.19	0.75	12
4.	Machia-making (Mechanised)	1	Borio	0.10	0.10	0.20	—	0.15	0.05	0.20	4
5.	Rope-making	2	Sahibganj and Rajmahal	0.15	0.25	0.40	—	0.30	0.10	0.40	6
6.	Tassar Reeling and Spinning	3	Rajmahal, Borio and Barhait	0.60	1.50	2.10	—	1.60	0.50	2.10	10
7.	Wood Packing Boxes	1	Sahibganj	0.25	0.30	0.55	—	0.41	0.14	0.55	5
8.	Pickles and Preserves	1	Sahibganj	0.40	0.25	0.65	—	0.49	0.16	0.65	5
9.	Honey Processing and Packing	1	Borio	0.15	0.25	0.40	—	0.30	0.10	0.40	3
	Mineral-Based										
1.	Brick Kiln	2	Rajmahal and Borio	0.60	2.50	3.10	—	2.30	0.80	3.10	90
2.	Stone Chips and Boulders	5	Mirzachauki, Taljhari, Tinpahar, Barharwa and Pathna	2.50	2.50	5.00	—	3.75	1.25	5.00	150

3.	Glass Pressed Wares	1	Rajmahal	9.85	5.15	15.00	—	11.25	3.75	15.00	227
4.	L.T. Insulators	1	Rajmahal	3.00	2.00	2.00	—	3.80	1.20	5.00	38
5.	State Pencils	1	Barharwa	0.07	0.08	0.15	—	0.12	0.03	0.15	5
6.	Plastic of Paris	1	Rajmahal	0.78	0.98	1.76	—	1.32	0.44	1.76	10
7.	Manglore Tiles	1	Rajmahal or Barharwa	1.45	0.78	2.23	—	1.67	0.56	2.23	38
8.	Paint and Varnish	1	Rajmahal or Barharwa	0.50	0.80	1.30	—	1.00	0.30	1.30	8
9.	Indigo	1	Rajmahal	2.50	3.00	5.50	—	3.90	1.60	5.50	20
	Live Stock Based										
1.	Lady Sandle and Chappals	1	Sahibganj	0.02	0.36	0.38	—	0.29	0.09	0.38	7
2.	Lady Fancy Bags and Novelty Items	1	Barharwa	0.47	0.75	1.22	—	0.92	0.30	1.22	16
3.	Bone Meal	1	Rajmahal	1.75	1.35	3.10	—	2.30	0.80	3.10	16
	Chemical-Based										
1.	Sodium Silicate	1	Rajmahal	2.70	1.50	4.20	—	3.15	1.05	4.20	15
2.	Calcium Carbonate	1	Rajmahal	5.24	1.73	6.97	—	5.23	1.74	6.97	26
3.	Barium Carbonate	1	Sahibganj	1.20	1.88	3.08	—	2.31	0.77	3.08	12
4.	Insecticide	1	Sahibganj	1.10	0.47	1.57	—	1.18	0.39	1.57	12
5.	Agarwatti	1	Barharwa	0.07	0.18	0.25	—	0.19	0.06	0.25	13
6.	Ghee and Butter	1	Barharwa	0.50	2.50	3.00	—	2.25	0.75	3.00	10

(Contd.)

APPENDIX I (*Contd.*)

1	*2*	*3*	*4*	*5*	*6*	*7*	*8*	*9*	*10*	*11*	*12*
7.	Tooth Powder	1	Barharwa	0.40	0.60	1.00	—	0.75	0.25	1.00	10
8.	Ice Cream and Ice Candy	1	Rajmahal	0.35	0.10	0.45	—	0.34	0.11	0.45	11
	Demand-Based										
1.	Agriculture Impliments	2	Borio and Barharwa	0.30	0.50	0.80	—	0.60	0.20	0.80	8
2.	Gate, Grills and Rolling Shutters	2	Sahibganj and Barharwa	0.30	0.30	0.60	—	0.45	0.15	0.60	8
3.	General Fabrication and Job Works	1	Barharwa	0.45	0.15	0.60	—	0.45	0.15	0.60	5
4.	Steel Almirah and Furnitures	1	Sahibganj	0.30	0.35	0.65	—	0.49	0.16	0.65	6
5.	Automobile Reparing Works	1	Barharwa or Rajmahal	0.90	0.15	1.05	—	0.79	0.26	1.05	8
6.	Builders Hard Wares	1	Sahibganj	0.80	0.26	1.06	—	0.80	0.26	1.06	25
7.	Bicycle Carrier	1	Sahibganj	0.12	0.35	0.47	—	0.35	0.12	0.47	8
8.	Bicycle Stand	1	Barharwa	0.25	0.31	0.56	—	0.42	0.14	0.56	10

9.	Bicycle Break Shoe	1	Sahibganj	0.10	0.30	0.40	—	0.30	0.10	0.40	9
10.	Corgated Paper and Boards	1	Sahibganj	1.50	3.75	5.25	—	3.94	1.31	5.25	25
11.	Hosiery Goods	1	Sahibganj	0.11	0.25	0.36	—	0.27	0.09	0.36	6
12.	Book and Register Binding	1	Barharwa	0.08	0.10	0.18	—	0.15	0.03	0.18	3
13.	Bicycle Reparing	4	Pathna, Taljhari, Barhait, and Tinpahar	0.04	0.16	0.20	—	0.15	0.05	0.20	8
14.	Ready made Garment	5	Rajmahal, Taljhari, Barhait and Tinpahar	0.25	0.50	0.75	—	0.56	0.19	0.75	15
15.	Radio and Transister Repairing	3	Rajmahal, Barharwa and Tinpahar	0.09	0.15	0.24	—	0.18	0.06	0.24	3
	Total	77		48.84	47.64	96.48	—	70.75	25.73	96.48	1019

Industries for Pakur Sub-Division for the Year 1990-95

Sl. No.	Name of the Units	No. of Units	Location	Investment in Lac.			Sources of Financed				Employment
				Fixed	Working	Total	State Govt.	Bank, B.F.C., N.S.I.C.	Own	Total	
1	2	3	4	5	6	7	8	9	10	11	12
	Agro-Based										
1.	Rice and Flour Mill (Huller Chakki Type)	5	Pakur, Hiranpur, Amrapara, Littipara and Pakuria	0.75	0.25	1.00	—	0.75	0.25	1.00	10
2.	Oil Mill	2	Amrapara and Hiranpur	1.10	1.00	2.10	—	1.60	0.50	2.10	10
3.	Chura Mill	2	Maheshpur and Littipara	0.40	0.50	0.90	—	0.68	0.22	0.90	10
4.	Bakery	2	Hiranpur and Amrapara	0.15	0.20	0.35	—	0.29	0.06	0.35	8
	Live Stock Based										
1.	Leather Goods (Shoes and Chappals)	3	Amrapara, Hiranpur and Pakur	0.18	0.30	0.48	—	0.36	0.12	0.48	15
2.	Bone Meal	1	Pakur	1.75	1.35	3.10	—	2.30	0.80	3.10	16

	Mineral-Based										
1.	Stone Chips and Boulders	15	Pakur, Maheshpur and Hiranpur	7.50	7.50	15.00	—	11.25	3.75	15.00	450
2.	Asbestos Pipes and Fitting	1	Pakur	0.72	0.60	1.32	—	0.99	0.33	1.32	20
	Forest-Based										
1.	Sizing of Wood	1	Pakur	0.30	0.50	0.80	—	0.60	0.20	0.80	5
2.	Wooden Furniture and Door and Window	1	Pakur	0.07	0.25	0.32	—	0.24	0.80	0.32	5
3.	Tassar Reeling and Spinning	4	Amrapara, Littipara, Hiranpur and Maheshpur	0.80	2.00	2.80	—	2.10	0.70	2.80	40
4.	Tassar Silk Weaving	2	Amrapara and Littipara	0.30	0.90	1.20	—	0.90	0.30	1.20	16
5.	Honey Processing and Packing	2	Amrapara and Littipara	0.24	0.20	0.44	—	0.33	0.11	0.44	20
6.	Machia-making (Mechanised)	1	Hiranpur	0.10	0.10	0.20	—	0.15	0.05	0.20	6
	Chemical-Based										
1.	Ice Cream and Ice Candy	1	Amrapara	0.35	0.10	0.45	—	0.34	0.11	0.45	11
2.	Tyre-Retreading and Resoling	1	Pakur	0.80	0.50	1.30	—	1.00	0.30	1.30	6
3.	Washing Soap	2	Hiranpur and Pakur	0.20	0.30	0.50	—	0.38	0.12	0.50	10

(Contd.)

APPENDIX I *(Contd.)*

1	2	3	4	5	6	7	8	9	10	11	12
4.	Rubber Balloons	1	Pakur	0.20	0.30	0.50	—	0.38	0.12	0.50	8
5.	Distilled Water and Battery Acid	1	Pakur	0.05	0.07	0.12	—	0.09	0.03	0.12	2
6.	Nail Polish	2	Pakur and Maheshpur	0.05	0.12	0.17	—	0.13	0.04	0.17	5
7.	Shoe Polish	2	Hiranpur and Pakur	0.31	0.25	0.56	—	0.42	0.14	0.56	12
	Demand-Based										
1.	Agriculture Impliments	2	Maheshpur and Hiranpur	0.15	0.25	0.40	—	0.30	0.10	0.40	4
2.	Iron Domestic Utensils	3	Hiranpur, Amrapara and Pakur	0.24	0.48	0.72	—	0.54	0.18	0.72	21
3.	Gate, Grill and Rolling Shutters	1	Pakur	0.15	0.15	0.30	—	0.23	0.07	0.30	4
4.	Automobile Repairing Works	1	Pakur	0.90	0.15	1.05	—	0.79	0.26	1.05	8
5.	Mechanical Repairing Works	1	Pukur	0.25	0.10	0.35	—	0.29	0.06	0.35	5

6.	Rewinding of Electric Motors and Battery Charging	1	Pakur	0.75	0.50	1.25		0.94	0.31	1.25	20
7.	Printing Press and Job Works	1	Pakur	0.35	0.20	0.55	—	0.42	0.13	0.55	6
8.	Agarwatti	1	Hiranpur	0.06	0.18	0.24	—	0.18	0.06	0.24	10
9.	Hosiery Goods	1	Hiranpur	0.11	0.25	0.36	—	0.27	0.09	0.36	6
10.	Electric Table Fan and Exhaust Fan	1	Pakur	0.75	1.00	1.75	—	1.31	0.44	1.75	20
11.	File Covers and File Boards	1	Pakur	0.25	0.20	0.45	—	0.34	0.11	0.45	12
12.	Rotary Screens and Eccentric Shafts	4	Pakur	2.00	1.00	3.00	—	2.25	0.75	3.00	20
	Total	70		22.28	21.75	44.03	—	33.14	10.89	44.03	821

Abstract of Industries Sub-Division for the Year 1990-95

Sl. No.	Name of the Sub-Division	No. of Units	Investment in Lac			Sources of Financed				Employment Generated
			Fixed	Working	Total	State Govt.	Bank B.F.C. N.S.I.C.	Own	Total	
1	2	3	4	5	6	7	8	9	10	11
1.	Dumka	71	30.43	35.11	65.54	—	49.29	16.25	65.54	626
2.	Deoghar	80	45.78	50.00	95.78	—	72.26	23.52	95.78	1025
3.	Jamtara	57	32.36	23.90	56.26	—	42.20	14.06	56.26	593
4.	Godda	70	36.37	36.52	72.89	—	55.04	17.85	72.89	734
5.	Sahibganj	77	48.84	47.64	96.48	—	70.75	25.73	96.48	1019
6.	Pakur	70	22.28	21.75	44.03	—	33.14	10.89	44.03	821
	Total	425	216.06	214.92	430.98	—	322.68	108.30	430.98	4818

Abstract of Industries Sub-Division-wise Based on Local Resources and Demand for the Year 1990-95

Sl. No.	Name of the Sub-Division	Agriculture-based	Mineral-based	Forest-based	Live Stock-based	Chemical-based	Demand-based	Total
1.	Dumka	20	6	13	3	8	21	71
2.	Deoghar	17	13	14	4	14	18	80
3.	Jamtara	14	8	4	3	9	19	57
4.	Godda	7	7	10	2	7	37	70
5.	Sahibganj	12	14	14	3	8	26	77
6.	Pakur	11	16	11	5	9	18	70
	Total	81	64	66	20	55	136	425

List of Possible Skill and Resource Based Cottage Industries which can be Established without Power by Local Women Especially Santhal Women

Sl. No.	*Name of Cottage Industries*
1	2
1.	Hand Pounding of Rice
2.	Chura-making
3.	Murhi-making
4.	Sabai-making
5.	Paper and Dalmote
6.	Pickles
7.	Sirka
8.	Honey Processing and Packing
9.	Machia-making
10.	Rope-making
11.	Cane and Bamboo Wares
12.	Toy-making
13.	Comb-making
14.	Bamboo Matting
15.	Tassar Spinning
16.	Tassar Reeling
17.	Tassar Silk Weaving
18.	Dona-Pattal-Making (From Sal Leaves)
19.	Datwan-making (From Sal, Neem, Karanj and Babool trees)
20.	Broom-making
21.	Thonga-making (out waste Paper)
22.	Hand Loom Fabrics
23.	Fishery Net
24.	Tailoring
25.	Knitting and Embroidery
26.	Ready made Garment
27.	Wool Knitting
28.	Doll and Guria-making
29.	Pottery

30. Stone Wares
31. Village Musical Instrument
32. Lac Ornaments
33. Paila-making
34. Dyeing and Printing
35. Painting
36. Book and Register Binding
37. Fancy Bags and Purses
38. Paper Toys
39. Gum, Harre, Bahera Collection (from Forest) and Processing

Sub-Division-wise and Block-wise Break-up for Financing the Rural and Urban Artisans for the Year 1990-95 under 20-Point Programme

Sl. No.	*Name of Block*	*Weavers*		*Shoe-Maker*		*Carpenter*		*Blacksmiths*	
		No.	*Amount*	*No.*	*Amount*	*No.*	*Amount*	*No.*	*Amount*
1	*2*	*3*	*4*	*5*	*6*	*7*	*8*	*9*	*10*
1.	**Dumka Sub-Division**								
1.	Dumka (Sadar)	50	50000	8	4000	5	2500	—	—
2.	Kathikund	45	45000	—	—	5	2500	5	5000
3.	Gopikandar	—	—	—	—	—	—	2	2000
4.	Ramgarh	10	10000	—	—	—	—	3	3000
5.	Jama	35	35000	5	2500	5	2500	—	—
6.	Saraiyahat	80	80000	—	—	—	—	—	—
7.	Jarmundi	70	70000	5	2500	5	2500	5	5000
8.	Masalia	60	60000	—	—	—	—	2	2000
9.	Sikaripara	30	30000	—	—	—	—	3	3000
10.	Raneshwar	20	20000	—	—	—	—	—	—
	Total	400	400000	18	9000	20	10000	20	20000
2.	**Godda Sub-Division**								
1.	Godda (Sadar)	100	100000	5	2500	5	2500	5	5000
2.	Poraiyahat	25	25000	5	2500	5	2500	5	5000
3.	Sundarpahari	40	40000	—	—	—	—	—	—
4.	Pathargama	80	80000	5	2500	5	2500	3	3000

5.	Mahagama	75	75000	2	1000	3	1500	2	2000
6.	Meharma	100	100000	3	1500	5	2500		
7.	Boarizore	40	40000	—	—	2	1000	2	2000
	Total	460	460000	20	10000	25	12500	17	17000
3. Deoghar Sub-Division									
1.	Deoghar (Sadar)	—	—	5	2500	5	2500	—	—
2.	Madhupur	20	20000	5	2500	5	2500	5	5000
3.	Mohanpur	60	60000	3	1500	2	1000	8	8000
4.	Sarath	10	10000	5	2500	3	1500	3	3000
5.	Sarwan	20	20000	2	100	—	—	2	2000
6.	Karaon	—	—	—	—	2	1000	2	2000
7.	Palazori	60	60000	5	2500	2	100	3	3000
	Total	170	170000	25	12500	19	9500	22	2300
4. Jamtara Sub-Division									
1.	Jamtara (Sadar)	20	20000	5	2500	4	2000	5	5000
2.	Narainpur	150	150000	4	2000	2	1000	3	3000
3.	Nala	25	25000	3	1500	2	1000	2	2000
4.	Kundhit	15	15000	5	2500	2	1000	2	2000
	Total	210	210000	17	8500	10	5000	12	12000
5. Sahibganj Sub-Division									
1.	Sahibganj (Sadar)	25	25000	5	2500	4	2000	3	3000
2.	Rajmahal	30	30000	5	2500	2	1000	2	2000

(Contd.)

1	2	3	4	5	6	7	8	9	10
3.	Taljhari	2	20000	—	—	2	1000	2	2000
4.	Barharwa	15	15000	4	2500	4	2000	2	2000
5.	Pathna	10	10000	—	—	—	—	2	2000
6.	Barhait	150	150000	—	—	2	1000	2	2000
7.	Borio	150	150000	5	2500	2	1000	2	2000
	Total	400	400000	20	10000	16	8000	15	15000
6. Pakur Sub-Division									
1.	Pakur (Sadar)	50	50000	5	2500	4	2000	5	5000
2.	Maheshpur	12	12000	3	1500	4	2000	3	3000
3.	Pakuria	38	38000	2	1000	2	1000	—	—
4.	Hiranpur	75	75000	5	2500	4	2000	5	5000
5.	Littipara	50	50000	2	1000	—	—	—	—
6.	Amrapara	25	25000	3	1500	2	1000	2	2000
	Total	250	250000	20	10000	16	8000	15	15000
1.	Dumka	400	400000	18	9000	20	10000	20	20000
2.	Godda	460	460000	20	10000	25	12500	17	17000
3.	Deoghar	170	170000	25	12500	19	9500	23	23000
4.	Jamtara	210	210000	17	8500	10	50000	12	12000
5.	Sahibganj	400	400000	20	10000	16	8000	15	15000
6.	Pakur	250	250000	20	10000	16	8000	15	15000
	Total	1890	189000	120	60000	106	53000	102	102000

(Contd.)

Sl. No.	Name of Block	Potters		Basket-Maker		Rope-Maker		Cocoon-Maker	
		No.	Amount	No.	Amount	No.	Amount	No.	Amount
1	2	11	12	13	14	15	16	17	18
1.	**Dumka Sub-Division**								
1.	Dumka (Sadar)	35	8750	10	2000	—	—	—	—
2.	Kathikund	30	7500	5	1000	—	—	710	142000
3.	Gopikandar	15	3750	5	1000	—	—	510	102000
4.	Ramgarh	15	3750	5	1000	—	—	—	—
5.	Jama	20	5000	5	1000	10	2000	—	—
6.	Saraiyahat	20	5000	5	1000	—	—	205	41000
7.	Jarmundi	25	6250	5	1000	—	—	—	—
8.	Masalia	15	3750	5	1000	—	—	—	—
9.	Sikaripara	15	3750	5	1000	—	—	500	100000
10.	Raneshwar	10	2500	5	1000	—	—	105	21000
	Total	200	50000	55	11000	10	2000	2030	406000
2.	Godda Sub-Division								
1.	Godda (Sadar)	25	6250	7	1400	—	—	100	20000
2.	Poraiyahat	20	5000	5	1000	—	—	—	—
3.	Sundarpahari	20	5000	5	1000	5	1000	300	60000
4.	Pathargama	10	2500	3	600	—	—	—	—
5.	Mahagama	15	3750	5	1000	—	—	—	—
6.	Meharma	—	—	2	400	—	—	—	—
7.	Boarizore	10	2500	3	600	—	—	—	—
	Total	100	25000	30	6000	5	1000	700	140000

(Contd.)

1	2	3	4	5	6	7	8	9	10
3.	**Deoghar Sub-Division**								
1.	Deoghar (Sadar)	50	12500	10	2000	—	—	—	—
2.	Madhupur	10	2500	5	1000	—	—	100	20000
3.	Mohanpur	10	2500	5	1000	—	—	—	—
4.	Sarath	10	2500	5	1000	—	—	—	—
5.	Sarwan	5	1250	2	400	—	—	—	—
6.	Karaon	—	—	3	600	—	—	—	—
7.	Palazori	15	3750	5	1000	—	—	—	—
	Total	100	25000	35	7000	—	—	100	20000
4.	**Jamtara Sub-Division**								
1.	Jamtara (Sadar)	45	11250	10	2000	—	—	—	—
2.	Narainpur	25	6250	7	1400	—	—	—	—
3.	Nala	10	2500	5	1000	—	—	—	—
4.	Kundhit	20	5000	8	1600	—	—	—	—
	Total	100	25000	30	6000	—	—	—	

(Contd.)

1	2	11	12	13	14	15	16	17	18
5.	**Sahibganj Sub-Division**								
1.	Sahibganj	30	7500	5	1000	—	—	—	—
2.	Rajmahal	20	5000	3	600	—	—	200	40000
3.	Taljhari	20	5000	5	1000	—	—	—	—
4.	Barharwa	30	7500	2	400	—	—	—	—

5.	Pathna	30	7500	2	400	—	—	200	40000
6.	Barhait	10	2500	3	600	—	—	100	20000
7.	Borio	10	2500	5	1000	15	3000	100	20000
	Total	150	37500	25	5000	15	3000	600	120000
6.	**Pakur Sub-Division**								
1.	Pakur (Sadar)	20	5000	—	—	—	—	—	—
2.	Maheshpur	15	3750	5	1000	—	—	200	40000
3.	Pakuria	25	6250	5	1000	—	—	—	—
4.	Hiranpur	35	8750	10	2000	—	—	400	80000
5.	Littipara	30	7500	5	2000	5	1000	400	80000
6.	Amrapara	25	6250	10	2000	—	—	620	124000
	Total	150	37500	35	7000	5	1000	1620	324000
1.	Dumka	200	50000	55	11000	2000	2000	1080	406000
2.	Godda	100	25000	30	6000	5	1000	700	140000
3.	Deoghar	100	25000	35	7000	—	—	1000	20000
4.	Jamtara	100	25000	30	6000	—	—	—	—
5.	Sahibganj	150	37500	25	5000	15	3000	600	120000
6.	Pakur	150	37500	35	7000	5	1000	1620	324000
	Total	800	200000	210	42000	35	7000	6670	1334000

Sl. No.	*Category of Artisans*	*Total No. of Artisans*	*Amount*
1	*2*	*3*	*4*
1.	Weavers	1890	1890000
2.	Shoe, makers, Carpenter and Blacksmiths, etc.	1373	464000
3.	Cocoon Rearers	5050	1010000
	Total	8313	3364000

Target Under I.R.D. Programme for the Year 1990-95

Sl. No.	Name of the Sub-division	No. of Blocks	No. of Artisans to be Assisted Including Tassar & Mulberry Rearers	Loan	Subsidy	Total
1.	Dumka	10	1500	450000	148500	598500
2.	Deoghar	7	1000	300000	99000	399900
3.	Jamtara	4	600	180000	59400	239400
4.	Godda	7	1000	300000	99000	399000
5.	Sahibganj	7	1000	300000	99000	399000
6.	Pakur	6	900	270000	89100	359100
	Total	41	6000	1800000	594000	2394000

Target Under TRYSEM Training Programme for the Year 1990-95

Sl. No.	Name of Sub-division	No. of Blocks	No. of Persons to be Trained	Estimated Expenditure on Training				Financial Assistance from Banks
				Stipend	Raw-Material	Monorarium to Master Crafts	Tools & Equipments	
1.	Dumka	10	150	15000	18750	7500	22500	300000
2.	Deoghar	7	105	10500	13125	5250	15750	210000
3.	Jamtara	4	60	6000	7500	3000	9000	120000
4.	Godda	7	105	10500	13125	5250	15750	210000
5.	Sahibganj	7	106	10500	13125	5250	15750	210000
6.	Pakur	6	90	9000	11250	4500	13500	180000
	Total	41	615	61500	76875	30750	9250	1230000

Target Under R.A.P. for the Year 1990-95

Sl. No.	Name of Subdivision	No. of Blocks	No. of Persons to be Trained	Estimated Expenditure on Training				Financial Assistance from Banks
				Stipend	Raw-Material	Monorarium to Master Crufts	Tools & Equipments	
1.	Dumka	10	100	10000	1250	5000	15000	200000
2.	Deoghar	7	70	7000	8750	3500	10500	140000
3.	Jamtara	4	40	4000	5000	2000	6000	80000
4.	Godda	7	70	7000	8750	3500	10500	140000
5.	Sahibganj	7	70	7000	8750	3500	10500	140000
6.	Pakur	6	60	6000	7500	3000	9000	120000
	Total	41	410	41000	51250	20500	61500	820000

APPENDIX II

ROLE OF VOLUNTARY ORGANISATIONS IN TRIBAL DEVELOPMENT

Voluntary organisations working in tribal areas or having centres of activity in such areas can be of good help in furthering tribal development programmes in these areas. Such organisations are being financed by the Ministry of Home Affairs and the Ministry of Social Welfare, besides State Governments. The extent of aid likely to flow to these organisations for tribal development from the Ministry of Home Affairs during the Sixth Plan may be of the order of Rs. 3.02 crores.

2. The types of activities which voluntary organisations working in tribal areas take up cover establishment of Balwadis and creches, tailoring and craft centres, adult education centres, functional literacy centres, nutritional programmes, mid-day meal centres and medical care centres. By and large, these organisations concentrate more on general programmes welfare than on family-oriented economic programmes. Some of these organisations have inducted tribal officials in their administration and have also taken in tribal members in the committee of management. It might be desirable to associate a field office of the State Government at the appropriate level.

3. Most of the organisations depend upon governmental assistance to a substantial degree for implementation of schemes taken up by them in the tribal areas, their own contribution being generally limited to 20 per cent. Organisations like Ramakrishna Mission have been doing good work in several interior tribal areas. The other all India level voluntary organisations (organisations having activity in or relating to more than one State) who have been assisted in good measure by the Ministry of Home Affairs include, among others the Nikhil Bharat Banbasi

Panchayat, the Servants of India Society, the Harijan Sevak Sangh and the Bharatiya Adim Jati Sevak Sangh.

4. While the source of income of most of the voluntary bodies is indigenous, there are some who are financed through donations and grants received from foreign individuals and institutions. In view of recent problems arising in some tribal areas, it would be desirable to subject the foreign assistance received by such organisations to strict check before permitting its utilisation in tribal area programmes. Wherever any foreign body individual intends financing programmes of welfare in such areas, the funds should be channelised through recognised all-India level voluntary organisations working in tribal areas after obtaining clearance of the Ministry of Home Affairs from the tribal angle. In such cases, the concerned State Government should also be kept in the picture.

5. The areas where voluntary organisations can contribute substantially are:

(1) ensuring active participation and involvement of the tribals in their welfare programmes;
(2) approaching the tribal problems and programmes from a closer perspective and implementing schemes of direct benefit among them;
(3) organising tribal voluntary workers and group leaders for social work; and
(4) taking up development programmes in interior and primitive tribe areas where on account of inaccessibility and lack of communication facilities the governmental programmes do not reach the lowest level. It has been conceded that governmental agencies may penetrate pretty little in some areas of activity where motivational coverage is important while the voluntary organisations may fare well in their effort.

6. One reason why optimal coordination of the activities of voluntary agencies with that of the State Governments has not been possible is the absence of institutional mechanisms to ensure such coordination. It has already been suggested in the Chapter on 'Primitive Tribal Groups' that voluntary agencies of the right type should be given a bigger role in implementation of

programmes for primitive tribes and one of the important duties of the concerned Project Officer, ITDP would be to periodically discuss involvement of these organisations and assist them in the approved programme of work for the primitive tribal group. A machinery for coordination is required, however, not only in respect of organisations working, or to work, in the primitive tribe areas but also for the tribal areas in general. It may be desirable to have a two-tier machinery for such coordination:

(1) at the ITDP level with the District Collector as the Chairman and the Project Administrator as its Convenor-Secretary; and
(2) at the State level with Secretary of the Tribal Development Department as the Chairman. While the first named coordination committee may meet more often, the committee at the State level should meet at least once in the early part of each financial year before grants and programmes of activity are allocated to such agencies.

7. We would suggest adoption of the following strategy during the Seventh Plan:

(1) Voluntary agencies of the right type having the required enthusiasm for the tribal problems should be encouraged to work in tribal areas. Agencies having a sense of involvement and a non-exploitative approach should, in particular, be encouraged.
(2) Programmes in primitive tribal areas and programmes requiring motivational approach besides programmes designed to raise economic levels of the tribal families be entrusted to such agencies. Programmes requiring employment of a highly qualified technical personnel and construction activities of substantial magnitude for which the State Government Departments already maintain well-established organisations may not be necessary to be entrusted to such agencies.
(3) To build up cadres of properly-oriented trained voluntary workers, organisations like the NIPCCD and the TRIs in the country should take on their training rolls

and workers of such agencies in their orientation training courses for which suitable course-contents should be formulated. Training of lady workers over a reasonable period of time should be insisted upon while releasing governmental grants.

(4) Funds channelised directly or indirectly through voluntary agencies working in tribal areas should come as far as possible from indigenous sources, including public donations. Utilisation of foreign assistance in such areas should be subject to scrutiny as suggested in para 4.

(5) Coordination between the voluntary organisations on the one hand and the governmental agencies on the other should be ensured by forming coordinating committees at the district and the State level as suggested in paragraph 6 above.

(6) In the interest of better coordination, as officer of the State Government of the appropriate level working in the tribal areas should invariably be taken in as member of the managing committees of the voluntary organisations working in tribal areas. Such representation would also be desirable at local level, at least at the block level.

(7) Voluntary organisations having women's wing should be encouraged for implementation of economic programmes for tribal women as suggested under the Chapter 'Development of Women and Children.'

APPENDIX III

TECHNOLOGY AND RESEARCH FOR TRIBAL COMMUNITIES

It goes without saying that spread of the appropriate level of technology into various fields of economic activities of the tribal communities is a prerequisite for their rapid advancement. It is however, well known that technology transfer is a complicated process and must take into account the existing social, cultural and economic milieu to be successful. The area of conspicious difference between the present level of development of the development community on the one hand and the tribal communities on the other has to be properly diagnosed and appreciated. Among other things, spread of improved technology to the tribal communities should specifically take note of the following:

(i) the existing economic base,
(ii) the agro-climatic condition of the tribal area,
(iii) the fauna, flora and the ecological environment, and
(iv) the occupational pattern.

In the present tribal context, any specific innovation should adequately recognise this vital consideration.

2. The subject spread of technology is a vast one and it is not possible to go into all aspects of improvement and spread of technology into all spheres of tribal life. We would, therefore, confine ourselves only to that aspect of spread of technology which will have a specific bearing on their economic condition and satisfy the following purposes:

(1) Improving the tribal economy by helping growth of production and processing of existing crop in the tribal

area and introduction of new crops both for subsistence and cash.

(2) Imparting variety and diversification into tribal produce/products in the sphere of agriculture and allied sectors, forestry and small industries.

(3) Raising living standards generally.

3. The above objectives will need a specific thrust in reorienting research programme for the tribal areas while formulating and implementing an action programme to spread and implement the new technological ideas and equipment into the tribal way of life. While researches in the country both original and adoptive have been done in almost all spheres of economic activity in tribal area farms and research gardens, a specific tribal orientation, as such, is necessary, particularly in the thickly tribal belt of Central, Central-eastern and the Central-western tribal belts. For the Himalayan and near-Himalayan regions in the North and the near equatorial regions in the South similar action would also be necessary.

4. The All India Co-ordinated Project on Tribal Area Research taken up under the auspices of the Indian Council of Agricultural Research has already taken up projects for research-*cum*-action programme in different centres in the tribal areas in the country. The research spheres include agricultural production, animal production, homestead vocations, home science and horticultural production. While there is a good number of regional research laboratories in the country, their contribution to tribal economy by way of research-*cum*-action programmes has been negligible. The same is more or less true of the Forest Research Institute. Government of India have been contemplating an Indian Council of Forest Research. This organisation, when it comes up, should pay special attention to spread and improvement of technology in tribal economy in the forestry and minor forest produce sector, in accordance with the broad purposes outlined above. The research institutes under the Department of Science and Technology have to examine the scope for reorienting their research programmes for the benefit of the Scheduled Tribe population as also the Council of Scientific and Industrial Research. Study and research into the health and nutritional

problems of the Scheduled Tribes needs looking into by the Indian Council of Medical Research.

5. We have listed out some of the areas in which upgraded technology can play a notable part incremental production. Put the list is merely illustrative and not exhaustive. We would, however, like to sound a note of caution in introduction of new technology. It is well known that different Scheduled Tribe communities are in different levels of socio-economic development. The differing socio-cultural backgrounds produce different ethos. The existing technological system of a tribal community can be both a product of as well as the prime mover of the socio-economic milieu. The single most important factor in transfer of new technology should be the acceptability and assimilative power of the tribal community. Cultural and religious practices having got inter-women through long usage with occupational and social patterns, the new technology must aim at a reasonable degree of compatibility. In other words, technology ritual convict and cultural incompatibility should be resolved to enable the new technology to succeed. The matter still requires deep sociological study with reference to a tribal community *vis-a-vis* the nature of the new technology. Both policy formulations and field translation have to be approached with perception and sensitivity.

6. Another important aspect is that while the programmes are implemented in the field through the medium of secoral schemes, it would have to be ensured that there is a fair degree of inter-sectoral technological consistency. A projectised approach would make for smooth technology transfer.

7. There is hardly any area or sector where new technology can fail to make impact. However, as already emphasised, a correct and appropriate level of technology will have to be discovered for each tribal situation in the concerned fields. Agriculture, horticulture, animal husbandary, small, village and cottage industries, forestry and health are the fields relevant in the present context. Adequate training of the tribals will help the process of technology transfer. There are certain national and regional institutes which can catalyse it.

8. For the spread of technology and research designed to further economic interest of the tribal community we would suggest as follows:

(1) Dry farming being the rule in vast tribal tracts of the country, research into introduction and multiplication of superior strains of pulses, oil-seeds, grains and other commercial crops suitable for different agro-climatic tribal regions should be given a boost.

(2) There are certain salutary agronomic practices amongst tribes in a country. For example, in the 'jholla' lands in Koraput plateau which constitutes the natural water-way of the hilly terrain paddy is sown before the first rains so that the roots become firm before serious on-set of rains. The paddy in the 'jholla' lands where substantial quantum of water flows for 8-9 months in a year is harvested late after the following though it goes down substantially in quantum. The manner in which better harvest of paddy is possible in such tracts and similar other agronomic practices prevalent amongst Scheduled Tribes in other areas should constitute a major field of research activity.

(3) *In situ* horticultural plantation in respect of mango and jack-fruit has caught up well in certain tracts inhabited by the Saoras and Dongaria Kondhs. Being simple in technique, a massive thrust can be given to the programme in all tribal areas in the country provided research on similar other horticultural species relevant to different tribal regions in the country is taken up.

(4) Lemon, orange and other citrus fruits have tremendous potential in the hilly terrains inhabited by the scheduled tribes as has been seen in the Ramgiri and Niyamgiri hills of Ganjam and Koraput districts. Inter-culture of ginger and pine-apple has also shown good prospects. Research and action plan to spread it and similar other practices in other tribal tracts appears to be very necessary.

(5) Evolving and spreading simple techniques of processing and preservation of guava, lemon, orange, pine-apple, banana seeds and beans which are harvested in very substantial quantity in a number of tribal areas in the country needs attention.

(6) Extraction of oil from sal, mahua, neem and kusum seeds is already in vogue in some tribal areas.

Improvement of the domestic processing procedure for value-addition and toxin-free extraction needs attention.

(7) Powdering, pulping, packaging and further processing of tamarind and myrobalan which are major tribal produce items have as yet not attracted much attention from technologists and researchers. They deserve special attention to improve tribal economy.

(8) Introduction of small gadgets/machines for baling and packing forest fodder grasses to make such grass marketable in nearby cities and towns (this has good scope in areas around Rourkela for example), rope-making from Sabai and other forest grass can substantially boost the income of the Scheduled Tribes depending on them for a living.

(9) Imparting knowledge on growing and processing of gum, resins and lacs after conducting adaptive research in different tribal areas can be a serious field of work.

(10) Improvement in design, methodology of working, chemical and other scientific treatment of tribal products on wood, bamboo and cane may increase both the earning and the employment potential in these sectors.

(11) Introduction of the technique of gur-making from palm, date-plam and Salapa in tribal areas where these species thrive appears necessary.

(12) Imparting instructions on simple techniques of milching of cattle and conversion of milk into curd, cheese and ghee (there are certain tribal areas where there is a cattle population but no milching is done) would be highly beneficial.

(13) Supplying tools and machines for reeling and weaving of yarn while spreading the technique of sericulture which has vast scope in the tribal tracts needs serious attention.

(14) The scope for introducing protein-rich nuts like soyabean and other type of beans in the tribal areas to improve the general health and nutritional standards of the scheduled tribes is an important area for study and action, besides research into the specific health and nutritional problems of the population.

(15) Methodology for scientific management and collection,

preservation and propagation of the herbal medicinal plants has to be perfected and spread amongst tribal population who practise this avocation.

(16) Introduction of simple tools and equipments for powdering, processing of cashew, Khair (catechu), bel (custard apple), mango-kernel and similar other tribal produce is likely to add to proficiency in occupation and income.

(17) Improvement of technology and diversification of designs and products in small and cottage industries and arts and crafts practised by Scheduled Tribes needs research as also action programme.

The respective national and state institutes of research must pay attention to these spheres. Though several research and action programmes have been going on in the country, to use them to the advantage of the tribals needs co-ordination at some level—such a co-ordination has been lacking so far. We suggest that the Tribal Research Institutes in the States be entrusted with this responsibility and the Research Advisory Committees for these institutes under the chairmanship of the Secretary-in-charge of Tribal Development liaise with the national and State level institutes in this sphere and formulate plans of implementation of the desired programmes in their respective context by establishing linkage with the development agencies in the State and the financial institutions. The Secretaries/Head of Departments of the Science, Technology, Forest, Agriculture, Industries and other concerned departments may be associated with the Committee.

APPENDIX IV

TRIBAL RESEARCH AND TRAINING INSTITUTE MAHARASHTRA STATE

1. Introduction

The Tribal Research and Training Institute, Maharashtra State, Pune has been established in the year 1962 under the centrally sponsored scheme during the Third Five Year Plan, in pursuance of orders contained in Government Resolution, Education and Social Welfare Department No. BCP-1062-M, dated 3rd May, 1962.

As a part of the strengthening of the Tribal Research and Training Institute, Pune, the whole-time Director to look after the working and administration of the Institute has been appointed and he has been declared as "Head of the Department" for all purposes, financial and administrative. The Institute is working under administrative control of the Secretary to Government and Tribal Commissioner, Social Welfare, Cultural Affairs, Sports and Tourism Department, Maharashtra State, Bombay.

The Tribal Research and Training Institute has been charged with Research, the responsibility of identifying tribal problems, research projects, Bench Mark Survey of Sub-Plan villages, Sub-Plan statistics, evaluation of Sub-Plan programmes and training of officials and non-officials working in Tribal Sub-Plan Area. Besides, the work of Annual Administration report of the Scheduled Area, caste ethnographic studies are also looked after by the Tribal Research and Training Institute.

2. Objectives and Functions

The main objectives of the Institute are to—

(a) Conduct research into the general and specific areas of economic activity affecting tribal life.

(b) Undertake pilot studies with a view to devising suitable schemes for the socio-economic development and amelioration of living conditions of tribals, keeping in view the customs and other specific features of particular tribal areas and groups.

(c) Maintain an effective "Data Bank" on the socio-economic aspects of tribal life, its collection and contents should subserve the objectives of the Tribal Sub-Plan/ Integrated Tribal Development Projects, as well as their periodical evaluation.

(d) Undertake case studies and sample surveys during the course of actual implementation of the schemes under the Tribal Sub-Plan, with a view to arriving at an objective understanding of the impact of schemes in operation as well as receptivity or otherwise of the tribals in such schemes.

(e) Undertake definitive studies in ethnographic and anthropological problems bearing upon the formulation of developmental schemes and their implementation.

(f) Act as the focal point for the collection and dissemination of Information in regard to tribal life and tribal economy. Generally this will have a three-fold purpose, viz.:

  (i) To educate the generality of the people (including Members of Legislative Assembly, Legislative Council and members of Government) in regard to the realities of tribal problems;
  (ii) To explain to the tribal beneficiaries and especially their leadership, the broad objectives and benefits of various schemes for their development and welfare; and
  (iii) To organise appropriate training programmes for officials and non-officials.

(g) Build up a Museum and Library on tribals.

(h) Any other task assigned by Government from time to time.

3. Governing Council

The Governing Council is constituted by the Government to advise on research and training matters, to watch the progress of the Institute and to ensure that it is functioning on right lines. It includes representatives of tribal M.L.As., concerned Heads of Departments and, Social Scientists. Generally the term of the council is for three years.

4. Research and Evaluation Projects Completed

Seventy studies have been completed by the institute since its inception. Some of the important research projects and evaluation studies are as under:

(1) Report on the evaluation of the scheme of eradication of Palemodi system.
(2) Report on the evaluation of the scheme of rehabilitation of shifting cultivators in Chandrapur district.
(3) Socio-economic survey of Katkaris of Kolaba district.
(4) Survey of Adiwasi sugarcane growers from the area of operation of Tapi Satpuda Sugar Factory in Dhule district.
(5) Survey of Adiwasi sugarcane growers from the area of operation of Panzarkhan Sugar Factory in Dhule district.
(6) Evaluation of the scheme of improved agricultural implements in Nasik district.
(7) Evaluation of the scheme of financial assistance for irrigation wells in Nasik district.
(8) Report on the working of F.L.C. Societies and its impact on tribals of Dhul district.
(9) Report on the forest privileges granted to S.Ts. its benefits and abuses.
(10) Report on the working of F.L.C. societies in Maharashtra and Gujarat and their role in tribal development.
(11) Monographic study of the Kolams.
(12) Monographic study of the Katkaris.
(13) Monographic study of the Halbas.
(14) Traits and characteristics of VJs. and N.Ts. of Maharashtra State.
(15) Brochure on traits and characteristics of S.Ts. of Maharashtra State.

(16) Report on the working of Ashram Schools in Maharashtra State.
(17) Report on education and communication of Tribal Development Block, Kurkheda.
(18) Report on education and communication of Tribal Development Block, Surgana.
(19) Report on education and communication of Tribal Development Block, Talasari.
(20) Report on education and communication of Tribal Development Block, Madh.
(21) Utilisation of Hostel facilities by Scheduled Castes and Scheduled Tribes in Maharashtra State.
(22) Education and communication in Tribal Development Block, Maregaon.
(23) Wastage and stagnation in primary and secondary schools of Peint and Surgana Tahsils of Nasik district.
(24) Report on the post-matric scholarships of Halba tribe students of Maharashtra State.
(25) Report on the Primary Health Centre, Kasa.
(26) Report on the Primary Health Centre, Dharni.
(27) Report on the Primary Health Centre, Mhaswad.
(28) Report on the Primary Health Centre, Ambegaon.
(29) Report on the Primary Health Centre, Surgana.
(30) Report on the Primary Health Centre, Rajur.
(31) Report on the Primary Health Centre. Etapalli.
(32) Leprosy problem in Chandrapur district.
(33) Study of Health and Nutrition problems of the Primitive tribes.
(34) Report on the Housing conditions and Housing schemes of Scheduled Tribes in Maharashtra.
(35) Gondi-Marathi conversational guide.
(36) Gondi-English conversational guide.
(37) Rapid survey of ten villages of Jawhar tahsil.
(38) Rapid survey of ten villages of Dahanu tahsil.
(39) Report on post-extension survey of Tribal Development Block, Ambegaon.
(40) Report on post-extension survey of Tribal Development Block, Dharni.
(41) Report on post-extension survey of Tribal Development Block, Mulgi.

(42) Evaluation of the scheme of Special Nutrition Programme in tribal areas of Maharashtra State.
(43) Evaluation report on the working of the scheme of supply of electric pumps to S.T. cultivators.
(44) Impact of urbanisation on Scheduled Tribes.
(45) Health condition of the tribal in Maharashtra State.
(46) महाराष्ट्रातील आदिवासी त्यांच्या सामाजिक व सांस्कृतिक जीवनाचे प्रश्न आणि कल्याणाच्या योजना।
(47) Alienation and restoration of land to Scheduled Tribes in Maharashtra.
(48) Evaluation of the working of Adiwasi Co-operative Societies in Maharashtra.
(49) Study of Bonded Labour in Thane district.
(50) Evaluation of the scheme of consumption finance in Maharashtra.
(51) Ethnographic notes on the Scheduled Tribes.
(52) Evaluation of the Ashram School Complex Scheme in Kinwat, district Nanded.
(53) A study of health services in selected Tribal Areas.
(54) Food habits of Adivasis in Maharashtra.
(55) Traditional Panchayat System in Tribal communities.
(56) Revision of schemes for the Backward Classes.
(57) Revision of Schemes for the Scheduled Tribes.
(58) New schemes and projects for the development of primitive tribes.
(59) Perspective Planning of Ashram Schools of Maharashtra.
(60) Study of the benefits accrued by the tribal people from Waghad Irrigation Project, Nasik and Surya Irrigation Project, Thane.
(61) Forest Labourers Co-operative Societies in Maharashtra and Gujarat: their significant in tribal development.
(62) Location survey of Ashram Schools in Maharashtra.

5. Integrated Area Development Projects Cell

In the year 1974, the Government in Social Welfare, Cultural Affairs, Sports and Tourism Department established the Integrated Area Development Projects Cell in the Directorate of Tribal Welfare, Pune. as well as in Social Welfare Department of Mantralaya, Bombay, to prepare the sub-plan and Integrated Area

Development Projects, as per the directions of Government of India. The cell from the Directorate of Tribal Welfare, M.S., Pune has been attached to the Institute since 1st April, 1977. The work done by the cell since that period is as under:

(1) Preparation of Integrated Area Development Project, Kinwat.
(2) Rationalisation of Scheduled Areas.
(3) Bench Mark Survey (in progress).
(4) Examination of Tribal Sub-Plan Area.
(5) Survey of locations of Ashram Schools in Maharashtra State and perspective plan.
(6) Extension of Areas—Additional Sub-Plan Area/Tribal Sub-Plan Area.
(7) Inclusion of the omitted villages.
(8) Adjustments of the Border area villages on the border having 50 per cent or more tribal concentration.
(9) Modified Area Development Approach and formation of pockets of 10,000 or more population with 50 per cent tribal concentration. This exercise has been done separately for enumerated and unenumerated tribal population.

6. Training Programme

A training wing has been established in the institute in 1968. The following orientation training programmes have been conducted:

Sl. No.	*Type of Training Course*	*No. of Courses Organised*	*No. of Trainees Benefited*
1	2	3	4
1.	Social Welfare Officer, Tribal Welfare Officers and Other Officers	4	41
2.	Extension Officers	12	229
3.	Tribal Youths	40	1,260
4.	Teachers of Govt. Ashram Schools	2	76
5.	Teachers from Government Balwadis	1	36
6.	Tribal couples	1	12
	Total	60	1,654

Thus various types of training programmes have been organised so far for the officials and non-officials working in tribal areas with a view to orient these persons with tribal life and culture; to acquaint them with the various schemes of tribal welfare; and to enthuse in them the spirit of service for this weaker section of the society.

7. Propaganda Camps

The Institute has organised (114) propaganda camps, through the media of film shows in tribal areas of Maharashtra State and thus efforts are being made to give publicity to the Tribal Sub-Plan programmes in the sub-plan areas of Maharashtra.

8. Caste Ethnographic Studies

The Institute offers advisory services to the State Government in respect of Scheduled Castes, Scheduled Tribes, Vimukta Jatis, Nomadic Tribes and other Backward Classes of Maharashtra. So far 200 ethnographic studies have been conducted by the Institute.

9. Scheduled Area Report and other Reports

The report on the annual administration of Scheduled Areas in Maharashtra is drafted by the Institute and submitted to Government in Social Welfare Department for approval and onward transmission to Government of India after its approval by the Governor of Maharashtra State.

Similarly, the information of Scheduled Tribes is collected from the concerned Departments and submitted to the Commissioner for Scheduled Castes and Scheduled Tribes, New Delhi of his annual report.

10. Library

There are about 4,000 books in the Library of the Institute on tribal problems and studies. The library is being used by the Post-graduate and the research students of the Universities and Officers of the Government Departments. The efforts are being made to organise the library on scientific lines. Besides the books, foreign and Indian journals on Sociology, Anthropology, Economics, Social Welfare, etc. are contributed. The statistical reports and census reports are also kept in the library.

11. Museum

There are about 600 exhibits in the Museum of the Institute on tribal life and culture of Maharashtra State.

The musical instruments, ornaments, tribal Gods and Goddesses, tribal painting, etc. are placed in the Galleries of the Museum. Some of the exhibits are very rare and valuable.

12. Expenditure

The expenditure on the Institute since 1974-75 is as under:

Year	*Plan*	*Non-Plan*	*Total*
1	2	3	4
1974-75	16,288	1,44,913	1,61,202
1975-76	79,782	1,40,827	2,20,609
1976-77	89,081	1,70,263	2,59,345
1977-78	1,93,119	1,85,785	3,78,904
1778-79	4,25,000	2,84,000	7,09,000
1979-80 (Provisional)	5,45,000	7,87,000	13,32,000

Organisational set up of the Tribal Research and Training Institute, Pune

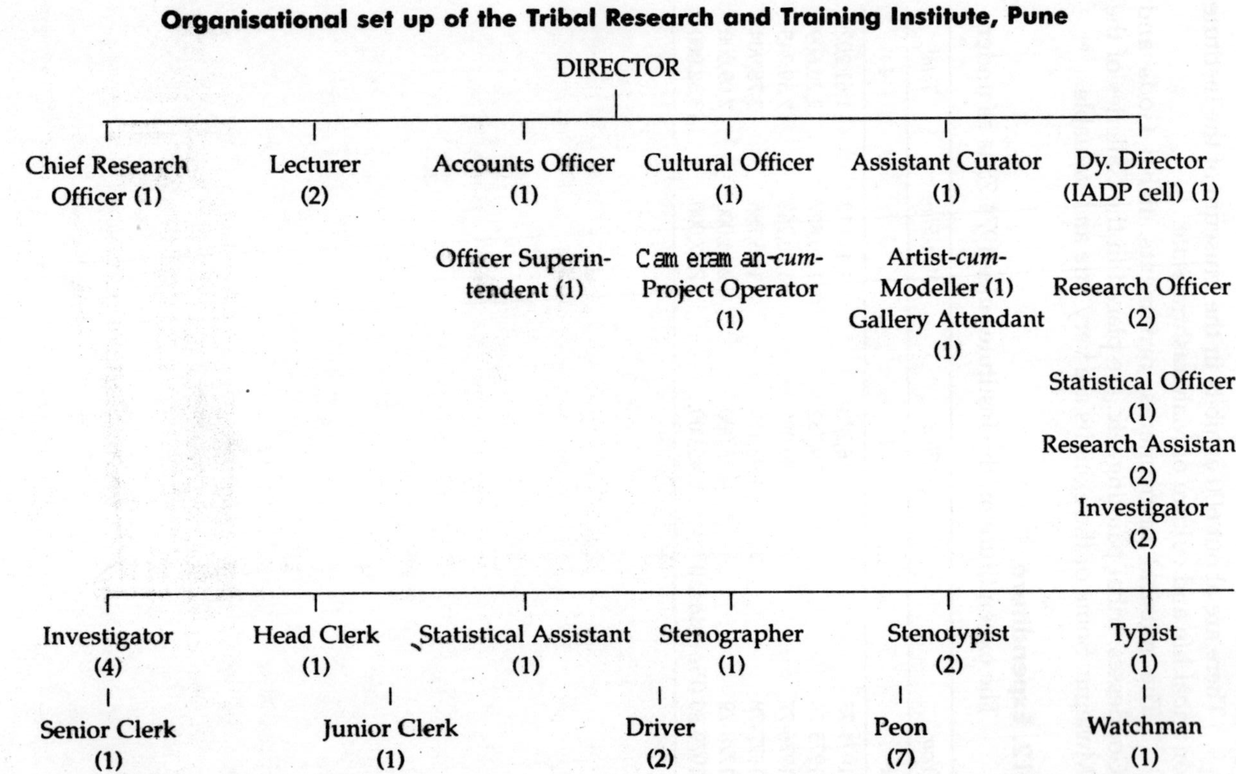

APPENDIX V

TRIBAL RESEARCH INSTITUTES

Introduction

To trace the origin and development of Tribal Research Institutes in the country one has to go back to the First Plan period. When formulating programmes for tribal development in First Plan, one of the major handicaps faced was the relative absence of data on the nature and magnitude of problems of different tribal communities and tribal areas. The need for orientation and training of personnel engaged in tribal development was also realised. The Committee on Special Multi-purpose Tribal Development Blocks and the Commissioner for Scheduled Castes and Scheduled Tribes had emphasised the need for material data and orientation and training of personnel. In order to overcome these difficulties, a beginning was made by starting a Tribal Research Bureau at Bhubaneshwar in 1953 (later renamed as Tribal and Harijan Research and Training Institute). Soon thereafter, Tribal Research Institutes were set up in Bihar (Ranchi, 1954), Madhya Pradesh (Chhindwara, now functioning at Bhopal, 1954) and West Bengal (Calcutta, 1955). The Committee on Special Multi-purpose Tribal Development Blocks (Elwin Committee) set up in 1958 stressed the need for setting up Tribal Research Institutes in States. The Committee, *inter-alia,* suggested that these Institutes should collaborate with the State Governments in an advisory capacity in all matters relating to tribal development. The Scheduled Areas and Scheduled Tribes Commission (Dhebar Commission, 1961) also stressed the importance of Tribal Research Institutes. The Study Team on Social Welfare and Backward Classes (Renuka Ray Team, 1954) and the Study Team on Tribal Development Programmes (Shilu Ao Study Team, 1969) also recognised the role of Tribal Research Institutes and suggested their strengthening.

2. During the Third Five Year Plan, it was decided that States having a tribal population of one million and above should get up a Tribal Research Institute. Accordingly, Tribal Research Institutes were set up in Maharashtra (Pune, 1962), Gujarat (Ahmedabad, 1962), Assam (Shillong, 1962 later as a result of bifurcation of Meghalaya from Assam the Institute was shifted to Gauhati), Andhra Pradesh (Hyderabad, 1963) and Rajasthan (Udaipur, 1964). Thus, by the end of the Third Five Year Plan, there were 9 Tribal Research Institutes. Lately, 2 more were added one each in Kerala (Calicut, 1971) and Tamil Nadu (Uthagamandalam, 1983) and a Cell at Lucknow in Uttar Pradesh (1971). Thus, by the end of 1983 there were 12 Tribal Research Institutes including Research Cell in Lucknow. The complete list of the Tribal Research Institutes is given in Annexure I.

Reviews

3. The working of the Tribal Research Institutes (TRI) was reviewed from time-to-time by Commissions/Committees such as the Committee on Special Multi-purpose Tribal Development Blocks (1960), the Scheduled Areas and Scheduled Tribes Commission (1960-61), the Study Team on Tribal Development Programmes (1969). A separate Study Team under the Chairmanship of Shri L.M. Shrikant was constituted in 1969 to review the working of the Tribal Research Institutes. The terms of reference of this Study Team were—(i) to examine the research and training activities, functions and actual working of the Tribal Research Institutes set up in previous plans; (ii) to explore the feasibility of including within the scope of their functions the problems of the Scheduled Castes and Denotified Communities in addition to the Scheduled Tribes; and (iii) to examine the need for setting up a Central Research and Training Institute for co-ordinating the activities of the regional institutes and for training personnel. The Team submitted its report in 1972. This Team *inter-alia* observed that the Tribal Research Institutes have to function in coordination with the Welfare Department. An Institute, however, should be able to undertake research in an objective and independent manner within the overall frame of policy directives and programme of research as determined jointly by the Department of Tribal Welfare and the Tribes Advisory Council and the Research Institute. The Institute should not have to obtain

clearance on matters of details or on issues pertaining to its day-to-day functioning. The role of Institute should be that of an objective adviser.

4. In recent times, that the role of the Tribal Research Institutes has been highlighted by the Parliamentary Committee on the welfare of Scheduled Castes and Scheduled Tribes in their twenty-first report submitted to Lok Sabha on 7th April, 1982. Conferences of Directors of the Tribal Research Institutes held in the Ministry of Home Affairs from time to time since 1979 also reviewed the functioning of Tribal Research Institutes.

5. In her inaugural address at the Conference of Directors of Tribal Research Institutes held on 4 May, 1984, Shrimati Ramdulari Sina, Minister of State for Home Affairs, advising the delegates said, "It is my suggestion that the Institutes, which are professionally competent, should render feed-back to State administration and the Ministry to formulate appropriate strategies for tribal development from time-to-time". Reiterating the full support of Government of India the Minister added: "I can assure that we will do all that is necessary to make Tribal Research Institutes viable to enable them to provide the professional input for implementation of tribal development programmes".

6. Since the adoption of the Tribal Sub-Plan strategy during the Fifth Five Year Plan period, the Tribal Research Institutes have assumed an important role in contributing to the developmental efforts and assisting the State administration in improving the socio-economic conditions of the weaker sections of the society, the Scheduled Castes and the Scheduled Tribes, by way of tendering advice as to how best inputs could be provided to achieve optimum results.

7. The important functions presently discharged by the Tribal Research Institutes are those related to planning, research, evaluation and training relevant to tribal development. Before discussing in detail these functions it would perhaps be appropriate to look at the structure, i.e., administration including staffing pattern and financing of these Institutes.

Administrative Set up

8. All the Tribal Research Institutes, except the one at Ahmedabad and the other at Uthagamandalam are under the

administrative control of the respective State Governments in matters of supervision, recruitment, financial control and programmes. The Tribal Research and Training Institute at Ahmedabad, is under the administrative control of Gujarat Vidyapeeth and that of Uthagamandalam under the Tamil University, Thanjavur.

9. In all the Institutes, except in the case of Cell in U.P., the Institute is headed by a senior class I officer designated as Director. Of the 11 Directors, 9 hold Ph.D. Degree.

10. The staffing pattern of the Institutes is not uniform. In general, the Director is assisted by Joint Director, Deputy Director, Research Officers and other supporting staff. Though in particular cases and at particular period the full complement of staff might not be in position, as in case of Kerala and Rajasthan, the Institutes are properly staffed. The details of staff sanctioned for individual Institutes is given at Annexure-II. It would appear therefrom, that next to Director, the post of Deputy Director is common to most of the Institutes. The Institutes of Assam and Madhya Pradesh have in between post of Joint Director and Rajasthan has Additional Director. Andhra Pradesh is having a post of Deputy Director-*cum*-Principal. The Institute of West Bengal is having post of Chief Planner and Assistant Planner. Some of the Institutes, such as Maharashtra, Gujarat and West Bengal have Museum Curator/Caretaker. The Institute in West Bengal is having specific posts for Movie Cameraman, Artist-*cum*-Photographer and Librarian.

11. Report of the Study Team on Tribal Research Institutes (1972) *inter-alia* observed that "for research work, the staff of an institute should have post-graduate and research qualifications. The existing staff should be given training in research methodology through short-term courses. Senior level research personnel should not only have post-graduate degree in Anthropology, Sociology or any other social sciences, but also perferably have a doctoral degree and publications to their credit as evidence of their research ability. The head of the Institute should be selected on the basis of published research work to his credit, academic background and training and experience in research *(op. cit.* 18-19).

Research Advisory Committee

12. With a view to keeping constant watch on the progress of work done by the Tribal Research Institutes, all the State Governments have constituted Research Advisory Committees. The Committee finalise the future programme of work, approve the Research projects and discuss the shortcomings and bottlenecks in implementation of the programmes. Importance of the role of research Advisory Committee has been emphasised from time to time in the meetings of the Directors of the Tribal Research Institutes held in the Ministry of Home Affairs.

13. In the meeting of the Directors of Tribal Research Institutes held in September 1979 it was felt that the Chief Minister or Minister-in-charge, Tribal Development should held the committee. Representatives from Universities, other academic institutes and Anthropological Survey of India as also non-officials should be included as members of the Committee. There should be regular and fruitful meetings of these Committees.

14. In the meeting of the Directors of Tribal Research Institutes held in October), 1980 it was noted that meetings of the Research Advisory Committee were not being held regularly and the need for regular meetings was stressed.

15. In the meeting of Directors of Tribal Research Institutes held in June, 1981 following points were emphasised regarding functioning of the Research Advisory Committee:

(i) The Advisory Committee should review the work of Tribal Research Institutes in the field of Research Planning, Evaluation and Training.
(ii) Director of Tribal Research Institute should act as Member-Secretary of the Advisory Committee.
(iii) Setting up of Committee to review follow up action.

Financing

16. The scheme of tribal research and training is included as a Centrally Sponsored Programme under the Backward Classes sector of the Plan. Prior to financial year 1979-80, cent per cent Central assistance was being given for the scheme of tribal research and training. Since the financial year 1979-80 the expenditure on the scheme is being shared between the States and the Centre on 50:50 basis. The Central outlay for the Sixth Plan is

Rs. 3.00 crores. It would appear from the Annexure III that the total amount released to States under research and training has increased from Rs. 15.80 lakhs in 1974-75 to Rs. 54.51 lakhs during the year 1983-84. An allocation of Rs. 70.00 lakhs has been made for the last year of the Sixth Plan, 1984-85.

Main Functions of Tribal Research Institutes

17. The Tribal Research Institutes are actively engaged in planning, research, evaluation and training.

Planning—The Institutes are actively associated in the preparation of tribal sub-Plan, i.e., delineation of Tribal sub-Plan and pockets of tribal concentration (MADA) and identification of primitive tribal groups. Tribal sub-Plan is under operation in seventeen States and two Union Territories. Pockets of tribal concentration numbering 245 have been delineated and 72 primitive tribal groups identified upto September, 1984. Five T.R.Is. also undertook universal Tribal Bench Mark Survey.

Training—The Tribal Research Institutes have a training wing with them. Regular training is imparted to the concerned State officials and officers from various departments to equip them with proper orientation and understanding of the way of life of the tribal people and problems of development in tribal areas.

A review of the various orientation training programmes undertaken by the Tribal Research Institutes would reveal that sizable work is being done by the Institutes in this sphere. Annexure IV gives training courses conducted by the Institutes during the Sixth Plan period. These training courses include subordinate staff as well as officers of various State departments directly responsible for administration and implementation of development schemes in the tribal areas. It would appear from the Annexure that Project Officers, District Officers, Extension Officers, Officers/Officials from Excise, Forest and Police Departments, School teachers. Tahsildars, etc., of the State government are regularly receiving orientation training in the Institutes. Besides members of Panchayat Samitis and Zilla Parishads, also get training from the Institutes. In addition to these usual orientation, training courses regularly conducted by Tribal Research Institutes, some Institutes have also taken up some other useful training courses for tribal leaders and harijan leaders (Kerala) Tribal Youth leadership training programmes

(Maharashtra); Training of organising cultural programmes, games and other extra-curricular activities in Ashram School (Maharashtra); Project implementation, monitoring and evaluation (Orissa); Research Methodology in Tribal Development Administration (Orissa); Training and Orientation of People's representatives at the grass-root levels (Rajasthan); Pre-service training to tribal graduates and under-graduates and those passed 12th standard (Maharashtra).

Orientation courses and imparting training to the persons (officials as well as non-officials) working in the tribal areas is one of the important tasks being performed by the T.R.Is. However, looking at the training programmes (Annexure IV) of the different Tribal Research Institutes during the Sixth Plan period, it seems imperative that Tribal Research Institutes should plan for extension of training programmes to offer opportunities for better familiarisation of problems in the tribal areas. It appears that presently only a few Institutes are continuing with their regular training programmes. Training programmes therefore, require an urgent attention and revitalisation in the States. Planned developmental process cannot afford to belittle the importance of such orientation and training courses. The Report of the Scheduled Areas and Scheduled Tribes Commission (Dhebar Commission) 1960-61 had no doubt attributed great importance to such training courses. The report observed that during the first two Five Year Plans the progress achieved in the welfare programmes for the Scheduled Tribes was short of expectations of the Commission both in physical achievement and quality and it concluded "Among the various causes for the inadequate progress of the tribal welfare schemes, the shortage of trained personnel is probable the greatest single factor" *(op. cit.,* 310). The report made it very explicit that success of any developmental programmes will be "largely conditioned by the approach of the official and non-official agencies, by their understanding of tribal culture and traditions, and on the appreciation of social psychological and economic problems" *(ibid)*. The report also presents elaborate scheme for training. It classified the various officials of the State Governments engaged in planning and implementation of the Tribal Welfare Programme into 5 broad categories viz., (i) Planning and Administrative Staff, (ii) Supervisory Staff who are expected to guide and direct the Field Workers, (iii) Technical non-field staff above and at the District level, (iv) Technical staff below District level, and (v) Field Staff.

The Twenty-seventh Report of the Commissioner for Scheduled Castes and Scheduled Tribes also recommended, "in order to give proper orientation to the personnel particularly to the lower level functionaries of Revenue, Forest, Agriculture, Cooperation Departments and other non-officials concerned with welfare of Scheduled Castes/Scheduled Tribes the T.R.Is. concerned should organise a comprehensive and realistic training programme." (1979-81 284).

Report of the Committee on Special Multi-purpose Tribal Blocks emphasising upon the training aspect of the personnel working in the tribal areas observed, "One of the major reasons why the development programme in the Multi-purpose Blocks has failed to adapt itself to local conditions is the lack of adequate training of the staff in the appreciation of tribal life and culture." (*op. cit.*, 40).

Seminars and Workshops—Besides conducting of training courses some of the Tribal Research Institutes have also organised seminars and workshops. TRI, Orissa (1981-82) organised a 'National level seminar on development aspects of tribal areas'. This seminar was sponsored by the National Committee on Development of Backward Areas, Planning Commission, New Delhi. TRI, Kerala (1983-84) has organised a seminar on 'Anthropological approach to tribal development administration'. TRI, Gujarat (1983-84) has organised a seminar on the theme of 'Prohibition and Tribals". Maharashtra Tribal Research Institute (1983-84) has organised workshops on Tribal Welfare Officers, Tribal Welfare Inspectors and Research Assistants in I.T.D.P. Orissa Tribal Research Institute has organised workshop on tribal development administration (1982-83), Workshops on scheduled castes development administration (1983-84), Workshop on preparation of project report for Project Administrators (1983-84). Tribal Research Institute, Rajasthan has organised a workshop on problems of applied nature and having direct relevance to the tribal development programme (1983-84). In 1982-83, Tribal Research Institute, West Bengal had organised an 'Essay and Debate Competition on Untouchability'. Besides this Institute had in 1982-83 also made an attempt in production of 16 mm documentary films on handicrafts of scheduled castes and scheduled tribes.

Research Studies—A look at the Research Studies (Annexure V) taken up by the Tribal Research Institutes shows that these very in range dealing with varied aspects of tribal life. These studies may broadly be categorised as under:

> 1. Demography, 2. Agriculture, 3. Dialects, 4. Health/ Nutritional Status, 5. Socio-Cultural Problems, 6. Economic Problems, 7. Educational Problems.

Most of the studies relate to either socio-cultural or economic problems of the tribals. Some of these studies relate to fertility, veneral disease, blindness, anthropometry, family planning, dietary, etc. Taking up of ethnographic studies of Scheduled Castes/Scheduled Tribes and bringing out monographs on them is a common programme taken up by different Institutes. Some of the research studies also attempt in understanding the specific problems of the tribal people and these are grouped as under:

Exploitation of Tribals—Exploitation of the weaker sections of the society by means of money lending, land alienation, bonded labour, etc. has drawn wider attention of the social scientists, planners and administrators alike. Some of the studies taken up by the Tribal Research Institutes on these aspects are—study of the impact of protective legislations in regard to land alienation, bonded labour, money lending, excise and forest policy (Orissa); study of exploitation of tribals by money lenders and its remedial measures (Rajasthan); nature and extent of indebtedness among the tribals in I.T.D.Ps. (West Bengal); study of land alienation (Andhra Pradesh); Study of bonded labour in Santhal Parganas District (West Bengal).

Displacement of Tribals—Displacement of tribals due to various developmental activities and their meaningful rehabilitation is another challenging task for the administration. Some of the studies undertakes by the Tribal Research Institutes on this problem are—Rehabilitation programme for tribals in submerged areas of Polavaram Barrage (Andhra Pradesh); study of displacement of tribals owing to installation of Industrial and Irrigation projects (Assam); study on displacement of tribals (West Bengal)-study of villages affected by NALCO project at

Damanjodi (Orissa); rehabilitation of displaced persons due to Kukad irrigation project in Pune district (Maharashtra); study of villages to be submerged in catchment areas of Narmada Dam (Gujarat).

Problems of Tribal Women Labourers— Some of the Tribal Research Institutes have also tried to study the problems faced by tribal women labourers—Problems of tribal women working in Industrial units of GIDC Estate Vapi (Gujarat); study of migrant women labourers in district Santhal Parganas—problems of their rehabilitation (Bihar); study of tribal women labourers engaged in various economic sectors (West Bengal).

Tribal Education—Studies taken up attempt to look into educational problems of tribal children like enrolment, drop out post-matric scholarships, working of Ashram schools, problems of tribal girl students, etc. Besides these the Institutes also prepare conversational guide, text books for primary stage, grammar, etc. of selected tribal dialects on an experimental basis.

Some of other studies on health/nutritional, socio-economic and religious aspects of tribal people are—Study of mal-nutrition including consumption of Kesari Dal (Bihar); Guinea worm—incidence *vis-a-vis* hand pump programme (Rajasthan); Impact of Gaon-Panchayat level cooperative societies and LAMPs on Tribals (Assam); Cooperative societies in Tribal areas with special reference to forest labourers cooperative society (Gujarat); Study of Social Forestry Programmes (Rajasthan); Poverty Line programme—a study of income pattern of tribals (Andhra Pradesh); Study of Psycho-socio-cultural Aspects of Denotified Tribal Societies (Orissa); Impact of Christianity on Tribals (Kerala); Impact of-Bhagat Movement on Tribal Population (Rajasthan). Some of the Tribal Research Institutes like that of West Bengal have made studies on Scheduled Castes regarding the problems of social disability and the crafts the Scheduled Castes are engaged.

Evolution Studies—It may be evident from Annexure V that evaluation of ITDPs/ITDAs is the most common evaluative study conducted by the different Tribal Research Institutes. Some of the other subjects which are normally to be found in the list of evaluation studies by the Institutes are—Co-operative Societies, LAMPs, Minor Irrigation Schemes, Ashram Schools, Post-matric Scholarships, etc. Institutes of Andhra Pradesh, Gujarat and

Maharashtra have taken up evaluation studies relating to dairy development programmes. Besides these, some of the evaluative studies which deserve mention here are, viz., socio-economic conditions of Scheduled Tribe beneficiaries under tassar culture programme (Andhra Pradesh), Evaluation study of Poultry Development (Gujarat), Evaluation study of credit facilities for purchase of oxen (Gujarat), Evaluation of impact of land survey and settlement operations in tribal areas (Orissa), Evaluation of plantation and other horticultural schemes (Orissa). Rajasthan attempted some useful evaluative studies of IRD programme, TADCF, ICDS, TRYSEM and Sahariya Development Project, etc.

It would be evident from the preceding account that the research and evaluation studies taken up by the different Tribal Research Institutes during the Sixth Plan period have attempted at looking into various problems relating to tribal life. However, the usefulness of the research/evaluation studies taken up by the Institutes may rightly be seen in the context of tribal sub-Plan strategy as these are not only closely associated with it, but have become an integral part of it in the course of time. In the context of multi-faced developmental schemes a quantitative and qualitative evaluation by Tribal Research Institutes would be necessary to take remedial measures. Some of the important programmes being implemented for accelerated development of Scheduled Tribes in Tribal sub-Plan, during the Sixth Plan are—

(i) Enforcement of various protective measures like law against alienation of tribal land, regulation of business of money lending, abolition of bonded labour, regulation of Inter-State Migrant Labour, review of forest, excise, credit and marketing policies.

(ii) Aiming to increase productive levels in agriculture, horticulture, animal husbandry, forestry, cottage village and small industries through increase in irrigation potential, introduction of modern technology and use of adequate inputs viz. improved seeds, fertilisers, etc.

(iii) Identification of tribal families living below the poverty line in the Tribal sub-Plan area and enabling them to cross the poverty line by rendering assistance under the various development programmes, viz., Integrated

Rural Development Programme, Drought Prone Area Programme, National Rural Employment Programme, Economic Rehabilitation of Rural Poor Programme, Employment Guarantee Affirmation Schemes, Hill Area Development and Tribal sub-Plan programmes.

(iv) Establishment of Ashram schools, girls' hostels, book banks for scheduled tribe students and making provision for adequate pre and post-matric stipends/ scholarships and taking up schemes of coaching and training the tribal boys for specific employment opportunities besides reviewing reservation of posts and services for Scheduled Tribes.

(v) Allotment of lands and developing the same for increasing production.

(vi) Allotment of house sites and assistance for construction of houses.

It would be evident by looking at the studies taken up by the Tribal Research Institutes during the Sixth Plan Period (Annexure V) that these included fairly varied schemes under operation in the tribal sub-Plan areas. However, the Tribal sub-Plan strategy during the Sixth Plan is marked with a shift on emphasis on family beneficiary-oriented programmes compared to the development of infrastructural facilities in Fifth Plan. This emphasis is not fully reflected in the selection of studies by the Institutes. It would have been certainly more advantageous had more studies on family beneficiary-oriented programmes been taken up. It would thus, be pertinent to quote observations made by Shrimati Ram Dulari Sinha, Minister of State in the Ministry of Home Affairs at the Coaference of Directors of Tribal Research Institutes held on 4th May 1984 wherein she emphasised on practical utility of the studies made by the Tribal Research Institutes and said, "In assessing the suitability of the programmes and accrual of benefits to individual families, the Tribal Research Institutes have an important role to play. We are not presently interested in academic research, which is in any case the universities and such other bodies are doing. I would emphasise that the Tribal Research Institutes should engage themselves more and more in practical studies which would assist the State administration in improving the programme content and implementation."

Emphasising on the objective value of the research/ evaluation studies taken up by various organisations, Second Report of the Commission for Scheduled Castes and Scheduled Tribes expressed gratification "to note that the Research Organisations, like Tribal Research Institutes, Anthropological Survey of India, University Departments, Bureau of Economics and Statistics, etc., have in addition to the conduct of sociological studies for the purpose of tracing the history of the tribals, their origin, their migration and their racial affinities which are important from academic point of view, have now started focussing equally their attention on the study of objective value of the welfare programme for the Scheduled Castes and Scheduled Tribes" (1979-80: 376).

In view of the practical aspect of the evaluation studies, the Ministry of Home Affairs have suggested some studies to each of the Tribal Research Institutes to be undertaken during 1984-85. A list of these studies is appended at Annexure-VI. It would appear therefrom that an attempt has been made to give due coverage to primitive tribal groups, MADA Pockets, Co-operative Society, Family beneficiary schemes besides usual study of ITDP. As stated earlier, it is envisaged that Tribal Research Institutes for improving the programme content and implementation of the development programmes for tribals should engage themselves in practical studies. Indeed, Tribal Research Institutes have done some useful evaluative studies in the past years. However, it is not known how far these studies are being utilised by the State administration in formulation and implementation of development programmes for the tribals.

Publication

18. Tribal Research Institutes publish the findings of their studies through books, mimeographed reports, bulletins, special numbers and journals. Some of these Institutes are also bringing out their journals. The title of the journals, place of publication and periodicity are given below:

Sl. No.	Name of Journal	Place of Publication	Periodicity
1.	Tribe	Tribal Research Institute and Training Centre, Udaipur	Quarterly
2.	Bulletin of the Cultural Research Institute	Cultural Research Institute, Calcutta	-Do-
3.	Bulletin of the Bihar Tribal Research Institute	Bihar Tribal Welfare Research Institute, Ranchi	Bi-annual
4.	Bulletin of the Tribal Research Institute	The Tribal Research Institute, Bhopal	-Do-
5.	Tribal	The Tribal Cultural Research and Training Institute, Hyderabad	-Do-
6.	Adibasi	Tribal Research Bureau, Bhubaneshwar	-Do-

19. It is observed that besides being published irregularly, there seems scope for improvement in the quality of contents. Other publications of the Institutes are also by and large irregular. Timely publication of these reports is imperative otherwise the data presented by them cannot be utilised in time and may loose its relevance.

Museum

20. The Tribal Research Institutes are also having a museum located in the Institute's building. The objective of setting up these museums is to collect artifacts connected with tribal culture in a systematic manner. The Institutes have collected specimens concerning material culture viz., hunting, fishing, agricultural implements, offensive and defensive weapons, utensils, basketry and pottery works, musical instruments, dress and ornaments, objects of art and sculpture, objects relating to magic and religion, etc. Folk tales and folk songs are also recorded and preserved in the museum. Photographs and documentary films depicting varied facts of the way of life of the tribals are also being taken and kept. Some of these museums like that of Ranchi, Bhubaneshwar, Chhindwara and Hyderabad have a fairly good collection

of specimens, charts, maps and plaster models. The system of arrangement of artifacts varies in different Institutes. The study team on Tribal Research Institutes (1972) found that there is no system of improving the skill of the technical staff of the museums in modern techniques of display, treatment and storage of exhibits. It would certainly improve the working if the museum curators are trained in Museology. The study team felt that "the museum of the Tribal Research Institutes should be manned by staff and arrangements should be made to provide in-service training to them." *(op cit.:* 65)

Quarterly Progress Reports

21. With a view to continuously monitor and assess the working of the TRIs, the Ministry of Home Affairs prescribed in September 1983 a quarterly progress report for these Institutes. A proforma for the report was also suggested by the Ministry. A review of these quarterly reports show that so far only the Institutes of Assam, Bihar, Gujarat, Orissa, Rajasthan, Uttar Pradesh and West Bengal have sent the quarterly progress reports for the quarter ending September, 1983 and only two Tribal Research Institutes, Gujarat and Rajasthan have furnished reports for the quarter ending December, 1983.

Conclusion

22. Except the Tribal Research Institute of Tamil Nadu, which is the latest (1983), most of the other Institutes have by now gained considerable number of years experience in the field of planning, research and training. As such these Institutes have become an integral part of the set up for planned development for the tribals. It is envisaged that these Institutes would take up a pragmatic and more objective stance and become viable for providing professional input to their respective State Governments for successful implementation of tribal development programmes.

23. Reviewing the general performance of the Tribal Research Institutes in the meeting of the Directors of Tribal Research Institutes held on 4th March, 1983, Shri N.R. Laskar, Minister of State in the Ministry of Home Affairs had observed in his inaugural address—"At present, the Tribal Research Institutes are mainly engaged in undertaking research studies on developmental problems of Scheduled Castes and Scheduled

Tribes, evaluation of programmes and training of officials. Some Institutes have done well in research, others in evaluation and some others in training. However, I do find that all Institutes are not putting in their best. I would emphasise that those lagging behind to make up and render a good account of ever assistance is available from the Central Government should be fully utilised by the State Governments so that the Tribal Research Institutes can establish themselves on sound footing. For the purpose the Institutes should be strengthened".

24. While making an appraisal nothing would be more apt than to quote Shrimati Ram Dulari Sinha, Minister of State (Home) at the conference of Directors of Tribal Research Institutes held on 4th May, 1984 while she said, "a review of the performance of individual Institutes reveals that while some Institutes have generally done useful work in some field, or the other, some Tribal Research Institutes have yet to properly organise themselves in many ways". Commenting on the latter category she advised that "such of the Institutes which have not done well must put in much more effort to properly organise themselves and discharge their functions creditably". Regarding full utilisation of the funds made available to the Tribal Research Institutes from the Central Government she observed. "It has been brought to my notice that the Tribal Research Institutes are not fully drawing the financial assistance available from the Ministry of Home Affairs. I am not aware of constraints for this. In any case, it is essential that the Institutes are not handicapped in any way in discharging their functions." Assuring the delegates from the Tribal Research Institutes the Minister reiterated that the Ministry of Home Affairs "will do all that is necessary to make the Tribal Research Institutes viable to enable them to provide the professional inputs for the implementation on tribal development and Scheduled Caste development programmes."

ANNEXURE—I

Tribal Research Institutes

Sl. No.	*State*	*Address*	*Year of Opening*
1	*2*	*3*	*4*
1.	Orissa	Tribal & Harijan Research-*cum*-Training, Government of Orissa, Bhubaneshwar-751014.	1953
2.	Bihar	Bihar Tribal Welfare Research Institute, Government of Bihar, Morhabadi Road, Ranchi-834008.	1954
3.	Madhya Pradesh	M.P. Tribal Research and Development Institute, Government of Madhya Pradesh, 35, Shimla Hills, Bhopal-2.	1954
4.	West Bengal	Cultural Research Institute, Sch. Castes & Sch. Tribes Welfare Department, Government of West Bengal, Pl/4, G.I.T. Scheme, No. VII M, V.I.P. Road, Kankurgachi, Calcutta-700054.	1955
5.	Maharashtra	Tribal Research Institute, Government of Maharashtra, 28, Queens Road, Pune.	1962
6.	Gujarat	Tribal Research & Training Centre, Gujarat Vidyapith, Ahmedabad-380014.	
7.	Assam	Tribal Research Institute, Government of Assam, New Sarania, Gauhati*-781003.	1962
8.	Andhra Pradesh	Tribal Cultural Research & Training Institute, Government of Andhra Pradesh, Ravindranagar Colony, H.No. 6-3-628/9, P.O. Kairatabad, Hyderabad-500064.	1963

*Separate institute for Assam set up in Gauhati after Meghalaya came into being. Earlier the Institute at Shillong functioned for the composite Assam.

(*Contd.*)

1	2	3	4
9.	Rajasthan	Manikya Lal Verma Tribal Research & Training Institute, Government of Rajasthan, Udaipur.	1964
10.	Kerala	Kerala Institute of Research, Training & Development Studies of Scheduled Castes and Scheduled Tribes, Government of Kerala, Kozhikode.	1971
11.	Uttar Pradesh	Directorate of Harijan & Social Welfare, Government of Uttar Pradesh Lucknow.	
12.	Tamil Nadu	Tribal Research Centre, Tamil University, Under fell Bungalow, Missionary Hill, Uthagamandalam, Tamil Nadu.	1983

ANNEXURE II

Administrative Set up of Tribal Research Institutes

Sl. No.	*Category/Designation*	*Andhra Pradesh*	*Assam*	*Bihar*	*Gujarat*	*Madhya Pradesh*	*Maharashtra*	*Orissa*	*Rajasthan*
1	2	3	4	5	6	7	8	9	10
1.	Director	1	1	1	1	1	1	1	1
2.	Additional Director, Joint Director, Dy. Director-*cum*-Principal, Dy. Director, Chief Planner, Chief Research Officer	9	2	2	1	9	2	2	3
3.	Research Officer, Assistant Director, Lecturer, Asstt. Research Officer, Cultural Officer, Museum Curator, Statistical Officer, Programme Officer, Planning Officer, Field Officer, Editor, Tabulation Officer, Cartographer	20	3	4	2	34	7	14	2
4.	Jr. Research Officer, Asstt. Museum Curator, Museum Caretaker, Investigator, Research Assistant	1	3	4	18	—	—	—	—

(*Contd.*)

ANNEXURE II (*Contd.*)

1	2	3	4	5	6	7	8	9	10
5.	Other Staff*	115	24	45	14	121	37	62	34
	Total sanctioned staff	146	33	56	36	158	59	122	40

*Office and other ministerial staff is included under item No. 5.

Notes: Kerala: The staff strength of the TRI, Kerala, consists of 1 Director who is assisted by 16 other gazetted officers, 12 non-gazetted officers and 6 other supporting staff.

Uttar Pradesh: A Research Cell has been opened in the Directorate of Harijan and Social Welfare, Lucknow, with 14 staff including 6 research workers.

West Bengal: Cultural Research Institute, Calcutta, is headed by a Director who is assisted by 1 Dy. Director, 1 Chief Planner, 1 Principal of the Training Wing. Other staff include 2 Asstt. Planners, 5 Research Officers, 14 Research Investigators. In addition there are Statistical Personnel, Artist-*cum*-Photograpber, Museum Caretaker and a Librarian.

ANNEXURE III

Research and Training Amount Released

(Rs. in lakhs)

State/U.T.	*1974-75*	*1975-76*	*1976-77*	*1977-78*	*1978-79*	*1979-80*	*1980-81*	*1981-82*	*1982-83*	*1983-84*	*Allocation for 1984-85*
1	*2*	*3*	*4*	*5*	*6*	*7*	*8*	*9*	*10*	*11*	*12*
Andhra Pradesh	0.85	1.00	3.00	4.00	2.00	3.00	3.85	4.50	7.55	5.00	—
Assam	—	1.00	0.50	0.65	2.50	2.00	4.50	2.25	6.60	10.00	—
Bihar	0.85	1.00	0.50	1.00	1.00	1.65	3.00	1.90	4.30	3.00	—
Gujarat	0.10	1.00	1.00	0.50	2.00	1.65	2.90	3.50	1.60	4.50	—
Himachal Pradesh	—	0.50	—	0.50	—	—	—	0.60	—	—	—
Karnataka	0.20	0.50	0.50	0.40	—	—	—	—	—	—	—
Kerala	0.60	1.00	2.00	2.00	2.00	1.00	3.75	8.00	12.00	10.00	—
Madhya Pradesh	3.10	3.50	1.11	1.25	2.00	7.20	4.50	4.00	2.00	2.00	—
Maharashtra	0.10	0.96	1.00	1.00	2.50	2.50	3.65	2.11	4.15	4.79	—
Manipur	0.10	—	0.25	0.45	0.50	0.25	0.30	0.50	1.00	1.10	—

(Contd.)

ANNEXURE III *(Contd.)*

1	*2*	*3*	*4*	*5*	*6*	*7*	*8*	*9*	*10*	*11*	*12*
Meghalaya	—	0.99	0.50	—	0.50	0.25	—	—	0.25	—	—
Nagaland	—	—	—	—	—	—	0.25	0.50	0.12	0.12	—
Orissa	3.60	4.00	2.50	3.00	2.00	3.30	5.95	3.70	6.57	4.19	—
Rajasthan	1.10	1.50	2.50	2.00	1.50	1.50	2.40	4.00	1.00	2.00	—
Tamil Nadu	0.10	0.50	0.53	0.50	0.50	0.30	0.50	0.30	0.15	0.65	—
Tripura	0.20	0.50	0.05	1.20	1.00	0.50	0.50	0.50	0.49	0.50	—
Uttar Pradesh	0.10	0.40	0.27	0.30	1.00	0.50	0.75	0.90	0.71	1.76	—
West Bengal	4.80	10.00	1.70	1.25	4.00	1.50	2.21	2.00	0.90	2.90	—
D and N Haveli	—	—	—	—	—	—	—	—	—	—	—
Mizoram	—	—	—	—	—	—	—	—	—	—	—
Total	15.80	28.35	17.91	20.00	25.00	27.10	39.10	39.26	51.39	54.51	70.00

ANNEXURE IV

SELECTED TRAINING COURSES CONDUCTED BY TRIBAL RESEARCH INSTITUTES DURING THE SIXTH PLAN PERIOD

1981-82
ANDHRA PRADESH

1. For development functionaries, Project Officers, District Officers and Extension Officers.
2. For special Deputy Collectors.
3. For Standing Committee members of Panchayat Samithis and Zilla Parishads.
4. Appraisal courses for Officers on MADA and primitive tribes.
5. Appraisal courses on issues of caste and community certificates for Tahsildars of Agency and non-Agency areas of Hyderabad.

1982-83

1. Peripatetic training programme for tribal leaders, Mandasa, Srikakulam District.
2. Management of Tribal Development Programmes for officials at Hyderabad.
3. Standing Committee members training course at Paderu Panchayat Samithi, Visakhapatnam.

1981-82
ASSAM

For Project Officers.

1982-83

For the Officials working in the tribal areas.

1983-84

For Officers working in the tribal areas.

1984-85

Sponsored by the Hill Area Department and conducted by the TRI, Assam. It was a Tribal Orientation programme for the Officers of various departments.

1982-83
GUJARAT

1. For Class I and II Officers working for Tribal sub-Plan Programmes.
2. For officials of the Gujarat State Forest Development Corporation.
3. For Officer trainees of Forest Ranger's College, Rajpipla.
4. For Class I and II Officers of Forest Department.
5. Peripatetic training programme (camp) organised at Vallabhpur in Rapar taluka of Kutch district—tribal group covered Koli and Bhil.
6. Peripatetic training programme (camp) organised at Mundra in Kutch district—tribal group covered Koli, Bhil and Pardhi.
7. Peripatetic training programme (camp) organised at Varvat in Dharampur taluka of Valsad district—tribal group covered Kokna and Dhodia.
8. Peripatetic training programme (camp) organised at Vansda taluk in Valsad district—tribal group covered— Kokna and Dhodia.

1980-81 AND 1981-82
KERALA

Training programmes as usual for in service personnel such as Village Officers, Voluntary Workers, educational institution staff.

1982-83

1. Leadership training for tribals.
2. For Village Officers.

1983-84

1. For the tribal leaders.
2. For harijan leaders.
3. For village officers.
4. For Tahsildars.
5. For Headmasters of Primary Schools.
6. For the Taluk Welfare Officers.
7. Language Orientation training to Officials working in tribal areas.

1983-84
MAHARASHTRA

1. Tribal youth leadership training programmes.
2. Foresters and Forest Guards.
3. Pre-service training to tribal graduates and under-graduates and those passed 12th standard.
4. Training to Ashram School Headmasters/Teachers.
5. Training of organising cultural programmes, games and other extra-curricular activities in Ashram Schools.

1980-81
ORISSA

1. Project Implementation, Monitoring and Evaluation sponsored by the Department of Personnel and Administrative Reforms, Ministry of Home Affairs New Delhi.
2. Tribal Development Administration sponsored by the Department of Personnel Ministry of Home Affairs, New Delhi.

1981-82

1. Project implementation, Monitoring and Evaluation.
2. Tribal development and culture for—Police, Excise and Forest Staff.

1982-83

1. Project Implementation, Monitoring and Evaluation.
2. Research Methodology in Tribal Development Administration (National level).
3. Tribal Culture and Development for Police Staff.
4. Organisation of training course on Tribal Development Administration at Kohima.

1983-84

1. Tribal Development Administration.
2. Research Methodology in Tribal Development Administration.
3. Project implementation, Monitoring and Evaluation (S.C. development programme).
4. Orientation courses on Tribal Culture and Development, Police, Excise and Forest staff.
5. A general course on special legislation for field officers of H and T W Department.
6. Organisation of course on tribal development administration of officers of Manipur.

1982-83
RAJASTHAN

1. Training and orientation courses for the tribal youth.
2. Training and orientation of people's representatives at the grassroot levels.

1982-83
WEST BENGAL

Organising Santhal Language training classes in different centres of West Bengal.

1983-84

Organising Santhal Language training classes in different centres of West Bengal.

ANNEXURE V

STUDIES (EVALUATION/SOCIO-ECONOMIC) UNDERTAKEN BY TRIBAL RESEARCH INSTITUTES DURING THE SIXTH PLAN

ANDHRA PRADESH

1. Study on Displacement of Tribals due to Medium Irrigation and Industrial Projects.
2. Study on Co-operative Movement among Tribals in Khammam District.
3. Study of General Qualifications Prescribed for all Posts in Tribal Areas *vis-a-vis* Available Manpower.
4. Study of Excise Policy in Tribal Areas.
5. Evaluation of Milch Cattle Scheme in Eturnagaram and Paderu Areas.
6. Evaluation of Integrated Tribal Development Agency, Visakhapatnam.
7. Study of sub-Plan at Macro-level.
8. Study of Land Alienation.
9. Venereal Diseases among Tribal.
10. Evaluation of Minor Irrigation Schemes in Adilabad District.
11. Adoption of Improved Animal Husbandry Practices in Integrated Tribal Development Agencies.
12. Assessment of Utilisation of Reservation in Employment for Scheduled Tribes.
13. Assessment of Utilisation of Reservation in Educational Institutes.
14. Assessment of Agricultural Programmes in Tribal Areas of Andhra Pradesh.
15. Dairy Development Programmes in Visakhapatnam District.
16. Milk Chilling Centres in Adilabad District.
17. Horticulture Programmes in Paderu ITDA, Visakhapatnam District.
18. Evaluation of Community Irrigation Wells in Tribal Areas.
19. Socio-economic Condition of S.T. Beneficiaries under Tassar Culture.
20. Health Status on Borders of Ashram Schools in Visakhapatnam District.
21. Evaluation of Post-Matric Scholarship Schemes among Scheduled Tribes.

22. Evaluation of Girijan Co-operative Corporation.
23. Fertility and Family Planning among Kolams of Adilabad District.
24. Study of Cattle Management in Tribal Areas of Andhra Pradesh.
25. Study of Structure and Functioning of sub-Plan at District Level—Case Study of West Godavari District.
26. Poverty Line Programme—A Study on Income Pattern of Tribals.
27. Rehabilitation Programme for Tribals in Submerged Areas of Polavaram Barrage.
28. Comprehensive Study of Social Structure with Special Reference to Controversial Tribes.

ASSAM

1. Field Studies in respect of Twenty Gram Panchayat Level Co-operative Societies and Two LAMPS in Hill Areas.
2. Rice-brewing by Tribals and Impact of Prohibition.
3. Field Studies in Respect of G.P.S.S.
4. Evaluation Study of an I.T.D.P.—Kokrajhar.
5. Study on the Displacement of Tribals due to Installation of Industrial and Irrigational Complexes.
6. Study on Socio-economic condition of the Kaibarttas—a Scheduled Caste in Assam.

BIHAR

1. Evaluation: Agro-economic Appraisal of Tribal Development Agency, Chakradharpur.
2. Study of Soil Conservation in Singhbhum District.
3. Study of Main Causes of Malnutrition Including Consumption of Khesari Dal.
4. Socio-economic Study of Mines and Quarry Workers.
5. Evaluation of Pump Sets Distributed in Srindega Meso Area, Ranchi District.
6. Land Alienation and Indebtedness Survey in the Non-sub-Plan Area.
7. Tribals of Dhanbad: A Socio-economic Study.
8. Study of Manki-Munda System.

9. Evaluation of I.T.D.P., Khunti.
10. Evaluation of Minor Irrigation Schemes.
11. Health Survey of Pahariyas.
12. Evaluation of Displacement due to River Valley Project.
13. Study of Pahariya Gram Sabha in Santal Parganas District.
14. Study of Bonded Labour in Santal Parganas District.
15. The Irrigation Need: An appraisal of Big Diameter Well in Chotanagpur.
16. Health Coverage in Tribal Areas.
17. Study of Migrant Women Labourers in Santal Parganas District: Problem of their Rehabilitation.

GUJARAT

1. Evaluation Study of Ashram Schools.
2. Evaluation Study of the Credit Facilities for Purchase of Oxen.
3. A Study of Structure and Functioning of Co-operative Societies in Tribal Areas, with special Reference to Forest Labourers Co-operative Societies.
4. A Socio-economic Study of Pomla (ST).
5. A Socio-economic Study of Bavcha (ST).
6. Problem of the Tribal Women Working in the Industrial Units of G.I.D.C. Estate, Vapi.
7. Socio-economic Survey of Important Scheduled Caste Communities in the State.
8. Evaluation Study of I.D.T.P.—(1) Dangs, (2) Dohad (Panchmahal), (3) Chotaudaipur, (4) Songadh.
9. Socio-economic Survey of Shenva (SC).
10. Socio-economic Survey of Turi (SC).
11. Evaluation of Poultry Development Programme.
12. Socio-economic Survey of a Backward Community— Borpi.
13. Evaluation Study of Tribal sub-Plan Programmes in Limkheda Taluk (Panchmahal).
14. Evaluation of Programmes of Component Plan for Scheduled Castes in Kheda District.
15. Socio-economic Survey of Sadhus (SC).
16. Socio-economic Survey of Chamar (SC).
17. Survey of Health and Sanitation Conditions in Tribal Areas.

18. Modern Industry and Tribals: A Study on Process of Industrialization in and around Atul Industry.
19. Study of Two Villages to be Submerged in the Catchment Areas of Narmada Dam.
20. A Study of Food and Nutrition among Tribals of Gujarat.
21. Tribal Labourers and Problem of Migration.
22. Land Alienation in Tribal Areas of Gujarat.
23. Milk Co-operative Societies in Tribal Areas: Impact on Tribal Economy.

KERALA

1. Evaluation of Ashram Schools.
2. Evaluation of I.T.D.Ps.—(1) Attapady, (2) Idukky, (3) Nilamber, (4) Wynad.
3. Land Alienation—a Restudy.
4. Displacement of Tribals by Large Projects.
5. Economic and Cultural Change in Tribes of Attapady.
6. Impact of Tribal Co-operative Societies in sub-Plan Areas.
7. Impact of Irrigation Facilities in Attapady.
8. Evaluation Studies on Certain Housing Schemes Implemented for Tribals of Wynad.
9. Evaluation of Tribal Balwadis and Nursery Schools in Wynad.
10. Drop out among the Scheduled Castes and Scheduled Tribes.
11. Impact of Award of Post-Matric Scholarships to Scheduled Tribe Students.
12. Culture change among the Washermen Castes of Kerala.
13. Evaluation Study on Certain Developmental Programmes already Implemented by the Harijan/Tribal Welfare Department.

MADHYA PRADESH

1. Evaluation Study of Minor-Irrigation Wells.
2. Evaluation of Representation of Scheduled Castes and Scheduled Tribes in the various Posts in the Government Services.
3. Evaluation of New System of Post-Matric Scholarships.
4. Survey of Socio-economic Condition of Tribal Women Affected by Bailadila Project in Bastar.

5. An Evaluation of Land Alienation in 15 Blocks of 15 Districts.
6. Socio-economic Survey of Fishermen in Tribal Blocks.

MAHARASHTRA

1. The Study of Rehabilitation of Displaced Tribal Persons due to Kukadi Irrigation Project in Pune District.
2. Evaluation Study of the Depachari Dairy Project in Tribal sub-Plan Area of Thane District.
3. The Study of Evaluation of Ashram School Complex Programme in Maharashtra State.
4. Evaluation of ITDPs—(i) Kasa (Thane District), (ii) Jawahar, (Thane District), (iii) Gadchiroli.
5. Study of Evaluation of Scheme of Electric Motor Pumps to Adivasi.
6. Study of Evaluation of Working of Adivasi Co-operative Societies in Maharashtra State—Some Case Studies.
7. Sociological Study of the Tribal Persons to be affected by Ichampalli Irrigation Project of Sironcha Tahsil, Chandra Pur District.
8. A Study of use of liquor by the tribal people in their socio-religious functions.
9. Study of Post-Matric Scholarships for Scheduled Castes and Scheduled Tribes.
10. Evaluation Report of Schemes under 'Nucleus Budget'—1981-82 in sub-Plan Area of Maharashtra State.
11. Evaluation of Schemes Implemented for the Development of Primitive Tribes in sub-Plan Area.
12. Evaluation of Government Backward Class Hostels and their Working in Maharashtra.
13. A Study on Socio-economic and Sociological aspects of the people in Akrani and Akkalkuwa taluka in Dhule District.
14. Socio-economic Survey and Model Rehabilitation Scheme for Tribal People affected by Bhopalpattnam Project Submergence.
15. Study of Primitive Tribes Ka-Thakur and Ma-Thakur of Thane District and Plan for their Development.
16. Socio-economic Survey of the Backward Tribes, i.e Ka and Ma-Thakur, Dhor Kolis, Kotlas and Bardas.
17. Study of Tribal Legislations in Maharashtra State.

ORISSA

1. Study of Bonded Labour in Phulbani District.
2. Study of Shifting Cultivation.
3. Study of Health and Nutritional Problems of Pauri Bhuiyans of Jaldih Board Area in Sundergarh District.
4. Study of Socio-economic Condition of Refugees and Tribes of Dandakaranya.
5. Study of Health and Genetic Problems of Kutia—Kondh of Belghar Area.
6. Study of Shifting Cultivation as Practised by the Hill Bhuiyans of Bonai.
7. Evaluation of Dug-Wells in Sub-Plan Area of the State.
8. Survey of Health and Nutritional States among the Juangs of Keonjhar and Gadabas of Koraput District.
9. Evaluation of Post-Matric Scholarships.
10. Evaluation of LAMPS in sub-Plan Area.
11. Evaluation of Seora Development Agency, Chandragiri.
12. Evaluation of ITDPs/ITDAs Objectives.
13. Evaluation of Insitute Plantation and other Horticultural Schemes.
14. Study of trafficking in Saora and Kondh Women of Ganjam and Phulbani Districts.
15. Study of Socio-economic condition of the Bauri/Bhoi caste in Puri, Cuttack and Balasore Districts.
16. Evaluation of Land Survey and Settlement Operations in Tribal Areas.
17. Study of Psycho-Socio-Cultural aspects of the denotified tribal societies.
18. Evaluation of Educational Institutions under Harijan and Tribal Welfare Department with Particular reference to the problems of wastage and stagnation.
19. Study of the impact of Protective Legislations in regard to Land Alienation, Bonded Labour, Money Lending, Excise and Forest Policy.
20. Evaluation of Poorest Families in Siripur Saora Village.
21. Land Tenure System in Areas Inhabited by the Koya, the Dongaria Kandha, the Saora and the Oraons.
22. Study of Economic Life with Particular Reference to Assets in Tribal Societies.

23. Study on Employment Potentiality among the Scheduled Castes in the Hinterland of Bhubaneswar.
24. Study of 20 Villages under SIDA Social Forestry Project (Balasore, Mayurbhanj, Keonjhar and Sambalpur).
25. Study of Tribals around BALCO Project in Keonjhar District.
26. Study of Villages affected by NALCO Project at Damanjodi.
27. Study of Health and Nutritional status of Tribals of Orissa.

RAJASTHAN

1. Sample Study of Land Records and Land Alienation.
2. Study of Exploitation of Tribals by Money-lenders and its Remedial Measures.
3. Study of Impact of Irrigation Facility Schemes, Problems and Solution.
4. Evaluation of ITDP, Banswara.
5. Impact of LAMPS on the Tribal Economy—A Case Study.
6. Study of Social-Forestry Programmes.
7. Performance of S.F.D.A. Dungarpur: A Study of Loaning to Tribals.
8. Indebtedness and Credit requirements in ITDP, Pratapgarh.
9. Study of Change in Agricultural Practices in a Tribal set up.
10. Study of Migration trends and New Employment Opportunities.
11. Study of Blasting Programmes of Wells.
12. *Sahariya Visistha Project Ka Mulyanakan—Hindi* (An evaluation of Sahariya Project).
13. Education Facilities of Scheduled Tribes in ITDP, Banswara.
14. Health coverage of Panchayat Samiti, Jhadol.
15. Impact of Special Nutrition Programme.
16. Evaluation of I.T.D. Programme.
17. Utilisation of Loans for Diesel Pump Sets.
18. Working of TADCF—An Evaluation.
19. Evaluation of ICDS Programme.
20. Evaluation of TRYSEM Programme.
21. Working of Ashram Schools.
22. Impact of Agricultural Extension Programme on Tribal Cultivators.
23. Guinea-worm Incidence *vis-a-vis* Hand Pump Programme.

WEST BENGAL

1. Evaluation of LAMPS.
2. Evaluation on Small Irrigations in ITDP Areas.
3. Study on Displaced Tribals.
4. Study on Enrolment and Drop-out Pattern of Scheduled Caste and Scheduled Tribe students reading in Primary Schools in ITDPs.
5. Progress of Secondary Education amongst the Scheduled Tribes in Comparison with non-Scheduled Communities of State (for 1980).
6. Socio-economic survey on Scheduled Caste Leather-working Communities.
7. Nature and Extent of Stagnation among the Scheduled Tribes and Other Communities in the Secondary Stage of Education.
8. Socio-economic Survey on the Families Engaged in Sweeping and Scavenging Occupations.
9. Study on the Achievement of Scheduled Caste and Scheduled Tribe hostellers in Comparison with the Day Scholars.
10. Evaluation of ITDPs of different Districts in General and ITDP, Binpur in Particular.
11. Study on Prevalence of Diseases among the Tribals of Tribal Contracted Areas and their Acceptance of Modern Medicine.
12. Nature and Extent of Untouchability in Different Pockets of West Bengal.
13. A Baseline Study of Tribal Market (Jubilee Market at Jhargram).
14. Study on Craft-practising Scheduled Castes of West Bengal.
15. Study on Drop Out, Stagnation in Post-Matric Stage amongst the Scheduled Caste and Scheduled Tribe Students.
16. Tribals and Minor Forest Produce (MFP) in Relation to LAMPS—An Evaluation.
17. Study on Identification of Scheduled Tribe Families Practising Traditional and Modern Crafts in ITDPs.
18. Socio-economic Study for Identification of the Problems of Tribal Women (Rural/Urban).
19. Case Studies in Relation to Functioning of Individual Schemes in ITDPs.

20. Nature and Extent of Indebtedness among the Tribals in ITDPs.
21. Identification of Resources and Problems in Areas Under Component Plan.
22. Educational Problems of the Tribal Girls at Various Stages of Education.
23. Study of Tribal Women Labourers Engaged in Various Economic Sectors (Agriculture, Industry—Tea, Colliery, Urban Construction, etc.).

ANNEXURE VI

EVALUATION STUDIES ENTRUSTED TO TRIBAL RESEARCH INSTITUTES DURING 1984-85

1. ANDHRA PRADESH

(i) Srikakulam ITDP.
(ii) Working of marketing societies in Paderu Taluk of Visakhapatnam district.
(iii) MADA programmes in Warangal district.
(iv) Primitive tribal group Kolam.
(v) Impact of special component plan in Medak district.

2. ASSAM

(i) Dhemaji ITDP.
(ii) Milch animals scheme and agriculture inputs scheme in one district.
(iii) Sericulture programme in one district.
(iv) Namsudhra community in Cachar district.

3. BIHAR

(i) Lohardaga ITDP.
(ii) Housing Scheme in Bhansa block.
(iii) Social forestry in one district.
(iv) Mal Paharia and Birhor primitive tribal groups.
(v) Dushadh community in one district.

4. GUJARAT

(i) Palanpur and Dharampur ITDP.
(ii) Milk Co-operative Societies in Dangs district.
(iii) Kotwalia primitive tribal group in Songadh district.
(iv) Madia community in one district.

5. KERALA

(i) Nilambur ITDP.
(ii) Wynad Co-operative Farming Society.

(iii) Bonded labour amongst Panyans.
(iv) Primitive tribal group Kadar.
(v) Impact of Special Component Plan in Palghat district.

6. MADHYA PRADESH

(i) ITDP, Petul and Gariaband.
(ii) Kamar primitive tribal group.
(iii) Irrigation well programme in one district.
(iv) Leather workers' programme in Nagodh.

7. MAHARASHTRA

(i) Sironcha ITDP in Gadchiroli district.
(ii) Supply of milch animals scheme in Dhulia district.
(iii) Primitive tribal programmes amongst Katkaria.
(iv) Rope-making amongst Malhar in one district.

8. ORISSA

(i) Keonjhar and Nilgiri ITDPs.
(ii) Supply of milch animals scheme in Keonjhar district.
(iii) Kadke irrigation project in Rairangpur ITDA.
(iv) Cane work amongst Kewat in Belgar Tehsil and Sabai grass in Baripada.
(v) Fishermen community in Puri and Ganjam district as also monograph on Dandasi.

9. RAJASTHAN

(i) ITDP, Dangarpur.
(ii) One Fishing Co-operative Society.
(iii) Diesel Pump distribution in one district.
(iv) Deepening of wells scheme in Udaipur district.
(v) Farm Forestry in one Block.

10. TAMIL NADU

(i) Kolli Hills ITDP.
(ii) Supply of Milch animals in Jawadhi hills.

(iii) Sericulture programme in Pachamalai district.
(iv) Bonded labour among Paniyans.

11. UTTAR PRADESH

(i) Kheri ITDP.
(ii) Irrigation Well programme in Kheri ITDP.
(iii) Rajis primitive tribal group.
(iv) Koltas in Jaunsar Bawar area.
(v) Construction of shops schemes under Scheduled Caste Component Plan.

12. WEST BENGAL

(i) Malda ITDP.
(ii) Piggery programme in Purulia and Bankura districts.
(iii) Lodha primitive tribal group.
(iv) Irrigation wells in Purulia and Bankura districts.

APPENDIX VI

SCHEME FOR AWARD OF RESEARCH FELLOWSHIP IN VARIOUS ASPECTS OF TRIBAL DEVELOPMENT

The Ministry of Welfare, in association with State Governments, will award a specified number of fellowships (not exceeding twenty-five only) annually with a view to encourage indepth study of the processes of socio-economic change in the tribal areas and of tribal communities particularly in the wake of the new developmental efforts. The fellowships will be open to scholars belonging to different disciplines like Anthropology, Sociology, Economics, Political Science, Agriculture, Medicine, etc. and who are registered for Ph.D. with a recognised University. A scholar belonging to any one of these disciplines will undertake a specific area for his study. This study will, however, keep in view the broad frame of the total socio-economic situation of the concerned community.

Field-work

2. It is expected that research scholar will spend adequate time as warranted by the nature of the study, in the village or villages which he may select for his field work. He will be, as far as possible, a participant observer during this period and will take part in the developmental programme in the concerned villages. This task will be defined keeping in view his background; it will, however, in no case be supervisory in character. Emphasis will be on actual first hand participation with the community. The precise assignment will be worked out by the local administration in consultation with the sponsoring Institute of higher learning and concerned guide.

Areas of Study

3. The broad areas of study have been indicated in Annexure I. They include the following facets:

(i) Analysis of the process of socio-economic change in the Tribal Areas.
(ii) Marginal and Pre-Agricultural Communities.
(iii) Shifting Cultivation.
(iv) Forests and Associated Areas.
(v) Industrial and Urban Context.
(vi) Land, Agriculture and Allied Activities.
(vii) Market, Credit and Co-operation.
(viii) Economic Infrastructure.
(ix) Social-Services—Health, Education, Other Aspects.
(x) Labour, Employment, Traditional Industry and Artisans.
(xi) Women in Tribal Economy.
(xii) Organisational Aspects.
(xiii) Socio-Cultural—Religious aspects during transition.

4. Subjects relating to the urgent problems in critical areas, like those around new industrial Complexes in the more backward regions and also those relating to the more backward tribal areas and communities will be given higher priority while granting scholarships. The itemisation under each facet is not aimed at defining precise subjects or title-heads of the research studies. A subject, which may be selected for study, may cover one or more of these aspects or could concentrate even on one of the many possible sub-regions under an item. The study, however, must be with reference to one or more specific field situations on the basis of which generalizations, if any, can be built up. These studies will be in clear contrast to library-oriented researches or research-based primarily on secondary data with only a small element of field work.

Period of Fellowships

5. The period of fellowship will be ordinarily 2 years which may be extended up to a maximum of 3 years, only on the basis of request by the State Government as well as recommendation of the guide.

Rate of Fellowships

6. The rate of fellowships and allowances for incidental expenditure for doctoral and post-doctoral work will be as follows:

POST DOCTORAL AND DOCTORAL FELLOWSHIPS

1. Value

(a) Post Doctoral

The amount of the post-doctoral fellowship will be Rs. 1,000 per month.

(b) Doctoral

The value of the doctoral fellowship will be Rs. 800 per month.

2. Contingency Grant

(1) The fellowships carry an annual Contingency Grant of Rs. 3,000 for post-doctoral and doctoral stages for meeting approved contingent expenditure connected with the research work such as stationery, typing, graphs and charts, journals, periodicals, travel expenses, etc. The fellowship grant can be increased upto Rs. 5,000 in case where, extensive field work or intensive computer work is involved. The contingency grant for the second year will be released only after receiving the copy of the thesis by the State Government from the candidate.

Procedure for Award

7. Candidates having the requisite qualifications may apply when advertisement calling for applications is issued by the Ministry to the heads of the Tribal Research Institute of the State in which the field work is proposed to be conducted, or to the Director. Tribal Welfare or equivalent officers in those States where there is no Tribal Research Institute. The applicant will be required to submit a brief synopsis of about 3 to 4 pages indicating the subject of his study, area for field investigation, time schedule for his work, etc. along with a copy of Ph.D. registration. It should also be accompanied by the recommendation of the Professor or other members of appropriate faculty who may be prepared to

accept him for research work under his guidance. The candidates employed in Government services should send a no-objection Certificate from the Competent Authority. The eligibility to draw the fellowship amount will be governed by respective Service Rules. The faculty and the university under which he will be working and the final degree for which the research work will be submitted should also be stated. An advance copy of the application may be forwarded to the Joint Director, (Research), Tribal Development, Ministry of Welfare, New Delhi. The Director, TRI/Director-in-charge of tribal Development of State Governments should forward all the applications received by them with the comments to the Ministry.

8. In respect of research fellows who are awarded Fellowship grants by the Ministry of Welfare through the State Governments should ensure that after completion of the stipulated period they must submit the thesis to the concerned Universities and copy of such thesis submitted to this Ministry for information. *If a candidate availing of the fellowship chooses to discontinue without completing the term or fails to submit the thesis on completion of the tenure he will be required to refund the fellowship amount drawn.* He will also execute a bond in favour of President of India, as prescribed.

9. The candidates selected for the award will be informed by the Ministry. The fellowship grant will be released by the concerned State Government after the selection list is provided to them by Ministry and with effect from the date the candidate actually accepts the award of fellowship. The award will have no retrospective effect.

10. The selection of the candidates for these awards will be made by a Selection Committee consisting of among other members a representative of the Planning Commission and from ICSSR/UGC/University, that will be set up for this purpose by the Ministry. After the selection, the list of the selected candidates will be sent to the State Governments. Efforts will also be made to intimate the candidates regarding such selections. *The Ministry of Welfare might stipulate the date by which the State Governments should intimate the date of joining of the candidates.* The arrangement will facilitate timely release of grants to the State Governments and disburse the fellowship grants to the candidates.

11. The total number of fellowships to be awarded each year will not exceed 25 out of which not exceeding 1/4th may be senior

and the remaining junior fellowships. The number, however, may be increased if more candidates are available for undertaking work in priority areas. Some universities may even sponsor more than one study in the same area so that a small multi-disciplinary group of research scholars may simultaneously study different facets of socio-economic life.

12. The arrangements for field work and precise assignment as a participant observer may be worked out in consultation with the local administration after the awards have been finalised.

ANNEXURE I

BROAD AREAS OF STUDY IN VARIOUS ASPECTS OF TRIBAL DEVELOPMENT

I. Process of Socio-economic Change in the Tribal Areas

1.1 Juxtaposition of the tribal and the modern socio-economic system—A dynamic analysis of their infraction and change.

1.2 Interaction of the modern formalised systems with the simple tribal societies in the early stages of economic development.

1.3 Traditional concepts of ownership of land, forest and other natural resources in tribal societies—Nature of conflict with new law and its consequences.

1.4 Changing social institutions in tribal areas under the impact of modern economic development.

1.5 A study of the quality of contact between modern civilisation and the more backward tribal areas.

1.6 The oral tradition of the tribal and the new world of 'written' authority.

1.7 Process of 'tribalisation' of early settlers in tribal areas.

1.8 Smaller tribal communities on the fringe of stronger groups—The dynamics of their socio-economic relationship.

1.9 Crisis in value systems, particularly concepts about morality in the context of the new confrontation with a different system and emergence of new demands.

1.10 Impact of the new laws particularly relating to land, and new social institutions on matrilineal and polyandrous tribal communities.

1.11 Excise policy in tribal areas—traditional custom, introduction of contract system by the British and its continuance attempts to change it, conflict of the tribal tradition with the new system, the excise contractor and his network, impact on the tribal economy, reformist movements—their genesis and results.

1.12 Tribal's concept of crime and justice.

1.13 Tribal in the law court.

1.14 Reformist movements in recent times.

1.15 Impact of new political processes on tribal society.
1.16 Study of tribal movements in recent times with reference to their political, social and economic implications.
1.17 Monetisation of tribal economy particularly in more backward areas—The process and its implications.
1.18 Changing consumption pattern and its impact on tribal economy.
1.19 Process of horizontal and vertical differentiation in a tribal society.
1.20 Dynamics of small growth centres in tribal areas and implication for tribal development.
1.21 Aspiration of different sections of the tribal society.
1.22 Parasites of tribal economy
1.23 Dependents of tribal economy.
1.24 Rehabilitation and settlement of large groups in backward tribal areas. Their impact on tribal economy.

2. Marginal and Pre-Agricultural Communities

2.1 Group studies.
2.2 Ecological systems—Study of states of equilibrium and the extent of disequilibrium.
2.3 Economic, social and ritual relationship of marginal communities with larger communities.
2.4 Subsistence economy of small communities.
2.5 Problem of health of declining communities.
2.6 Nomadism as a system for optimal utilisation of scarce resources.

3. Shifting Cultivation

3.1 Shifting cultivation—Its sociological, economic and ecological aspects.
3.2 Shifting cultivation as a way of life-implication and change.
3.3 Shifting cultivation—A comparative study of practices in different regions.
3.4 Economics of shifting cultivation.
3.5 Economics of shifting villages.
3.6 A study of directed change amongst shifting cultivators.

4. Forests and Associated Areas

4.1 Inter-dependence of forests and tribal economics.

4.2 Traditional concepts of ownership of forests and the methods of self-management of these resources by the tribal communities.
4.3 Rights and privileges of tribal communities in forests and their produce Historical perspective, principles and practice.
4.4 Forest villages and their economy.
4.5 Policies of working and utilisation of forest resources and their impact on tribal economics.
4.6 A study of 'nistar' management in tribal areas.
4.7 Economics of minor forest produce like tassar, lac tamarind, myrobalan, etc.
4.8 Exotic plantations in the tribal areas and their impact on wild life and tribal economy.
4 9 Wild life and tribal economy,
4.10 Forestry Development Corporation, their concept, organisation and working.

5. The Industrial and Urban Context

5.1 Perception of the process of industrialisation by the tribal society and the industrial centre.
5.2 Initial impact of an industrial complex—displacement, rehabilitation.
5.3 Economics of industrial location in the more backward areas and non-recognition of traditional rights.
5.4 Social consequences of industrialisation—Conflict, reaction and final solution.
5.5 Economic consequences of industrialisation to the tribal community in the zone of its influence.
5.6 Consolidation of the industry and its consequences to hinterland tribal economy.
5.7 Social, economic and skill discontinuities and their consequences for the tribal and core economics.
5.8 Rigidities of the industrial frame and its consequences to the tribal economy.
5.9 Unorganised tribal labour in organised industrial sector.
5.10 Problems of adjustment of tribal labour in the organised sector.
5.11 Supporting services in industrial complexes in tribal areas.

5.12 Labour organisations and the place of tribal.
5.13 Place of tribal in small urban and semi-urban areas.
5.14 First generation tribal in the urban setting.
5.15 Condition of tribal labour in search of jobs in urban areas.
5.16 Tribal labour under contractors outside their original places.

6. Land, Agriculture and Allied Activities

6.1 Different tenure systems and traditional concepts of land ownership with special reference to their implications for land alienation.
6.2 Management of land in traditional tribal societies.
6.3 Study of implementation of land reforms and land settlement operation in tribal areas.
6.4 Land alienation studies.
6.5 Agricultural practices as a part of the social rhythm-implications.
6.6 Traditional agricultural practices in tribal areas and the rationale of traditional land-use pattern.
6.7 Agricultural development programmes, their relevance to the tribal economy; successes and failures.
6.8 Problems in adoption and adaptation of modern agricultural practices.
6.9 Traditional system of irrigation in tribal areas.
6.10 Irrigation—problems of adopting intensive irrigated agricultural practices.
6.11 Big irrigation projects—change in land-use pattern and benefit to the tribal community.
6.12 Economics of irrigation in marginal and sub-marginal lands.
6.13 Aspects of animal husbandry problems.

7. Market, Credit and Co-operation

7.1 Monetisation of the tribal economy.
7.2 Traditional concept of money-lending.
7.3 Money-lender—His place and role in the traditional tribal economy.
7.4 Tribal markets—A complex socio-economic phenomenon.
7.5 System of communication in the tribal society—Role of markets.

7.6 Aspects of marketing of agricultural and minor forest produce—Practices, experience and possibilities.
7.7 Co-operation and a preliterate society—problems and prospects.
7.8 Co-operation, credit and pre-modern agricultural practices.
7.9 Co-operation, systems in tribal areas—structure, functioning and other aspects.
7.10 Dynamics of co-operative leadership in tribal areas.
7.11 Problem of indebtedness—Its socio-economic implications.
7.12 Bonded labour.

8. Economic Infrastructure

8.1 Economics of road development in the sparsely populated areas.
8.2 Impact of road development on tribal economy in the more backward areas.
8.3 Sources of energy to a tribal household.
8.4 Rural electrification and its impact on tribal development.

9. Social Services—Health

9.1 Traditional medicinal systems in the tribal society.
9.2 Medicinal herbs and plants in tribal areas.
9.3 Acceptance of modern medicine—problems and projects.
9.4 Special health and nutritional problems.
9.5 Traditional diet and its food value.
9.6 Changing diet in the tribal society with change in the ecological system.
9.7 Source of drinking water of tribals adaptation of tribal physiology and programmes for solving the problem.

10. Social Services—Education

10.1 Process of learning in the tribal society and modern educational system.
10.2 Language barrier and process learning.
10.3 Problems of a tribal child in early schooling.
10.4 Tribal youth in early college and high school years.
10.5 Psychological constraints of tribal youth between the traditional society and the new educational system.
10.6 Position of educated tribal youth in a tribal village.

10.7 Educational planning and administration in tribal areas—various facets and their impact on education.
10.8 Tribal dialects.

11. Social Services—Other Aspects

11.1 Dynamics of social service development in the tribal areas with reference to tribal development.
11.2 Social security system in tribal communities.
11.3 Adaption of a tribal dwelling to the climate and physical conditions.
11.4 Tribal settlements—their design and rationale.
11.5 Colonisation—A study of schemes and their economic system; finance.
11.6 Regrouping of tribal habitations as a strategy for social services.

12. Labour, Employment, Traditional Industry and Artisans

12.1 Labour in the tribal economy—forms, concepts and attitudes.
12.2 Traditional tribal craftsmen.
12.3 Traditional household skills amongst the tribals—the problem of their survival.
12.4 Technological innovation amongst the tribal communities.
12.5 Technological innovation amongst the tribal artisans.
12.6 Problem of irrelevance of traditional skills amongst some tribal groups.
12.7 Landless agricultural labour in areas of mixed tribal population.
12.8 Study of tribal migrations between different territories.
12.9 Traditional forms of mobility of tribal labour—origin, process and impact.
12.10 Barriers in the mobility of educated/uneducated tribals from rural and from smaller to bigger places.
12.11 Entrepreneurship—The problems of initiation in small modern activities.

13. Women in Tribal Economy

13.1 Family in a tribal society.
13.2 Social status of the tribal women.

13.3 Role of tribal women in the economic life of the tribal community.
13.4 Financial and social responsibility in bringing up a child is a tribal community.
13.5 Role of women in decision-making in marketing and agricultural operations.
13.6 Changing role of tribal women with socio-economic change and its implication for their social and economic status.

14. Organisational Aspects

14.1 Traditional leadership in tribal communities—their system of self-management of secular, social and religious matters.
14.2 New institutions and the traditional leadership.
14.3 Problems of complex administration and simple society.
14.4 Administration as a system in the backward tribal areas.
14.5 Mutual perception by the tribal community and the administrative system.
14.6 Social and economic hierarchy in a traditional tribal society.
14.7 Quality of contact between the administration and the simple tribal community.
14.8 The new emerging tribal leadership in rural areas.
14. 9 Youth organisation in tribal societies.
14.10 Working of the District Councils in the north-east.
14.11 Panchayat Raj in the tribal areas.
14.12 Voluntary organisations in the tribal areas.
14.13 Administrative innovation, past and present, for tribal areas.
14.14 Management of common property and community assets in the tribal society.
14.15 Impact of uniform administrative policies on the tribal society and economy
14.16 Personnel system—selection, training and piecemeal.

15. Socio-cultural-religious Aspects during Transition

15.1 World-view of the tribal societies in different settings.
15.2 The life and work of tribal poets (pre-literato tradition).
15.3 Tribal art in wood, stone, mental and wall decorations.
15.4 Tribal socio-religious complexes.
15.5 Tribal festivals and their significance in the tribal economic cycle.

15.6 Tribal Folklore.
15.7 Tribal Cosmology.
15.8 Religion and economic development in the context of simple tribal societies.
15.9 Changing material culture and its impact on tribal development.
15.10 The tribal family—an economic and social unit.

Bibliography

Books and Journals

Archer, W.G., The Hill of Flutes, Love and Poetry in Tribal India.

Bodding, P.O., A Santhal Dictionary, also 1935-36.

——, Santal Folktales, Vols. I, II and III.

——, Traditions and Institutions of Santal Benagaria, 1916.

Bose, Nirmal Kumar: Tribal Life in India.

Elvin V., The Aboriginals, Bombay, 1940.

——, The Religion of an Indian Tribes, 1955.

Haram, K., Traditions and Institutions of the Santals, 1887.

Mackkphail, J.M., The Story of Santals.

Man, E.G., Santalia and the Santals, Calcutta, 1807.

Mazumdar, D.N., Affairs of a Tribe.

——, Races and Culture in India, Allahabad.

Mazumdar, D.N. and Madan, T.N., An Introduction to Social Anthropology 1907.

Sachhidananda, Profiles of Tribal Culture in Bihar, Calcutta, 1965.

——, The Tribal Village in Bihar.

Vidyarathi, L.P., Bihar Ke Adibasi, Patna, 1960.

——, Dynamics of Tribal Leadership in Bihar.

——, Education in Tribal Bihar, 1955.

——, Urbanisation and Changing Pattern of Social Life in Cultural Contours of Tribal Bihar, Calcutta, 1964.

Vidyarthi, L.P. and Roy, B.K., The Tribal Culture in India, Delhi, 1977.

Vidyarthi, L.P., The Peasant Organisation in India (A Case Study of a Voluntary Organisation in Tribal Bihar), Ranchi, Council of Social and Cultural Research, 1977, p. 40.

Reports and Journals

A Draft Perspective Plan, Bihar, 1978-79, Bihar State Planning Board, Patna.

Annual Plan, 1966-67, 1967-68 and 1968-69.

Annual Sub-Plan for Tribal Areas of Bihar, 1980-81, 1982-83, 1983-84, 1984-85, Government of Bihar.

Approach to Tribal Development in the Sixth Plan—A Preliminary Perspective, Vol. XVII, Ministry of Home Affairs, New Delhi.

Bihar Through Figures, 1979, Government of Bihar, Patna.

Bulletin of the Bihar Tribal Welfare Research Institute, Vol. XII, Nos. I and II, Government of Bihar, Patna.

Census of India, 1961, 1971, 1981.

District Credit Plan, Santal Pargana, 1983-85, State Bank of India.

District Gazeteer of Santal Pargana, 1938.

Draft Annual Sub-Plan for Tribal Areas of Bihar, 1984-85, Government of Bihar, Patna.

Draft Fifth Five Year Plan, 1974-79, Planning Commission, New Delhi.

Draft Five Year Plan, 1978-83, Planning Deptt., Government of Bihar, Patna.

Draft Medium Term Sub-Plan for Tribal Areas of Bihar, 1978-83, Parts I and II, Government of Bihar, Patna.

Draft Perspective Plan for Bihar, 1978-89, Bihar State Planning Board.

Draft Sub-Plan for Tribal Region of Bihar, 1974-77, 1974-79, Government of Bihar.

Economic and Political Weekly, Vol. VIII, Nos. 4 to 6, 1973, and Vol. XIII, Nos. 6 to 7, 1978, Bombay.

Five Year Plans, First, Second, Third, Fourth, Fifth and Sixth, Planning Commission, New Delhi.

Reports of the Commissioner for Scheduled Castes and Scheduled Tribes, 1973-74, 1974-75, 1975.76, 1977-78, 1978-79 and 1979-80, New Delhi.

Social and Ceremonial Life of the Santals, Vol. 59.

The Santal Rebellion—M.I.I. Vol. XXV, No. 4.

Index